SLAVERY BEHIND THE WALL

Cultural Heritage Studies

UNIVERSITY PRESS OF FLORIDA

Florida A&M University, Tallahassee
Florida Atlantic University, Boca Raton
Florida Gulf Coast University, Ft. Myers
Florida International University, Miami
Florida State University, Tallahassee
New College of Florida, Sarasota
University of Central Florida, Orlando
University of Florida, Gainesville
University of North Florida, Jacksonville
University of South Florida, Tampa
University of West Florida, Pensacola

SLAVERY BEHIND THE WALL

An Archaeology of a Cuban Coffee Plantation

THERESA A. SINGLETON

Foreword by Paul A. Shackel

University Press of Florida
Gainesville · Tallahassee · Tampa · Boca Raton
Pensacola · Orlando · Miami · Jacksonville · Ft. Myers · Sarasota

Printed in the United States of America on acid-free paper

This book may be available in an electronic edition.

20 19 18 17 16 15 6 5 4 3 2 1

Library of Congress Cataloging-in-Publication Data
Singleton, Theresa A., author.
Slavery behind the wall : an archaeology of a Cuban coffee plantation / Theresa A. Singleton ; foreword by Paul Shackel.
pages cm — (Cultural heritage studies)
Includes bibliographical references.
ISBN 978-0-8130-6072-9 (acid free paper)
1. Slaves—Cuba—Social conditions. 2. Slavery—Cuba—History. 3. Coffee plantations—Cuba—History. 4. Plantation life—Cuba—History. 5. Material culture—Cuba—History. 6. Social archaeology—Cuba. 7. Excavations (Archaeology)—Cuba. 8. Cuba—Antiquities. I. Shackel, Paul A. author of introduction, etc. II. Title.
HT1076.S56 2015
306.3'62097291—dc23
2015004632

The University Press of Florida is the scholarly publishing agency for the State University System of Florida, comprising Florida A&M University, Florida Atlantic University, Florida Gulf Coast University, Florida International University, Florida State University, New College of Florida, University of Central Florida, University of Florida, University of North Florida, University of South Florida, and University of West Florida.

University Press of Florida
15 Northwest 15th Street
Gainesville, FL 32611-2079
http://www.upf.com

To my Cuban colleagues and friends, especially to
Lisette, Sonia, Mahé, Anicia, Dania, and Adrián

Contents

List of Illustrations

Figures

Tables

Foreword

While U.S.-Cuban relations have been far from normal, a few U.S. scholars have been allowed to study and work in Cuba. Therefore, Theresa Singleton's groundbreaking work *Slavery behind the Wall: An Archaeology of a Cuban Coffee Plantation* is a pioneering effort that connects prominent U.S. archaeologists to a country that has been off-limits to the majority of Americans for about a half century. Singleton's work makes available an important narrative that expands our knowledge of plantation life in the Caribbean and broadens our perspective of enslavement and landscapes in Cuba.

Singleton provides an important context for plantation life and enslavement in Cuba. Her study shows the development of the early Cuban economy and the role of the plantation and its connection to the larger Atlantic world. Singleton's work moves skillfully between the site of Cafetal Biajacas and the larger context of coffee and sugar plantations in the Caribbean. She creates a compelling story of the enslaved, who were forced to live behind a walled enclosure, and she uses objects from archaeological excavations to tell their story.

Plantation archaeologists in the United States will find a comparison of the institution of slavery to be of great interest. For instance, the laws that governed slavery in Spain were based on the thirteenth-century codes of the Castilian king, Alfonse X. As under previous Islamic law, all people were born free and enslavement was an unnatural state justified as a consequence of war or the refusal to accept a conqueror's religion. Spanish slave codes allowed enslaved people to keep family cohesion, buy their freedom, and sue their masters for mistreatment (Deagan and MacMahon 1995:6). While enslavement in the Caribbean was much harsher, Cuba had slave codes derived from these Spanish origins, and the enslaved had some (although very few) legal rights. For instance, they could bring their masters to court.

Cafetal Biajacas is unique because it has a massive masonry wall built around a settlement of detached slave houses, thereby limiting access inside and outside. This wall is a primary focus of Singleton's study. While we do not know if this wall was built to comply to a slave code following the 1825 slave rebellion, it impeded slave movement and, possibly, limited opportunities for the enslaved persons within the enclosure to engage in trade. Singleton uses archaeologically recovered materials to delve into a discussion about the uses and meaning of the enclosure. Walls compel us to think about social relations and space. I have found Ross Samson's (1992:26–44) study of medieval European walls relevant for examining the plantation enclosure. Walls separate spaces into inside and outside. Walls remove ambiguity in the landscape. They control movement and define meaning as subjects enter or exit spaces defined by walls. Since they can symbolize authority, walls can separate individuals and invoke social tension. In this case, the plantation enclosure defines private ownership of the enslaved, and it is part of the everyday negotiations that create these social relations.

The question at Cafetal Biajacas is: Was the wall built primarily to keep the enslaved people in? Or was it constructed to keep others out? Could it serve both functions? Does it convey other symbolic meanings on the plantation landscape? The investigation of the walled community has proved quite challenging because the walled enclosure appears to be an anomaly among extant ruins of former Cuban plantations. The archaeological signature of this walled compound is quite different from other Caribbean and U.S. plantations. Examining the everyday material culture, Singleton observes that while the wall functioned to inhibit movement, it also facilitated other activities that were obscured by the wall. There is a relatively small quantity of household objects and a significant amount of artifact recycling of sugar molds and tobacco pipe bowls. This archaeological signature provides some clues regarding the effectiveness of this enclosure and how the enslaved made use of their surrounding landscape and material culture.

Whoever controls the public memory of events will control the historical consciousness that interprets those events. Cuba has embraced its plantation history, and two plantation districts are UNESCO World Heritage Sites. The country also celebrates slave rebellion and slave runaways, and the events are represented on the landscape in monuments. Museum exhibitions of Cuban slavery focus on the brutal methods of slave punishment and the long hours of working in the fields. What is often missing in the public memory of plantation life is an understanding of the daily practices and cultural life of enslaved Cubans on plantations that are part of Cuban culture today, such as cuisine, music and dance, or items of adornment. Theresa Singleton's archaeology takes an important step to make these contributions of the enslaved part of the national narrative.

Paul A. Shackel

References

Deagan, Kathleen, and Darcie MacMahon

1995 *Fort Mose: Colonial America's Black Fortress of Freedom*. Gainesville: University Press of Florida/Florida Museum of Natural History.

Samson, Ross

1992 "Knowledge, Constraint, and Power Interaction: The Defenseless Medieval Wall." In *Meaning and Uses of Material Culture*, edited by Barbara J. Little and Paul A. Shackel. *Historical Archaeology* 26(3):26–44.

Preface and Acknowledgments

I embarked on this journey in November 1996 when I traveled to Cuba for the first time. On that trip, I went to two coffee plantations (both of which I have since revisited), an excavated cave site once occupied by slave runaways, and a "drumming" (a ritual of Santería religion) in a rural area of Matanzas province. At that time, I had no idea that my visits to these diverse spaces would somehow come together and contribute to the substance of this book.

Two years later, again in November, I visited for the first time the site of Santa Ana de Biajacas, the subject of this book, with a group of archaeologists from the Gabinete de Arqueología [Department of Archaeology], a division of the Office of the Historian for the City of Havana that served as the host institution in Cuba for my undertaking this project. I thank Dr. Eusebio Leal Spengler, historian for the City of Havana, for providing me the opportunity to conduct this research through his prestigious organization.

Several members of the small group with whom I visited Cafetal Biajacas became the long-term members of the project team to whom this book is dedicated: Lisette Roura Álvarez, Sonia Menéndez Castro, Karen Mahé Lugo Romera, Anicia Hernández González, Dania Hernández Perdices, and Adrián Labrada Milán. Their unwavering support of me and this project is greatly appreciated. They have always come through for me even when they did not always agree with how or understand why I did things the way I did things.

When in 1999 we began archaeological investigations at Cafetal Biajacas (which we call El Padre as the site is known today), I immediately became hooked on the research potential of the site but worried that the project would be a major undertaking that required a lot of time and many resources. The funding of field research in Cuba is difficult because of the U.S. trade embargo. Federal funding sources that typically support archaeological research (the National Science Foundation, the National Endowment for the Humanities, and the Fulbright Program) are unequivocally prohibited from funding research in Cuba.

I therefore gratefully acknowledge the financial support I received from various alternative sources: the Scholarly Studies Research Grant, a competitive funding source for Smithsonian Research staff. I began this research during my tenure as a Research Curator at the Smithsonian Institution; start-up research funds I received when I began working at Syracuse University; the H. John Heinz Family III Fund Grant Program for Latin American Archaeology; a faculty research grant through Syracuse University's Maxwell School's program in Latin America and Caribbean Studies; and numerous Appleby-Mosher grants also from the Maxwell School. I am similarly thankful for archival research funds provided me through a New-York Historical Society Fellowship and through a Library Scholars Summer Grant, David Rockefeller Center for Latin American Studies, Harvard University.

Notwithstanding limited financial resources, the project team accomplished a substantial amount of field research thanks to numerous volunteers who assisted us in various capacities. The volunteers were not the stereotypical North American shovel bumps but world-class professionals: artists, photographers, cartographers, conservators, engineers, and more. I especially acknowledge the following individuals for their specific contributions: Jorge Ponce Aguilar worked with us almost every field season from the very beginning and became an unofficial member of the project team; Amilkar Feria Flores also worked several seasons and developed the initial concept and preliminary drawing for the proposed reconstruction of the plantation featured in chapter 4; Néstor Martí Delgado worked with us in 2000 and took most of the field photographs that year. Also in 2000, Mark Hauser, then an advanced graduate student, and Stephan Lenik, then an advanced undergraduate in the Department of Anthropology, Syracuse University, came to Cuba to assist me and mapped the site. Jorge Garcell Domínguez and Ernesto Fong Arévalo undertook all the subsequent field mapping of the site. Ramón González Caraballo of the Department of

Geosciences, Instituto Superior Politécnico José Antonio Echeverría (ISP-JAE), offered his expertise for the geophysical prospecting of the site, and his student Orlando R. Carraz Hernández conducted the geophysical field study of the site gratis.

Roger Arrazcaeta Delgado, director of the Gabinete de Arqueología (Division of Archaeology), advised and helped me in many ways and joined the team in the field, beginning in 2004, to study the ruins of the great house. He sent Acelia Rodríguez Bécquer in 2001 to record and analyze the traces of mural art found on all the interior walls of the great house. Claudia Roessger, a native of Germany, assisted Acelia in the painstaking task of reconstructing the decorative motifs in these murals. I am very grateful to Roger for his foresight in getting the mural art recorded before it further deteriorated and to Acelia and Claudia for doing this very tedious job.

Unfortunately, I do not have a complete list of all the individuals who assisted in the fieldwork or in some aspect of the archaeological research and analysis, particularly those who worked on the project in my absence, when I was unable to travel to Cuba. I nonetheless acknowledge their contributions as well as those of the following individuals: Carlos Alberto Hernández Oliva, Beatriz Antonia Rodríguez Basulto, Ivalú Rodriguez Gil, Antonio Qúevedo Herrera, Fidel Navarrete Quiñones, Jorge Luis García Báez, Aldo Primiano Rodríguez, Juan Carlos Méndez Hernández, Alejandro Ramírez Anderson, Alejandro Torres Collazo, Babette Forster, Rolando Barroso Gutiérrez, Germán Barroso Gutiérrez, Francisco Simanea Vidal, Melanie Pilecki Estrada, Carlos J. Sentmanat Vázquez, Maickel Cáceres, and Osvaldo Jiménez.

I consulted with several archaeologists working in Cuba during the course of this project and in some cases visited the sites where they had worked or were working at the time of my visits. Among them, I thank Lourdes Domínguez González, Gabino La Rosa Corzo, Enrique (Kiko) Alonso (deceased), Roger Arrazcaeta Delgado, Silvia T. Angelbello Izquierdo, Odlandyer Hernández de Lara, and Alexa Voss for their valuable advice and insight and for sharing their research with me.

The investigation of primary documentary sources greatly benefitted from the contributions Leida Fernández Prieto made to this project. She located the estate records for the plantation and other records in the

Archivo Nacional de Cuba [Cuban National Archives]. Manuel Barcia brought several important documents to my attention, shared aspects of his work with me, and read an early draft of the manuscript for this book. Rosalía Oliva provided helpful tips and answered a lot of my dumb questions on doing research in the Cuban archives. I appreciate the assistance I received from the archivists of Archivo Nacional de Cuba and the Archivo Histórico Provincial de Matanzas when I used those repositories.

Acknowledgement is also due the archivists who graciously assisted me, sometimes on very short notice, with the stateside collections of Cuban materials I consulted including Baker Library, Harvard School of Business; Bristol Historical Society, Rhode Island; Hagley Museum and Library, Delaware; Houghton Library, Harvard University; Library of Congress; Long Island Studies Institute; Hofstra University, Rare Books and Manuscripts; Massachusetts Historical Society; National Archives of the United States; New York Academy of Medicine; New-York Historical Society; New York Public Library, Division of Manuscripts; and Rhode Island Historical Society.

Many archaeology colleagues in North America and elsewhere demonstrated their interest in this project in useful and generous ways. Over the years, they reviewed proposals and draft manuscripts of this book and other publications on this project, offered suggestions, and wrote letters of support for research grants. These individuals include Douglas Armstrong, L. Antonio Curet, Shannon Dawdy, Christopher DeCorse, Steve Mrozowski, Robert Paynter, and Daniel Schávelzon. I thank Paul Shackel for his comments on the manuscript and for his interest in including my book in the University Press of Florida Cultural Heritage Studies series. I thank Patricia Samford and James A. Delle for their comments on the manuscript.

I also thank past and present graduate students in the Department of Anthropology, Syracuse University, with whom I discussed many ideas and from whom I learned a great deal as they pursued dissertation projects on slavery, plantations, African diasporas, and related topics. These students include Matt Reeves, Mark Hauser, Sam Spiers, Hadley Kruczek-Aaron, Natalie Swanepoel, Lori Lee, Lori Stahlgren, Elizabeth Kellar, Heather Gibson, Francois Richard, Liza Gijanto, Dwayne Scheid, Stephan Lenik,

Helen Blouet, Shannon Dunn, Marcos Torres de Souza, Samantha Rebovich, Paôla Schiappacasse, Holly Norton, Cathy LaVoy, Sarah Shroud, William Werner, Wes Willoughby, Maria Fernanda Boza Cuadros, Zachary Beier, Paul Noe, and Jessica Bowes.

Colleagues in disciplines other than archaeology have been extremely helpful. I owe a debt of gratitude to Michael Mason who persuaded me to undertake archaeological research in Cuba and with whom I made my maiden voyage there in 1996. Although the collaborative project we envisioned did not work out, I am grateful he encouraged me to go beyond the Anglophone world to study the African diaspora. I also thank Michael for introducing me to Enrique Sosa Rodríguez with whom I consulted at the inception of this project. Sadly Sosa passed away shortly thereafter. He forewarned me that doing this project would present numerous challenges, but he believed that it would be an important and worthwhile effort. All these years I have clung to his words, particularly when doing this research became unusually difficult.

I am particularly appreciative to Dale Tomich who shared with me his research on Brazilian coffee plantations. He also invited me to participate in the Harpur College Dean's Workshop "Built Environments of Atlantic Slavery" at the Fernand Braudel Center at SUNY Binghamton in 2007. There I met architectural historian and classicist Charles Burroughs who, in turn, put me in touch with Paul Niell, an art historian of Latin America. Both Charles and Paul introduced me to the neoclassical architecture of Cuba. Paul Niell read and commented on an earlier draft of chapter 4, and it is much improved as a result of his input.

Learning about coffee culture was an important aspect of this research and, at times, became an obsession for me. My understanding of nineteenth-century coffee production was greatly enhanced by my observing all phases of coffee production and processing at present-day farms and processing facilities. My deep gratitude goes to Victor Camilo Bencosme, a resident of the Dominican Republic, who contributed to my thinking about this project in many ways. His enthusiasm for it sometimes overshadowed my own. In the Dominican Republic, he took me to coffee farms, coffee factories, and coffee fairs. He even persuaded his Dominican relatives in San Juan, Puerto Rico, to take me to visit a coffee plantation near

Ponce. He has been a very devoted friend and companion from whom I have learned a great deal about the Spanish Antilles as a whole. I hope we will one day be able to travel to Cuba together to visit Cafetal Biajacas.

On another personal note, I gratefully acknowledge the two Cuban families who welcomed me into their homes and with whom I developed strong friendships. In Havana, I extend warmest appreciation to Frances Séra and her husband, Arsenio, and to their family members Judith, Isbeth, Getrudis, Javier, Osvaldo, and recent additions. At the site of the coffee plantation, I offer equally earnest thanks to Consuelo and Ismael and to their daughter, Aleida, and her husband, Francisco, who completely opened their homes to our team. We camped near their houses, and they let us use their homes to shower, cook, watch television, and play dominos until the early morning hours. I thank Francisco for working with us every season in the field research, and I thank Orestes, Aleida, Yarita, and Yeny for assisting us in many ways that made our field experience enjoyable.

Special appreciation goes to Genaro Vidal, whom we met on our second visit to the cafetal. He grew up around the ruins of the site, and provided us with his recollections of them, particularly the locations of plantation buildings that have since been razed. He has passed away but will always be remembered for his interest in the archaeological work at Cafetal Biajacas. I enjoyed his site visits and learned a great deal from him about the afterlife of Cafetal Biajacas.

As for my own family, I thank them for their support and especially for their understanding my missing Christmas holidays beginning in 2002, when the team began doing December field research during my semester breaks. Of all my family members, my sister Rosalind, both my greatest cheerleader and my harshest critic, was most interested in this project. I truly regret that I did not complete it before her untimely death in 2009. Yet in large part, it was her death that made me realize that the time had finally come to bring this project to closure.

Preparing the computer-drawn illustrations and photographs for this manuscript was a major undertaking and, I appreciate Joseph Stoll of Syracuse University's Cartographic Laboratory for developing the final drawings of maps and for creating many of the illustrations. I greatly appreciate his patience with me and his putting up with my constant revisions. I am also very grateful to David Broda of the Syracuse University Photo and

Imaging Center, who scanned countless slides and other images related to this project.

The writing of this book has taken considerably longer than I anticipated. There were many false starts. I often felt paralyzed, unable to think and write about the project because I had so few artifacts, postholes that did not make sense to me, and a massive wall that enclosed the slave houses. My insecurity about the research, unfortunately, was often reinforced in scholarly encounters at conferences and invited lectures. I kept telling myself for years that I needed to do more research, conduct more fieldwork, find additional written sources. When these were no longer options, I finally came to realize that there was a lot I could say about one, but the most spectacular, artifact at Cafetal Biajacas—the massive wall—and how it might be related to the paucity of artifacts, even to the postholes that made little sense. This has been a long journey for me, full of challenges, self-doubts, and small successes. But it is a journey I will always cherish for the many things it taught me. I thank everyone who played a role in nurturing the project and bringing this book to fruition.

1

Introduction

The Object World of Cuban Slavery

Cuban historian and economist Ramiro Guerra Sánchez titled his memoir of the former coffee plantation Jesús Nazareno *Mudos testigos* [Silent Witnesses]. This referred to the still-living fruit trees—mangos, zapotes, and mamoncillos [Spanish lime]—presumably planted when the coffee plantation was established. These trees can grow to be quite large and live over a century. Guerra estimated that the trees were between 120 and 130 years old, possibly older, at the time he wrote his account in the 1940s.

When Jesús Nazareno, located east of Batabanó near the south coast of Mayabeque province, was in operation, fruit and other trees lined the *guardarrayas* [avenues and footpaths in between rows of coffee trees] providing shade and protection to coffee shrubs and beautifying the plantation. For Guerra ([1948] 1974:28), the trees epitomized the former beauty and grandeur of the Cuban *cafetal* [coffee plantation] and formed the most important tangible vestiges of the former plantation. The longevity of the trees, Guerra reasoned, made them capable of witnessing everything that had occurred at Jesús Nazareno since its establishment in the early 1800s. Thus they provided a testament to the richness of the land and, by extension, the richness of the history.

Had Guerra been an archaeologist, he might have considered the standing ruins and buried remains at Jesús Nazareno significant vestiges capable of providing information on past activities. Guerra ([1948] 1974:51–53) described the buildings, but he considered the trees to be far more significant.

Archaeological remains, and even the trees, are not merely silent testaments to the past; they were once active parts of it. They are the residue of things—from built landscapes to beads—produced, consumed, abandoned, or discarded by the people who lived and worked at these places. Archaeologist Ian Hodder has argued persuasively for more than three decades that "material culture does not just exist. It is made by someone. It is produced to do something. Therefore, it does not passively *reflect* society; it creates society through the acts of social agents" (Hodder and Hutson 2004:6). Artifacts are human constructs that inform us on many aspects of social life. Their significance, however, is neither inherent nor universal but socially constructed. Thus objects can be perceived in many ways depending on their context. Sometimes they are taken-for-granted tools used in everyday tasks; at other times they are manipulated into powerful or evocative symbols. In these and other cases, artifacts are integral to society.

Over the years, archaeologists as students of material culture have variously applied, debated, and refined their approaches to understanding the roles that objects play in social life. Some archaeologists, following the long-standing anthropological interest in exchange and trade, view objects as commodities, emphasizing the production, consumption, or exchange of such items. Others focus on how stylistic or utilitarian attributes of objects are used to meet specific economic or social needs. Still others emphasize the ways objects are imbued with socially constructed meanings that are deployed in diverse cultural expressions. Proponents of materiality urge archaeologists to combine these foci into broader analyses of the interrelationships of objects and people. Approaches to materiality are concerned with the characteristics of objects and how people engage with the objects and are shaped by those experiences (DeMarrais, Gosden, and Renfrew 2005:2). Simply put, materiality examines the effect of objects upon the people who use them. Lynn Meskell (2005:7) identifies several ways to begin archaeological analyses of materiality that include looking at the object world in archaeological and historical contexts, tracing the biographies of things and examining the deployment of objects in historical and contemporary practice. With the goal of contributing to the archaeologies of the African diaspora and of plantations, the following study combines analyses of object characteristics, traces the biographies of select objects, and examines the deployment of imbued objects to understand the object world of slavery on nineteenth-century Cuban coffee plantations.

Framing a Study around a Wall

A massive masonry wall built around a settlement of detached slave houses, known as *bohíos*, is the primary artifact under investigation in this study.[1] Located at the site of the former coffee plantation Santa Ana de Biajacas, the wall measures 11 feet high, 27.5 inches thick, and encloses an area of 1.7 acres. From the first day I visited the plantation site in November 1998, the wall intrigued me. As a student of slavery in North America, I had never read of slaveholders containing enslaved people in such a way, if, indeed, that was the primary purpose of the wall. From that day onward, I found myself pondering several questions: Was the wall built to keep the workers in? To keep others out? Or both? Did it serve purposes other than restricting slave movement? What was life like for the people living inside the enclosure? How did they respond to living within it? What did building such an imposing wall convey about the master-slave relationship at this particular plantation? And about the larger slave society of which Cafetal Biajacas was a part? These questions inspired my research, frame this study, and inform the themes of several chapters.

Although these are simple, straightforward questions, investigating them has proved quite challenging because the wall enclosure at Cafetal Biajacas appears to be an anomaly among the ruins of Cuban plantations. Moreover, the practice of enclosing detached slave houses within a wall was not a customary way of housing laborers, although this practice is described in an ordinance and alluded to in other nineteenth-century documents. These documentary sources indicate that the primary purpose of such walls was to contain slave laborers at night to prevent them from running away or from leaving the plantation to engage in activities unauthorized by slaveholders. While this explanation satisfied my initial presumption about the wall, it belies two unanswered questions. Why did the owner of Cafetal Biajacas not build walls around the slave houses at his sugar plantations, particularly at the one located only a few miles away, where the workers also lived in bohíos? If restricting slave movement was the primary purpose of the wall, why did so few slaveholders in Cuba choose this option to house slave workers when nocturnal departures and running away from the plantation were frequently voiced planter concerns? These questions point to the need to consider additional factors for why the wall was built and how it was used and perceived.

Archaeologists have increasingly questioned interpretations based solely upon presumed functions of artifacts, because such interpretations often obscure how objects are used as cultural expressions or are manipulated in social relations. A plethora of studies have examined symbolic use and multiple meanings of objects, but two have been particularly useful to me, both in developing my interpretation of the wall and in organizing this narrative. They are Ian Hodder's (2006) *The Leopard's Tale: Revealing the Mysteries of Çatalhöyük* and Patricia Samford's (2007) *Subfloor Pits and the Archaeology of Slavery in Colonial Virginia*. These vastly different studies, one based in Neolithic Turkey and the other in eighteenth-century Virginia, share the common goal of framing their investigations and analyses around a puzzle.

In *The Leopard's Tale*, Hodder's puzzle concerns the frequent depiction of leopards (or other wild cats and wild animals) in paintings and relief art and the absence of bones from these animals at the site of Çatalhöyük. In the process of his investigation, Hodder (2006:13) provides a thought-provoking account of life in this remarkably well-preserved Neolithic town. Using ethnographic analogies, Hodder unravels the values, taboos, and restrictions he proposes were part of "an elaborate symbolic world" of the site's inhabitants.

In a similar vein, the puzzle of the wall enclosure frames my study, but the investigation reveals various ways elite Cuban planters used the built environment to create showplaces and impose a hierarchical social order while controlling slave laborers by employing either one of two ways of housing them: bohíos [detached houses] or *barracones* [multiunit quarters].

Cuban slaveholders debated which of the two forms of housing was preferable for controlling workers. Advocates for bohíos reasoned that these slave-built detached houses promoted family formation, independent production, and the acquisition of personal property—incentives that could potentially reduce slave rebelliousness. On the other hand, slaveholders favoring barracones believed these buildings prevented workers from leaving their quarters at night, which in turn suppressed rebelliousness. Enslaved laborers in Cuba had their own vision for their quarters. They built crop storage areas for their own produce in both forms of housing and made their living areas private places where they prepared and consumed food and beverages they shared with others as well as participated in social and religious activities.

Patricia Samford's study examines subfloor pits—holes dug below the floor boards of slave houses in Virginia. These features have puzzled archaeologists for decades, and various proposals have been offered as to how they were used for the storage of food, personal items, or pilfered goods. Through a detailed analysis of 103 pits, in which she carefully recorded location, size, and contents, Samford suggests that some pits were used as spiritual spaces—shrines devoted to the ancestors. Her study inspired me to look beyond what appears as the obvious function of the wall enclosure—containment of enslaved workers—to consider additional possibilities.

Both Hodder's and Samford's studies have their strengths and weaknesses, but they challenge archaeologists to broaden the scope of how to think about objects and to consider various interpretative possibilities for them. In this study, I argue that the wall enclosure served as more than a functional device to control slave movement. It fulfilled a powerful symbolic role, perhaps even an aesthetic one, but it became a source of conflict and compromise between the enslaver and the enslaved. Without a doubt, the wall succeeded in obstructing some slave activities, but it also appears, rather unexpectedly, to have facilitated others.

Analyzing the dialectical relationship between the slaveholder and slave workers at Cafetal Biajacas is the broad theme of this study. Most studies of slavery examine some aspect of the dialectical relationship between the enslaver and the enslaved. Archaeologist Randall McGuire (2007:74) explains in the dialectic the entities that make up the whole of society are not expected to fit comfortably; instead, they lie in relational contradictions because they emerged from the fact social categories are defined by and require the existence of their opposites. Slavery, for example, defines both slaveholders and the enslaved, and both are necessary for slavery to exist, yet they are opposites.

Georg W. F. Hegel coined the concept "master-slave dialectic" (also translated as "lordship and bondage") in *The Phenomenology of Mind*, published in 1807. Through an allegorical narrative, Hegel describes the encounter of two self-conscious individuals who engage in "a struggle to death" until one enslaves the other. The enslaver, now dependent upon the enslaved person for his or her livelihood, produces nothing. The enslaved person produces something of value, but the master owns it; however, through his or her work, the enslaved person acquires knowledge of nature that the master cannot achieve. Thus the master's control of the enslaved can never be absolute or complete. Hegel's insight into the limitations of the master's control over the enslaved figured in subsequent analyses of power relations. Karl Marx and other social thinkers extrapolated and expanded upon Hegel's dialectic to analyze a variety of asymmetrical social relations, particularly class struggles. With the rise of studies on planter hegemony, slave resistance, and relations of power, the master-slave dialectic acquired increased prominence in slavery studies of the Americas. Some scholars emphasized the conflictive character of this social relation while others emphasized the compromising character of it (Morris 1998:983).

Hegelian scholars claim, however, that Hegel drew his understanding of slavery from the ancient Greek philosophers, most notably Aristotle. But revisionist scholarship suggests Hegel's dialectic may be more applicable to slavery in the Americas than previously thought (Buck-Morss 2009:48–50; Fischer 2004:24–33). Susan Buck-Morss (2009:42–48) posits that Hegel's reference to slavery was taken from current events—the slave rebellion on Saint-Domingue (Haiti)—rather than slavery in the classical world. She suggests Hegel followed the unfolding events of the Haitian Revolution (1791–1804) in the German publication *Minerva*, a political periodical that all German intellectuals would have read. The journal featured periodic updates on the slave rebellion, and when Hegel wrote *Phenomenology* in 1805 and 1806, it was Haiti's first year as a new nation. Considering the impact of that revolution on slavery in the Americas, and on Cuba in particular, the revisionist scholarship on Hegel's master-slave dialectic presents an opportunity to reconsider its application in an archaeological study of Caribbean slavery.

Like all social theories, the Hegelian dialectic has been subjected to critique from various perspectives (Fischer 2004:24–33). When applied to archaeological studies, however, it offers a way of seeing the world and thinking about how material culture can be used to interpret it (McGuire [1992] 2002:93). Because the Hegelian dialectic makes social relations the key to studying society, it provides insights into the ways in which material culture is used to "establish, mediate, or disrupt" these relations (Demarrais, Gosden, and Renfrew 2005:2). This dialectical analysis aims to understand the roles plantation space, slave living conditions, and cultural practices played in the struggles and negotiations between enslavers and the enslaved. The wall enclosure, as a multivalent artifact, serves as the point of entry for analyzing these conflicts, particularly the opposing meanings and usages of the wall for both enslaver and enslaved.

The slaveholder used the wall for at least two purposes: first, to control slave movement while keeping outsiders out, and, second, as a way to distance and "other" enslaved people, that is, to reinforce their subservient status. In all slave societies, fear of slave flight and rebellion motivated slaveholders to restrict slave movement. The laws, policies, and practices implemented to check slave mobility have been broadly referred to as "geographies of containment" (Camp 2004:6), and the wall enclosure provides an example of this form of containment executed in the built environment. Othering, another slaveholder practice frequently executed in the built environment, is well documented for many North American settings (Ellis and Ginsburg 2010) but heretofore not interpreted on Cuban plantations. Enslaved workers at Cafetal Biajacas subverted the slaveholder efforts to restrict their movement and to subjugate them by creating "rival geographies" (Camp 2004:7), spaces where they socialized and possibly concealed activities such as gambling, imbibing, harboring slave runaways, or practicing their African religions.

Central to this work is the analysis of plantation space. Space is becoming an important analytical framework in slavery studies, prompting a historian of the southern United States to write, "Space mattered: places, boundaries, and movement were central to how slavery was organized and to how it was resisted" (Camp 2004:6). Slavery in the Americas has always been examined within defined geographic parameters, but the current spatial trend utilizes concepts of social space (Bourdieu 1985:723–24; Lefebvre 1991:73–92) to examine how slaveholders, slave workers, and others imagined, made, and used space to attain both similar and competing goals. In slavery studies, space has formed the context for the examination of gender, class conflicts, social networks, and resistance, among other topics.

Archaeology contributes to the analysis of social space through the investigation of tangible sites once occupied by plantation residents, bridging the enormous gap between how spaces were imagined, particularly in elite ideologies, and how they were actually lived. James Delle (1998) pioneered this type of inquiry by using archaeological, cartographical, and written sources to examine the relationships between intended design of space and the actual use of space at three Jamaican coffee plantations. His study focuses on how plantation spaces were negotiated during slavery and redefined after emancipation. This analysis of plantation space builds upon Delle's work and examines how plantation spaces were imagined, created, consumed, and lived from the vantage points of planters, visitors, and enslaved workers on Cuban coffee plantations.

Through the deployment of neoclassical architecture and landscape design, Cuban planters envisioned their plantations as earthly paradises with beautiful gardens, guardarrayas, orchards, grand avenues leading to great houses, and commanding vistas of the surrounding area. Coffee plantations became renowned for their beauty, and for many travelers to Cuba, visiting a cafetal was an obligatory destination. Travel diaries often support that the intended design of Cuban planters was actually implemented.

Evidence for how enslaved Cubans perceived these landscapes is unfortunately more limited and requires some degree of speculation. Juan Manzano, who wrote the only known Cuban slave narrative, recounted two horrific incidences on a coffee plantation in which he referenced designated plantation spaces. Additional slave perspectives are inferred from archaeological remains in conjunction with a variety of documentary sources: planter correspondence, travel diaries, and reports from the Spanish colonial officials. Through the careful reading of these sources, insights are gained as to how enslaved workers appropriated and reinterpreted planter-dominated spaces and created spaces of their own.

Slave resistance is a significant theme of this work. Many archaeologists embrace James C. Scott's (1985, 1990) broad conception of resistance, which can range from individual transgressions to organized revolts. Everyday practices, as Michel de Certeau (1988:xix) asserts, are "tactical in character" and are ways the subjugated become victorious over the dominant. These everyday maneuvers were pervasive in enslaved peoples' lives, and enslaved Cubans, like oppressed peoples elsewhere, exercised notions of *power* to challenge the authority of slaveholders and their emissaries in many different ways.

Until quite recently, the historiography of Cuban slavery has devoted more attention to organized and overt forms of slave resistance—conspiracies, revolts, and marronage (processes of slave flight, self-liberation, and survival)—than to subtle forms of protest. Manuel Barcia (2008:7) traces this tendency to the political discourse of revolutionary Cuba (post-1959), which encouraged studies of marronage and slave revolts, analogously linking Cuban revolutionaries to slave rebels, who fought against their masters for over 400 years of colonial domination. Struggle and resistance are also prominent themes extended to the public interpretation of Cuban pre-Columbian archaeology (Berman, Febles, and Gnivecki 2005:48) and in archaeology of the African diaspora (Singleton and Torres de Souza 2009:465). Barcia has undertaken the first study of Cuban slavery to evaluate the wide range of slave resistance in Cuba from violent to disguised, nonviolent forms. These various forms of resistance are examined in this work, and whenever possible, the role of material culture in acts of resistance is considered.

Certainly there was more to slavery than power struggles. Numerous archaeological studies over the four past decades have investigated a variety of themes: identity formation, crafting activities, culinary practices, use of domestic space, religious beliefs, and household production and exchange. Relations of power, however, should not be overlooked in analyzing these and other aspects of slave life. Many slaveholders intruded upon and attempted to control most aspects of enslaved peoples' lives, and it is rather naïve to suggest otherwise. The Cuban slaveholder discourse on managing enslaved people went beyond debates about providing food, clothing, and shelter. Like slaveholders elsewhere in the Americas, Cuban planters exerted their control in family formation, child rearing, and many aspects of everyday life. Although they were often unsuccessful in their efforts to repress slave activities, their domination was always a potential obstruction to slave action.

Planter domination is often overlooked in archaeological studies of slave household economy. The increased emphasis on the ability of enslaved peoples to acquire personal and household items via trade often diminishes the tremendously oppressive conditions under which these activities took place. The fact that they were able to produce goods for sale, participate in various venues of exchange, and accumulate money or non-real property is truly remarkable in a system of chattel slavery. Slave independent production and trade, pursued with or without the permission of slaveholders, point to contradictions within slave societies. A dialectical approach to study of slavery allows us to evaluate areas of compromise and conflict between enslavers and enslaved in this and other realms of activity.

Cuban planters encouraged independent production, but some unscrupulous planters and managers found ways to exploit and benefit from this modicum of opportunity granted to enslaved workers. Any analysis of slave independent or own-account production and exchange should consider the circumstances under which these activities took place as well as the advantages and disadvantages for both enslaver and enslaved. When considered from the perspective of the master-slave dialectic, the outcome for enslaved people may not appear as beneficial as many studies assume.

Like all archaeological studies of slavery, this work contributes to our understanding of quotidian or everyday life in the quarters. This is one of the few archaeological studies of a Cuban plantation that focuses primarily on slave activities and material life. The archaeological study of Cuban plantations dates to the 1960s, if not earlier, around the same time similar research began in the United States. But, with a few exceptions, most of the Cuban research has emphasized the study of standing ruins of plantation buildings with minimal excavations (Bernard Bosch, Blanco Conde, and Rives Pantoja 1985; Domínguez 1986, Domínguez González 1991). While these excavations yielded artifacts related to slave life, the question of how workers lived was secondary to the recovery of detailed information on the construction of their living quarters and other plantation buildings.

Archaeological research at the site of Cafetal Biajacas provides the most extensive excavations conducted at slave settlements in recent times. What stands out at this site is the relatively small quantity of household objects (considering the amount of excavations) as well as the significant amount of artifact recycling—from sugar molds to tobacco pipe bowls. These findings suggest enslaved Cubans had considerably less access to trade than other slave societies investigated in the Americas. Could the wall enclosure have played a role in restricting slave access to trade? Planters sought to prevent workers from leaving plantations at night to exchange goods at nearby taverns and shops. Although planters were unsuccessful in eliminating this so-called clandestine trade, the wall enclosure and similar buildings that were locked at night may have reduced it.

As an examination of enslaved Africans and their descendants in the

Americas, this study contributes to the archaeology of the African diaspora. The African heritages of enslaved peoples in the Americas constituted vital sources for the creation of the cultural lives of enslaved peoples. Uncovering archaeological evidence of African influences in the material culture of slavery has been an important objective since the inception of this research. But, as many other efforts have encountered, the interpretation of African-influenced practices from archaeological sources of enslaved peoples has proven quite challenging, and this study is no exception.

Archaeologists in the southern United States have increasingly recovered discrete deposits of artifacts in and around the living areas of enslaved peoples that are often identified with the religious practices of various African cultural groups. These intentional caches of artifacts are sometimes compared with the *prendas* [religious altars] of Congo-Cuban religion (Brown and Cooper 1990; Fennell 2007). But no discrete deposits containing objects associated with prendas were recovered from Cafetal Biajacas, and such finds appear to be rare on Caribbean plantations in general. At other Cuban sites, however, presumed African-derived religious artifacts have been found in Cuban slave burials (Domínguez 1999) and in caves once occupied by slave runaways (Garcell Domínguez 2009; Hernández de Lara, Rodríguez Tápanes, Arredondo Antúnez 2012:105–6).

Although the assemblage at Cafetal Biajacas did not yield clear evidence of religious practices, objects like the machete—an indispensable tool for agricultural work—were highly symbolic and imbued with multiple meanings among Afro-Cubans. The recovery of a sizable number of machetes within the wall enclosure could point to the religiosity as well as to the resistance of the enslaved laborers at Cafetal Biajacas.

Another way in which an African heritage may have influenced the material culture at Cafetal Biajacas is in the construction of slave-built bohíos, light-frame, thatched roofed houses, that appear to have been constructed according to the preferences of the slave residents. The bohío, however, is an amalgam of cultural traditions. Both the term and its emergence in the Antilles originated from indigenous Americans. Later, Africans and Europeans appropriated and modified it to suit their needs. Cuban scholars (García Santana 2000:12; Roura Álvarez and Angelbello Izquierdo 2007:137) recognize the bohío as a product of transculturation—a process of interaction among diverse cultural traditions—resulting in its transformation over the past five centuries. But specific African contributions to this house form have only been nominally considered in Cuba.

Other examples of African-influenced material culture come from written rather than archaeological sources examined for this study. These sources suggest that enslaved Cubans made extensive use of highly perishable materials (that do not persist in the archaeological record) to make items similar to those used in Africa: the use of gourds for household utensils and musical instruments; seeds strung together as jewelry; palm leaves twisted into basketry and hats. The paucity of ceramic and glass objects recovered from excavations at the slave settlement of Cafetal Biajacas may in fact be related to a greater reliance upon, perhaps even a preference for, these highly perishable materials for making personal objects.

The findings and interpretations offered in this book raise questions: How representative is the single case study of the larger society for which it is a part? And at what spatial scale of analysis is this study directed? I have struggled with these questions from the very beginning and made concerted efforts to examine other plantations in the general vicinity of Cafetal Biajacas. This is not just an analysis of one isolated plantation. It examines the larger area of coffee plantations located on the rolling lowlands of western Cuba, with special reference to the area east of Havana and west of the city of Cárdenas in Matanzas province (figure 1.1). This is the area Fredrika Bremer (1853:2:387) referred to as the "paradisiacal regions of the Caffetal to the east of Havana" during her trip to Cuba.

Cafetal Biajacas and neighboring plantations were part of Matanzas jurisdiction prior to 1878 when the island was subdivided into provinces for the first time. This area attracted many North American settlers and visitors whose correspondence and unpublished diaries located in archives in the United States supply underutilized resources on Cuban slavery. These primary sources along with Laird Bergad's economic history of Matanzas suggest it was different from other coffee producing areas of Cuba and the Caribbean. For example, Bergad (1990:34) found that in some districts of Matanzas, larger numbers of workers were utilized on coffee plantations than on sugar plantations, which goes against the general assumption that sugar required greater labor demands than coffee. My analysis supports his claim and offers reasons to account for this more intensive use of labor

Figure 1.1. Area of western Cuba examined in this work. Depicts locations of cities, towns, plantations, and nineteenth-century districts within present-day provinces. Drawn by Syracuse University Cartographic Laboratory.

in the grassy plains of Matanzas compared with the highlands of eastern Cuba or on other Caribbean islands. The soil and topography in Matanzas, while ideal for sugar production, required planting considerably more coffee trees to produce coffee yields comparable to trees planted at higher elevations. More significantly, limited water resources compelled planters to apply laborious dry methods of coffee processing. These practices therefore demanded more laborers than typically found on coffee plantations elsewhere in the Caribbean.

Whenever possible, coffee production and slavery are examined from a hemispheric perspective in which local developments are compared and contrasted to broad global patterns. But this is primarily a study in microhistory. Microhistory is defined in so many ways that some proponents for it claim it lacks a precise definition (Brooks, DeCorse, and Walton 2008:4–6). In this work, I follow the methodological definition for microhistory, "a meticulous layering of disparate sources concerning the same people," proposed by historians of Cuba Louis A. Pérez Jr., and Rebecca Scott (2003:vii). Archaeological findings are layered with diverse documentary sources in order to illuminate the lives of the people who were forced to live behind a wall at Cafetal Biajacas. Yet, despite the wall, this study demonstrates that Cafetal Biajacas had much in common with nearby coffee plantations with similar slaveholdings whose owners belonged to the planter elite.

Archaeological Study of Cuban Slavery and Plantations

Like plantation archaeology in the United States, the first archaeological studies of Cuban plantations sought architectural restoration of the buildings and grounds. Fernando Boytel Jambú (1961:29–30) recounted how he began his initial study of La Isabelica, a nineteenth-century French-owned coffee plantation outside of the city of Santiago, in 1930. In 1959, a few days after the victory of the Cuban revolutionaries, efforts began to restore the site and develop it into a plantation museum. The museum is still in operation today, and La Isabelica lies within the UNESCO World Heritage site entitled Archaeological Landscape of the First Coffee Plantations in Southeast Cuba, in the provinces of Santiago de Cuba and Guantánamo. Other archaeological investigations of plantations predated the Cuban Revolution, but little seems to be known today about them.[2]

Manuel Moreno Fraginals, in his classic study, *El Ingenio: complejo económico social cubano del azúcar*, briefly refers to the excavations of Cuban archaeologist Rudolfo Payarés Suárez at coffee and sugar plantations in the former province of Havana (now Artemisa and Mayabeque provinces, see figure 1.1). Moreno Fraginals (1978:2:30n34) noted that numerous tools were recovered, particularly machetes that were twice as heavy as those of today. Payarés also worked alongside Ernesto Tabío, a prominent archaeologist of Cuban prehistory, on a survey of coffee plantations in the Sierra del Rosarios in Pinar del Río, the westernmost province of Cuba. They located, identified, and recorded 17 cafetales, and their report contains valuable descriptions, maps, and detailed drawings of select ruins (Tabío and Payarés 1968). In the late 1970s, Payarés undertook some archaeological work at Triunvirato, a sugar plantation in Matanzas province and the center of a major slave rebellion in 1843 that is remembered today by a monument to the slave rebels (Barcia 2012:7; Hernández de Lara, Rodríguez Tápanes, and Arredondo Antúnez 2012:32, 42).

In 1970, the Cuban Academy of Sciences investigated Ingenio Taoro, a sugar plantation in Cangrejeras, a town located within La Habana, the province of the city of Havana. Excavations focused on a slave cemetery, the first investigation of this kind in Cuba and possibly in the Caribbean as whole (Domínguez 2005:62). Limited excavation was also undertaken in the *patio* of a large barracón that may have housed as many as 224 slave laborers plus Chinese indentured laborers and other plantation personnel totaling approximately 300 residents within this huge building (Domínguez 1986:276).

Study of La Manuela, a coffee plantation near Ramiro Guerra's Jesús Nazareno, began as an effort to determine if the site's ruins were those of a cafetal and to establish the name and owners of it (Bernard Bosch, Blanco Conde, and Rives Pantoja 1985:4–9). Consequently, the project developed more as an archaeology of archives rather than field archaeology. Published in 1985, *La Manuela: Arqueología de un cafetal habanero* is one of the first monographs on a specific Cuban plantation containing archaeological data. Although the field investigations consisted primarily of collecting information on extant ruins, La Manuela is an important case study because it was one of the largest coffee plantations in what is now Mayabeque province. With over 160 enslaved laborers (Bernard Bosch, Blanco Conde, and Rives Pantoja 1985:117), La Manuela employed nearly twice as many workers as most coffee plantations in this region.

Since investigations began at Cafetal Biajacas in 1999, Cuban archaeologists have explored several plantations in central and western Cuba. From 1999 to 2007, Silvia T. Angelbello Izquierdo conducted a study of San Isidro de los Destiladeros in the Valle de los Ingenios [Valley of the Sugar Mills], a major sugar-producing district of central Cuba of the nineteenth century located near the town of Trinidad founded in the sixteenth century (Roura Álvarez 2006:212). Together, Trinidad and Valle de los Ingenios form a UNESCO World Heritage site (Scarpaci and Portela 2009:90–95). Angelbello Izquierdo directed her investigation toward rediscovering the original spatial organization and subsequent modifications made to San Isidro during its transformation from the use of a *trapiche* [an animal-powered sugar mill] to a steam-powered mill. In addition to the examination of the industrial complex, excavations unearthed the foundations of a long, narrow barracón, sometimes referred to as a *nave*.

In 2006, el Castillo de San Severino Museo de la Ruta del Esclavo [San

Severino Fort Slave Route Museum] in the city of Matanzas sponsored archaeological testing of La Dionesia, a cafetal established by French immigrants around 1820 (Hernández de Lara 2010). Located in the Canímar valley of Matanzas Province, La Dionesia lies within an area selected for the creation of a national park opened to public visitation, particularly for the promotion of tourism. The archaeological research involved mapping, study of extant ruins, surface collecting, and subsurface testing to identify the locations of structures lacking aboveground ruins, including the barracones, coffee dryers, and plantation bell. No structural remains of the barracones were identified, but artifacts associated with slavery, such as slave shackles, were recovered.

Gabino La Rosa Corzo, renowned for his studies of *cimarrones* [slave runaways], conducted historical and archaeological testing at coffee plantations such as Santa Brigada (shown in figure 2.1) near Cafetal Biajacas in the 1980s. In 2009, he undertook field research at Angerona, the best known and reputedly the largest coffee plantation in all of Cuba. Cornelio Souchay, a German immigrant, established the plantation located southwest of Havana near the town of Artemisa in 1813 (La Rosa 2012:16). Most of the archaeological work focused on the slave settlement, which from a purely visual inspection resembles the wall enclosure at Cafetal Biajacas (Singleton 2001:103). La Rosa identified three construction phases of the slave settlement, an observation which corrects much of the misinformation and speculation of the site.

Lisette Roura Álvarez, a member of the project team for Cafetal Biajacas, is undertaking an ongoing project in the Sierras del Rosarios (west of Angerona) at Cafetal San Pedro. She has completed three field seasons and her investigations have focused on the great house and a nearby service building.

Plantation archaeology has figured prominently in Cuban historical archaeology (defined here as the archaeology of the modern world), and specific findings from the studies summarized above are discussed throughout this work. Although the objectives of Cuban plantation archaeology have varied widely, Cuban archaeologists often see the study of plantations as industrial archaeology. This perspective is perhaps due to the strong influence of historical materialism—a Marxist theory that privileges economics as the driving force in the ways societies are organized and in development of all forms of social thought. Historical materialism has been particularly influential in the pre-Columbian archaeology of revolutionary Cuba (Davis 1996:168). Cuban plantation archaeology tends to emphasize the economic and technological development of plantations rather than the lives of plantation residents. While projects in industrial archaeology increasingly focus on the study of the people associated with industries (Casella and Symonds 2005), industrial archaeology often emphasizes technological development, the economics of industries, or industrial landscapes rather than the laborers (Shackel 2011:2).

My research at Cafetal Biajacas, however, was undertaken as part of "el projecto etnia Afrocubana" [the Afro-Cuban ethnicity project] with the Gabinete de Arqueología, Office of the Historian for the city of Havana. The project aimed to study Afro-Cuban culture through archaeology, and so the investigation of slavery at Cafetal Biajacas was framed within the archaeological study of the African diaspora and not within industrial archaeology.

Researching Santa Ana de Biajacas

The research undertaken on Cafetal Biajacas combines archaeological investigations with the study of diverse historical sources including maps, a variety of records created by Spanish colonial officials in Cuba, voluminous estate records generated over a 15-year period (1838–53) of administrating the estate after the owner's death in 1838, correspondence and other documents of North American coffee planters, and travel diaries. Archaeological investigations undertaken from 1999 to 2009 consisted of surveys and mapping, geophysical prospecting, excavations of more than 473 1 m × 1 m units along with uncovering the foundations of a service building (possibly a kitchen), and limited excavation within the ruins of the great house. The archaeological fieldwork is examined at length in discussions of specific loci within the plantation.

The historical research unfolded just as slowly as the archaeological study and followed a somewhat circuitous route. After the first field season established that archaeological evidence of slave quarters and artifacts of the cafetal era was recoverable from within the wall enclosure, a historian joined the project and undertook archival research on Cafetal Biajacas between 2000 and 2002. She located the estate records mentioned above and other primary sources on the cafetal and Cuban coffee production in general. For the most part, account books or other records kept by planters and managers of Cuban plantations during the first half of the nineteenth century have not survived to the present. While the estate records contained a great deal of information about the plantation, they only documented the last eight years, 1838–46. Therefore, it was necessary to find a way to work backward from this well-documented period. A few earlier, but sporadic, documents on Cafetal Biajacas did help to fill in some gaps. Inferences were also drawn from records of other coffee plantations in nearby districts, particularly those owned by North American planters.

After a review of the primary sources on Cafetal Biajacas and those of North American planters, I conducted archival research at the Archivo Nacional of Cuba (ANC) in Havana in 2006 and 2007 to gather information on slavery during the first half of the nineteenth century, keeping an eye out for specific references to slave housing, provisioning, slave independent production, and slave resistance. For several years during the course of this project, the Archivo Histórico Provincial de Matanzas (AHPM) was closed, and when it reopened, I undertook research there in 2009. My goal was to gather information on slavery in the vicinity of Cafetal Biajacas, and I found records concerning slave runaways, but many of the records I wanted to examine were unavailable.[3] A final trip to the Cuban archives planned for 2011 was cancelled when my request for a research visa was denied. This forced me to work with historical research already undertaken and rely more on published primary and secondary sources than I originally planned. But in the end, these resources exceeded my expectations in pursuing the research objectives for this study.

Despite considerable archival research, I still lacked descriptive information on many material aspects of plantation life to ground my interpretations of the archaeological data. For this kind of information I turned to travel diaries. Because of Cuba's location at the crossroads of principal sea lanes of the Caribbean Sea and the Gulf of Mexico, Cuba became a well-visited destination for travelers during the nineteenth century when travel literature was at its peak (Pérez 1992:xxv–xxvi). Consequently, the travel literature on Cuba is very rich and, in spite of the characteristic flaws of travel writing, Cuban travelogues often describe aspects of material culture not found in any other written sources (Sarmiento Ramírez 2006:304–14).

Piecing together these disparate historical sources with the archaeological findings proved challenging, but it was necessary to tell the story of the people who lived behind the wall. Archaeological and historical research contributed equally to this project and, in most cases, complemented each other. Archaeological interest brought attention to the site, and archaeological research yielded data on the lives of the enslaved laborers that could not be found in any written source. On the other hand, the historical research provided information on the composition of the enslaved community at Cafetal Biajacas, and on some of their actions that are not recoverable from archaeology. In this respect, this study in historical archaeology is entirely interdisciplinary.

This book is organized into nine chapters. This chapter presents the research questions, theoretical and analytical premises, and background of the research project at Cafetal Biajacas. Chapter 2 briefly describes the historical and environmental setting of Cafetal Biajacas, focusing on the Spanish colonial period (1511–1898) and on the owner of the coffee plantation, Ignacio O'Farrill y Herrera, his family, and his other plantations. Chapter 3 describes the nineteenth-century coffee economy of western Cuba and examines Cuban coffee production, planters, and the circumstances that led to the downfall of Cuban coffee. Chapter 4 delves into the spatial practices implemented in the built landscape of many Cuban coffee plantations and explores how the built landscape was used to subjugate enslaved Cubans physically as well as symbolically. Using both archaeological data and documentary sources, I propose a reconstruction of the central plantation settlement, known as the *batey* in Cuba, for Cafetal Biajacas. Chapter 5 traces the origin of the two categories of slave housing used on Cuban plantations and the planter discourse for using each type. This discussion provides the backdrop for interpreting the wall enclosure as an approach to slave housing that combined elements of both categories of slave housing.

The ethnic and gender composition of the enslaved residents at the plantation and the various ways they were provisioned are discussed in chapter 6. Chapter 7 presents the interpretation of the quotidian life and cultural practices of the enslaved residents based on analyses of artifacts recovered from the enclosure. In chapter 8, the slave resistance at Cafetal

Biajacas informs evaluation of the master-slave relationship at the cafetal and offers general insight into the kinds of slave actions Cuban slaveholders tolerated and those they did not. Concluding the book, chapter 9 discusses the broad implications of this case study beyond western Cuba while affirming its specific contribution to local Cuban archaeology and heritage.

2

Locating Cafetal Biajacas

In 1829, Ignacio O'Farrill, the owner of Santa Ana de Biajacas, described his property Biajacas in a legal document as a *cafetal potrero* [a coffee plantation with a stock-raising farm], "compuesto de treinta caballerías de tierra en la Hacienda Cayajabos, situado en el Partido de Cabezas, jurisdicción de Matanzas" [consisting of 30 *caballerías* (about 1,000 acres) in Hacienda Cayajabos, located in the district of Cabezas in the jurisdiction of Matanzas] (ANC Salinas 1829b:1671). This description refers to territorial divisions of the colonial period that do not exist today, and it dates prior to the 1870s when the island was first subdivided into provinces. Geopolitical territories of Cuba changed periodically throughout the island's history and continue to change. To understand the relationship of earlier geopolitical divisions to modern-day Cuba, it is necessary to describe and depict these locations on maps. Cafetal Biajacas today is in the province of Mayabeque, established in 2010, formerly the eastern portion of Havana province. It is located 75 km southeast from the city of Havana and 11 km southeast from the town of Madruga.

This chapter provides important background information necessary for understanding the larger contexts of which Cafetal Biajacas was a part. It is intended to briefly introduce Cuba to readers unfamiliar with the island nation, focusing on issues and themes that have direct bearing on Cafetal Biajacas, specifically, and on coffee plantations and slavery in western Cuba more generally. Summaries are provided on the natural environment, the Spanish colonial period (1511–1898), colonial geopolitical divisions referred to throughout this work, and Ignacio O'Farrill's family history and plantations.

Natural Setting

Cuba is the largest of the Western Antilles and occupies 50 percent of all the land mass in the form of islands within the Caribbean region. Cuba is actually an archipelago consisting of the island of Cuba (104,945 sq km or 40,520 sq mi), the island of Juventud (2,200 sq km), and over 4,000 small islands and keys (3,715 sq km or 1,435 sq mi). In total, the land surface of Cuba is 110,860 sq km or 42,830 sq mi, slightly smaller than the state of Pennsylvania. The distance from east to west is 1,250 km or 777 mi (Gebelein 2012:3–4).

The land surface is primarily flat or rolling with the exception of three major mountain ranges: Sierra de Organos and Sierra de Rosario in Pinar del Río, the westernmost province of Cuba, at elevations between 300 and 700 m; the Sierra Trinidad and Sierra Guamuhaya (also known as Escambray) in the provinces of Cienfuegos, Villa Clara, and Sancti Spíritus in central Cuba, where the elevations are between 500 and 1,500 m; and the Sierra del Maestra at 300 to 2,000 m in the southeastern extremity of Cuba, the highest elevations on the island. Areas of lower elevations, 120 to 400 m, called *alturas*, are also found sporadically throughout the island. The Alturas del Norte de la Havana-Matanzas, consisting of hills and plateaus, is such an area in western Cuba. It contains several diverse natural subregions, including the Alturas de Bejucal-Madruga-Coliseo where Cafetal Biajacas is located (Gutiérrez Domech and Rivero Glean 1999:16–20, 27, 43–46, 117–20).

Cafetal Biajacas lies along the southern fringe of the Alturas de Bejucal-Madruga-Coliseo (hereafter Alturas B-M-C), an area of rolling hills, plateaus, and low-lying mountains extending approximately 120 km (74 mi) from the town of Bejucal in Mayabeque province, moving east to Coliseo in Matanzas province (see figure 1.1). This area encompasses 1,425 sq km, with elevations varying between 120 and 320 m (Gutiérrez Domech and Rivero Glean 1999:32). The topography consists of karsts—irregular limestone formations produced by the gradual erosion of limestone from acids found in organic materials.

Karst formation is an important feature of the Cuban physical landscape found throughout the island. Two general types of karst are characteristic of the Alturas B-M-C: (1) *mogotes*, steep conical slopes rising abruptly either singularly or in chains from surrounding alluvial plains and valleys and (2) karst plains containing caves, underground channels, sinkholes, and a rough ground surface (Iturralde-Vinent 1967:208–9; Seale et al. 2004). During the plantation era, slave runaways sought refuge in these caves and rock shelters. The runaways in the Alturas B-M-C were particularly attracted to those within the Sierras del Grillo, located just northeast of Madruga. These hills are among the highest in the Alturas B-M-C at 321 m (1,053 ft) and are difficult to climb; consequently, runaways were able to elude capture for substantial periods of time. Except for runaways, El Grillo has been uninhabited because the terrain is not suited to agriculture (La Rosa Corzo 2005:163).

Average median temperature is 22–24° C (72–75° F), and annual rainfalls range from 1,400 to 1,800 mm (55 to 72 in) in the Alturas B-M-C. Abundant rainfall combined with arable soils has made this a rich agricultural zone that today produces sugar and various fruits and vegetables. The Madruga area is at the higher range for rainfall with the vast majority of its rainfall as much as 1,000 to 1,200 mm (39 to 47 in) occurring during the rainy season from May to October. In the nineteenth century, the area was prone to frequent hurricanes (Gutierrez Domech and Rivero Glean 1999:33). The hurricanes of 1844 and 1846 devastated many of the coffee plantations in the area including Cafetal Biajacas.

Soil maps of Cuba reveal a mosaic of soil colors and textures. Within the Alturas B-M-C alone, soils include dull gray mixtures with calcium carbonates, rich dark humus, alluvial deposits, and a series of red, ferrous-oxide clays known as Colorado de Matanzas found extensively in Artemisa, Mayabeque, Matanzas, and Santa Clara provinces, as well as in a few areas of eastern Cuba (ICGC 1978:36–37; Gutiérrez Domech and Rivero Glean 1999:33). The Colorado de Matanzas series—a fine-grained texture clay capable of almost complete absorption of generous rainfall—is one of the most important soils in Cuba because of its durability under long-term cultivation. In the 1920s, two soil scientists of the United States found successful production of sugarcane in red soil fields cultivated for 100 years with little or no fertilizer (Bennett and Allison 1928:96–99). They proclaimed with a few notable exceptions that there are no soils in the United States "like the productive and very extensive Matanzas red soil, either physically or chemically" (Bennett and Allison 1928:1). A French Canadian team of soil scientists similarly concluded that the red Matanzas soils were ideal for sugar cultivation (Guerra Sánchez [1948] 1974:27–28n1).

Early-nineteenth-century sugar planters, however, may have been unaware of the agricultural potential of the red soil for sugar cultivation. Abiel Abbot (1829:44, 139), a traveler from the United States to Cuba in 1828, observed on plantations well within the zone of Colorado de Matanzas that black soil was preferred for cane and red soil for coffee. By the mid-nineteenth century, both districts Abbot had visited were exclusively devoted to the production of sugar cane. Cafetal Biajacas contained both red and black soils, but coffee appears to have been the only cash crop produced there when it was a coffee plantation (ANC Galletti leg. 934, no. 6). Until very recently, sugarcane has been planted over most of the area once part of the plantation in both black and red soils, but since 2007 the land is being used increasingly to cultivate diverse subsistence crops, including cassava, corn, *malanga* [cocoyam] peanuts, sweet potatoes, tomatoes, and papaya. Cuban red soils are also highly praised for producing these crops.

Due to long-term agriculture in the area, most vegetation in Alturas B-M-C is the result of human activities—agricultural fields, pastures, and fruit trees, with some secondary vegetation emerging in abandoned fields. The exception is found in the Sierras del Grillo where forests and thickets on hill slopes are protected and offer prospects for botanical study of seminatural vegetation, plants occurring primarily from ecological factors. Human activities have similarly diminished native fauna of the region, particularly to species believed to be predators of farm animals. Three characteristic native animal species are *jutía conga* or Cuban hutia (*Capromys pilorides*), a rodent resembling a guinea pig, *majá de Santamaría* (*Epicrates angulifer*), the Cuban boa, and *Anolis lucius*, a small lizard (Gutiérrez Domech and Rivero Glean 1999:33).

Four Hundred Years of Spanish Colonialism

Christopher Columbus landed on Cuba on October 28, 1492, at a harbor near the eastern tip of the island and reputedly described the pristine landscape as "the most beautiful land the human eye has beheld" (Cantón Navarro 2001:15). Although Spanish settlement of the island did not begin until two decades later, Cuba would eventually become "Spain's pearl"—its richest possession of the Caribbean. Colonization of Cuba began in 1511 under the command of Diego Velázquez y Cuellar, a prominent landowner in Hispaniola, who led 300 men to conquer and establish the first permanent Spanish settlements. Velázquez rapidly subjugated the aboriginal population through violence and brute force and became the first Spanish governor of Cuba. By 1515, seven Spanish settlements had been founded: Baracoa (1511), Bayamo (1513), Sancti Spíritus (1514), Trinidad (1514), Havana (1515), Puerto Principe (1515), and Santiago de Cuba (1515). All these towns were located where today there are major cities, and they were probably chosen because of the close proximity to aboriginal communities who could provide labor for the Spaniards (Cantón Navarro 2001:24). In each town, the first plots were used for a central plaza with a church, a town hall, and a garrison. Town dwellers were provided with plots to build their houses; forests, pastures, and watering places were for common use. Remaining lands within the colony were distributed by the local representatives of the Spanish Crown, *vecinos*, who farmed out smaller portions of the land, *encomiendas*, based upon the beneficiary's influence and position within the social hierarchy (Gott 2004:17).

Settlers were granted land in usufruct; they could profit from using the property, but the Spanish Crown retained ownership. Amerindians, both native to Cuba and from nearby islands, were enslaved to provide a workforce for the encomiendas. Brutal treatment drastically reduced their numbers, and in 1542 the Spanish Crown abolished the encomienda system. By that time, many of the first Spanish immigrants to Cuba had left in search of gold in Mexico and Peru. For the next 200 years, Cuba developed into a sparsely populated colony of cattle and pig ranches and small-scale farms, some of which produced sugar and tobacco—staple crops that would later bring prosperity to the island. Africans replaced Amerindians as the primary workforce for many of these enterprises. Havana and Santiago flourished as port cities servicing ships passing to and from mainland Spanish America.

Cuba underwent major economic and social transformations under the reigns of the Spanish Bourbon monarchs, Carlos III (1759–88) and his son, Carlos IV (1788–1808), who enacted a succession of reforms from 1765 to 1789 designed to make Cuba a profitable colony. The last of these reforms promulgated in 1789 opened the island to foreign slave merchants who traded directly between Cuba and Africa. This action set in motion Cuba's transformation from a society with enslaved laborers to a slave society. Between 1790 and 1866, when slaving either had been abolished or was declining in most of the Caribbean, Cuba imported over 780,000 Africans to labor on plantations and farms, and it became the largest slave-importing colony of the Spanish Empire (Bergad, García, and Barcia 1995:29–38). A particularly large concentration of enslaved Africans found themselves on plantations in Matanzas jurisdiction. In 1817, 49.5 percent of all Matanzas inhabitants were enslaved, increasing to 57.9 percent in 1827 and 62.7 percent in 1841. In districts of Matanzas where the only economic activity was staple crop production, the enslaved population constituted 70 to 89 percent of the total population (Bergad 1990:67).

The Bourbon Reforms opened up possibilities for the development of a Cuban plantation economy, but the Haitian Revolution (1791–1804) created the opportunity for Cuba to become the leading plantation economy of the Caribbean in the nineteenth century. The Haitian Revolution ended the prominent position that Saint-Domingue, France's richest colony, held as the world's leading producer of coffee and sugar. Within a relatively short period, Cuba filled this void. Yet the idea of transforming Cuba into a plantation society preceded the Haitian Revolution. In 1789, Francisco Arango y Parreño—a member of Havana's elite, a student of the Enlightenment, and the Cuban equivalent of Adam Smith—lobbied Spain to permit the development of a Cuban agricultural economy based upon slave labor (Tomich 2003; Van Norman 2013:37–38). Although Arango y Parreño represented the interests of a very small segment of Cuban society (S. Johnson 2001:125–29, 187–88), he paved the way for Cuba's meteoric rise in the nineteenth-century world market. Through his leadership of the Sociedad Económica de Amigos del País of Havana [Economic Society of Friends of the Country] founded in 1793, Arango y Parreño promoted the idea of a Cuban economy independent of Spain and of making Cuba a center of achievement (Carley and Brizzi 1997:80).

The resurgence of slavery in the nineteenth century in areas formerly marginal to the world economy, as was the case for Cuba, is referred to as Second Slavery (Tomich 1988). Cuba prospered as a plantation economy, becoming the world's leading producer of coffee from 1817 to 1830 (Ramírez Pérez and Paredes Pupo 2004:40–47) and of sugar from the

1830s onward. Despite Spanish treaties with Britain to end slaving, the Cuban slave trade persisted until 1866 when Spain finally resolved to end it through a royal decree (Bergad, García, and Barcia 1995:33). Twenty years later, in 1886, slavery was finally abolished in Cuba.

The explosion of Cuba's plantation economy boosted the growth and trade at port cities, and by 1850 Havana was among the ten busiest ports of the world. After Cuba received access to free trade, the United States became Cuba's major trade partner and financier. Increased trade followed increased settlement of Americans in Cuba, and significant numbers of Cubans established themselves in North American cities (Gott 2004:68). Advocates for the annexation of Cuba to the United States anticipated the end of Spanish rule when the United States offered to purchase Cuba from Spain in 1848 and again in 1854. But Spain refused to sell.

By the mid-nineteenth century, many Cubans, frustrated with the restrictive Spanish colonial structures, concluded that Spanish control stifled Cuba's productive capacities (Pérez 1990:14–15). A few Cuban progressives had spoken out earlier against Spanish rule, but the conservative elite of Cuba reasoned they needed Spain's support to maintain slavery and to crush any slave revolts (Gott 2004:52). A growing desire for independence accelerated as Cuban landowners found themselves increasingly contributing to the Spanish tax burden and paying for an empire that Spain was having difficulty financing (Gott 2004:73). The Cuban struggle for independence lasted for 30 years (1868–98), resulting in two wars, and finally in 1898, with intervention by the United States, Spain was forced to withdraw from Cuba.

Colonial Territorial Divisions

Cafetal Biajacas was formed from Hacienda Cayajabos, an early form of land grant in Cuba dating to the sixteenth century. Designed for a sparsely populated stock-raising economy, these land grants were of two types: *hatos* for cattle and *corrales* for pigs. Both were called haciendas and consisted of large circular properties. A hato, the larger of the two, was 1,684 caballerías or approximately 56,582.4 acres; a corral was 421 caballerías or 14,145 acres (Bergad 1990:4–5). The large circular land grants generated considerable disputes because boundaries for a particular hato or corral were poorly defined. Additionally, center points for the circles were sometimes established too close to existing grants, thus resulting in a pattern of overlapping land grants. These problems can be seen in the placement of both the cafetal and potrero Biajacas outside the surrounding circles instead of being inside one (shown in figure 2.1, drawn on the basis of Pichardo's maps).[1] Whether this was a misrepresentation of the cartographers is unknown, but this example highlights the problems of establishing boundaries for the circular land grants. In the final analysis, the hacienda system proved inadequate to meet the demands of a growing population desirous of expanding the agricultural potential of Cuba.

In the late eighteenth century, *demolición* began, a process of breaking up and converting haciendas into private parcels, although a royal decree making private property legal in Cuba was not officially sanctioned until 1816 (Bergad 1990:25). Luisa Herrera, the mother of Ignacio O'Farrill, purchased a portion of Hacienda Cayajabos in 1783 from Tomás Cepero (ANC ML leg. 1149). The amount of land Herrera purchased is not given in this index to land transactions, but it is very likely that it included more land than the 1,000 acres that came to be cafetal potrero Biajacas. In 1794 and 1795, José Ricardo O'Farrill, Ignacio O'Farrill's older brother, purchased 53 caballerías in the Arrabal de Madruga [outskirts of Madruga]. The O'Farrills established numerous plantations near the town of Madruga that were part of other corrales as shown in figure 2.1. Although the hacienda system became obsolete with the development of private landownership, references to hatos and corrales continued to be used in land transactions well into the nineteenth century.

By 1800, Cuba was subdivided into three *departamentos* [departments]: Occidental, or western, Central, and Oriental, or eastern. Each department was subdivided into *jurisdicciones*. Within each jurisdicción or *tenencia de gobierno*, as they were also called, were *partidos* or districts. Partidos were further subdivided into *cuartones*. Figure 2.2 shows the location of Cafetal Biajacas in the partido of Cabezas and within the jurisdicción of Matanzas. It also shows surrounding jurisdicciones and partidos. The original map from which figure 2.2 is derived shows the annexation of the cuartón Cayajabos in 1856 to the partido of Madruga. Previously cuartón Cayajabos belonged to the partido of Ceiba Mocha in Matanzas jurisdicción (ANC GSC leg. 1129, no. 41699). This cuartón included several coffee planta-

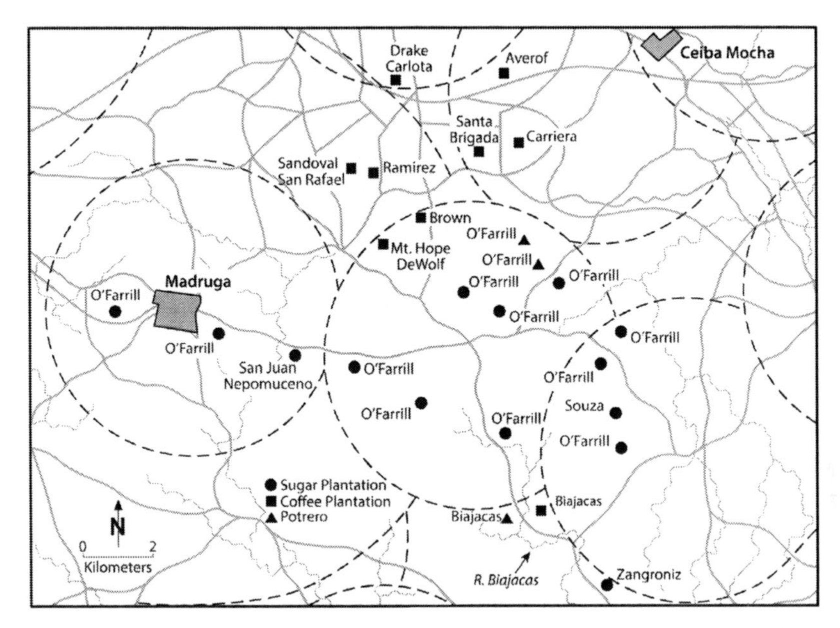

Figure 2.1. Plantations and farms near Madruga within early circular land grants from which these properties were established. Drawn by Syracuse University Cartographic Laboratory.

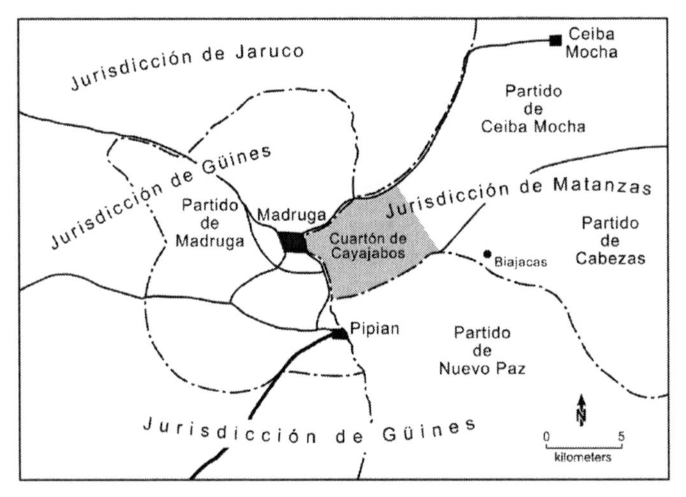

Figure 2.2. Cafetal Biajacas within 1856 territorial divisions when Cuartón de Cayajabos was annexed to the partido of Madruga, Güines jurisdiction. Cafetal Biajacas remained in Cabezas, Matanzas jurisdiction. Adapted from original map in ANC GSC leg. 1129, no. 41699 [1856]. Drawn by Syracuse University Cartographic Laboratory.

tions: Carlota, Mount Hope, San Rafael, and Santa Brigada among others as well as Ignacio O'Farrill's sugar plantation San Juan de Nepomunceno, all of which were located in the vicinity of Cafetal Biajacas.

In addition to the hierarchy of territorial divisions, properties were assigned to jurisdictions for different administrative purposes: *judicial*, *gubernativo* [governmental], *eclesiástico*, and *militar* (Figueras 1959:78–79). The territorial designations for these varied purposes did not necessarily coincide with each other. For example, cafetal potrero Biajacas belonged to the partido of Cabezas in Matanzas jurisdiction for judicial and governmental purposes, to the *parroquia* [parish] of Madruga for ecclesiastical purposes, and to Comandancia de Armas [armed command or squadron] of Madruga for its military designation.

The partido of Madruga for which the town of Madruga was the center, however, belonged to the jurisdicción of Güines (as shown in figure 2.2). Additionally, the Administración de Rentas Reales [administration of royal income] charged with keeping account of all income-producing property listed the Cafetal Biajacas, and after its demise, the lands that once belonged to the coffee plantation, on registers under the partido or parroquia of Madruga (ANC GSC leg. 871, no. 29460; ANC GG leg. 562, no. 27528). Therefore, the Cafetal Biajacas was as much a part of the partido of Madruga as it was of the partido of Cabezas. Since the early nineteenth century, Cafetal Biajacas, known today as Cafetal del Padre, was closely linked to Madruga even when it was part of Matanzas jurisdiction.

Established in 1803, the town of Madruga appears to have initially developed around abundant mineral waters that became a popular place for bathing. Juan Manzano ([1840] 1996:127]) wrote in his autobiography of his enslavement that he accompanied his female slaveholder to Madruga so she could enjoy the baths. In 1822, authors of the bylaws for the town boasted that Madruga contained three clothing stores, three bakeries, two inns, two pharmacies, six taverns, and several warehouses, and highly profitable coffee and sugar plantations were located nearby (ANC GSC leg. 871, no. 29460). The O'Farrill family owned 6 of the 11 sugar plantations, 2 of 9 coffee plantations, and 6 of the 29 *potreros*—pasturelands—around Madruga listed in the 1822 report. In addition to their sizable property holdings near Madruga, the O'Farrills became well known for their philanthropy to the town.

Ignacio O'Farrill's Family and His Plantations

The progenitor of the O'Farrill family, Richard O'Farrell y O'Daly (as the surname was spelled before it was Hispanicized), born on the island of Montserrat in the Eastern Caribbean of Irish parents, came to Cuba in 1715. He represented the South Sea Company of London, a business engaged in the slave trade that received an *asiento*, a monopoly granted by the Spanish Crown, for 30 years to supply enslaved Africans to Spanish American colonies. O'Farrill established slave barracks in Havana and Santiago and soon after became known for supplying slave workers to landowners in Cuba (Ely [1963] 2001:47). He married María Josefa de Arriola, the wealthy widow of Miguel Ambulodi, who owned several sugar plantations near Havana (González-Ripoll Navarro 1999:140). As landownership was a privilege linked to holding an office in the colonial regime, María also acquired land through her family. Her father, Bartolomé de Arriola y Valdespino, had been the Contador Mayor del Tribunal de Cuentas for Cuba [senior auditor of the court of accounts], and her uncle, Agustín Arriola, served as mayor of Havana in 1710 (González-Ripoll Navarro 1999:140).

Richard and María had two children: Juan José (1721–79) and Catalina (1723–96). The fortune Richard amassed from the slave trade and María's family sugar landholdings made it possible for Juan José to establish Santo Cristo de la Vera Cruz, one of the largest sugar plantations in eighteenth-century Cuba with approximately 100 enslaved laborers (González-Ripoll Navarro 1999:141). Both Juan José and Catalina married wealthy landowners with titles and privilege. Juan married Luisa María Herrera y Chacón (?–1806), who was the daughter of IV Marqués de Villalta and the widow of Martín Recio de Oquendo, the son of I Marqués of Real Proclamación. The union of Juan and Luisa produced 11 children, of which Ignacio O'Farrill was the seventh (Cornide Hernández 2008:497).

The offspring of Juan José and Luisa also married into important Havana families and, in some cases, they married close family members. Their sons held important military and official posts in Cuba, but only Gonzalo O'Farrill (1754–1831), educated in France, lived in Spain and worked directly with Spanish monarchs. He held several posts under Carlos IV and was appointed minister of war under Fernando VII. After Fernando's abdication and Napoleon Bonaparte's invasion of Spain, King Joseph

Bonaparte reappointed Gonzalo minister of war. Following Napoleon's invasion, Fernando VII ordered the governor of Cuba to strip all supporters of the French party of any titles and to confiscate their properties in 1809. This decree also resulted in the expulsion of French immigrants from Cuba a few months later (Ramírez Pérez and Paredes Pupo 2004:35–36). Consequently, Gonzalo lost his Cuban properties and only received a small annual pension from the proceeds garnered from the auction of them. After Fernando VII reclaimed the Spanish throne in 1813, Gonzalo moved to Paris and never returned to Spain or Cuba (Cornide Hernández 2008:500).

Like their parents and grandparents, the O'Farrills continued to invest in land and slave laborers and owned numerous plantations not just near Madruga but in several jurisdictions in western Cuba. They lived in lavish homes; particularly notable are the extant houses of José Ricardo O'Farrill (1749–1842) and Rafael O'Farrill (?–1845) in Habana vieja [Old Havana]. José Ricardo's house, built in the first decade of the 1800s, was one of the earliest neoclassical houses in Havana as shown in figure 2.3 (Carley and Brizzi 1997:111). Rafael O'Farrill modeled his house after that of José Ricardo, his older brother and father-in-law (he married his brother's daughter), and today the building functions as Hotel Palacio O'Farrill (Cornide Hernández 2008:502–3).[2] Jacinto de Salas y Quiroga, a Spaniard who visited Cuba in 1839, identified the O'Farrills as belonging to the opulent class of sugar planters (1840:94).

Compared with his brothers, little has been written about Ignacio O'Farrill (1757–1838) whom genealogist María Teresa Cornide Hernández (2008:501) refers to as the "rara avis" [rare bird] of the family because only he dedicated his life to religion. Ignacio O'Farrill was a Catholic priest, a subdeacon, and a professor of philosophy. In keeping with the rest of his family, he owned between 350 and 400 enslaved persons, three plantations, a two-story house in Havana (ANC MRH leg. 142, no. 2662), and other land he inherited from his parents, some which he sold (ANC AGT leg. 170, no. 16; ANC Salinas 1829a:244).

Ignacio's three plantations included La Concordia, a sugar plantation in Tapaste partido about 37 km from Havana, a property his mother, Luisa Herrera, awarded to him and his brother Gonzalo after her death (ANC Protocolo Salinas 1788). Ignacio acquired the other half of La Concordia

Figure 2.3. José Ricardo O'Farrill's house in Old Havana, circa 1800–1810, presently houses the headquarters for the Archdiocese of Havana. Photograph by Lisette Roura Álvarez.

in 1809 when Gonzalo's properties were confiscated and sold. San Juan de Nepomuceno, another sugar plantation, began as an investment opportunity Ignacio purchased in 1807 with another priest, Ignacio Méndez, and in 1812, Méndez sold his portion of the ownership to O'Farrill, who become the sole owner of it (ANC Salinas 1829b:1671). Santa Ana de Biajacas was his only coffee plantation and the place where he resided and later died in 1838. Unlike the two sugar plantations, Ignacio provided no information as to how or when he acquired the cafetal, except that he owned it *libre de todo gravamen* [free of all liens] in 1829 (ANC Protocolo Salinas 1829:1671). Perhaps his mother gave him some of the property she acquired in 1783. It is also unknown when Ignacio began planting coffee at Cafetal Biajacas.

Following the downward spiral of Cuban coffee that began in the mid-1820s, Ignacio developed financial difficulties. In 1829, he undertook several transactions that involved borrowing money against his properties, including his enslaved laborers. He borrowed 60,000 pesos against the value of his three plantations: 25,000 pesos from each of the sugar plantations and 10,000 pesos from Cafetal Biajacas to pay money he owed his *refaccionarios* [factors—merchants who supplied credit to planters that were usually repaid from profits obtained from crop harvests] (ANC Salinas 1829b:1671).[3] He also mortgaged 10 enslaved workers who labored in the potrero of Biajacas for 2,000 pesos to pay a debt he owed to Juan Armazy (ANC Salinas 1829d:1262–63).

By the time of his death, Ignacio had amassed considerable debt, which delayed the settlement of his estate. To make his estate profitable to pay off Ignacio's debts, the administrators of his estate decided to relocate the enslaved laborers who were "los más sanos, jóvenes adultos y aptos para el trabajo" [the healthiest, young adults, and most fit for work] at Cafetal Biajacas to Ignacio's sugar plantations. Forty of them were assigned to San Juan de Nepomuceno, and 20 to La Concordia (ANC Galletti leg. 240, no. 1, pieza 3). The remaining 17, most of whom were either old or infirm, continued to work at the cafetal and produced coffee until the hurricanes of 1844 and 1846 destroyed the plantation.

For an unknown period Cafetal Biajacas lay in ruins (ANC Cotés leg. 227, no. 7), but by 1862, the property had been subdivided into 33 *sitios*, small subsistence farms (ANC GG leg. 562, no. 27528). The known written sources on Cafetal Biajacas end in the 1860s, although the site of the cafetal continued to be designated on maps throughout the twentieth century and became known as "cafetal del padre" [the father's coffee plantation]. This study examines the period from approximately 1815 to 1846 when the site of Cafetal Biajacas was operating as a coffee plantation.

3

Cuban Coffee Sector

William S. Deall of Ticonderoga, New York, arrived in Cuba in January 1822 seeking opportunities in Cuba's booming economy. Deall anticipated that his uncle, John Latting, a co-owner of an import-export house based in Matanzas City, would assist him in establishing some type of business venture of his own. While acclimating to Matanzas society, he contemplated the prospect of becoming a coffee planter, and in a letter to sister Carolina dated May 1, 1822, he described the rapid development of coffee plantations in Matanzas: "The country around Matanzas for three or four miles is not of the first quality, but there is an extensive and fertile country in the rear which is scarcely in cultivation within three years 70 new coffee plantations have commenced within 20 miles of this [city of Matanzas]. In [a few] years, the land here may rival the Havana sugar and can be purchased much cheaper. A man only needs a few thousand dollars for capital and moderate views to make himself comfortable." Only two months after writing the letter, Deall died from "black vomiting" (yellow fever), before he realized his goal of becoming a *cafelero* [coffee planter] or a *comerciante* [a merchant or trader] (Latting Family Papers, box 1, folder C).

Many other recent immigrants from the United States, England, France, and Germany, however, would join established Cuban planting families, like the O'Farrills, to develop the Cuban coffee sector during the first half of the nineteenth century. As the title indicates, this chapter delves into the economic landscape of Cuban coffee production. It examines the rise and fall of coffee in Cuba, how the crop was produced, and how the labor used to produce it was organized. When applicable, coffee farming in western Cuba is compared with other areas of Cuba and the Caribbean to suggest some of the unique aspects of coffee culture in Matanzas jurisdiction.

Coffee in the Plantation Economy of Cuba, 1790–1850

French expatriates fleeing from Saint-Domingue to Cuba during the Haitian Revolution (1791–1804) are often credited with the introduction and expansion of Cuba's coffee industry. French immigrants played a significant role in developing Cuban coffee production, particularly in the Sierra de Maestra in eastern Cuba (Portuondo Zúñiga 1992) and Sierra de Rosario in western Cuba (Ramírez Pérez and Paredes Pupo 2004). The initial experimentation and incentive to produce coffee in Cuba, however, originated outside of Havana.

As early as 1748, references to a cafetal in Wajay, a present-day suburb of Havana, suggest coffee cultivation had begun (Gordon y Acosta 1896:9; F. Pérez de la Riva 1944:7). Twenty years later, the office of captain-general (the highest-ranking governing official in Cuba) reported on March 8, 1768, that many owners of haciendas in the Havana jurisdiction were engaged in the commercial production of coffee (ANC GSC leg. 1158, 1768). In the same year, coffee planters received a waiver on export duties of coffee (F. Pérez de la Riva 1944:7–8, appendix 1:307–8). In 1790, Cuba exported 185,000 lbs (92.5 tons) of coffee to ports in Spain, at a time when only five or six plantations were solely devoted to coffee production (F. Pérez de La Riva 1944:8).

The Haitian Revolution ended Saint-Domingue's reign as the world's leading producer of coffee and sugar. Historian William van Norman (2013:38) argues, however, that the revolution affected coffee and sugar differently. The newly established nation of Haiti was unable to produce sufficient sugar exports to compete on the world market. This void in the availability of sugar caused prices to rise sharply, which in turn stimulated sugar production in Cuba. During the 1830s, Cuba became the world's leading producer of sugar.

The situation, however, was different with Haitian coffee. Although the revolution drastically reduced prerevolution production levels, Haiti continued to produce sufficient coffee exports to stay competitive on the world market from 1821 to 1844. In fact, Haitian coffee competed directly with Cuban coffee in the United States, Cuba's largest market from 1821 to 1830 (Marrero 1985:11:136n40).[1] Thus, while the Haitian Revolution facilitated the sugar boom in Cuba, its effect on coffee, though important, was far less significant than sugar. Its primary impact on Cuban coffee resulted in the migration of French coffee planters from Saint-Domingue to Cuba who contributed to the growth of the coffee sector (van Norman 2005:60–62).

Despite competition from Haiti as well as other producers, coffee production dramatically increased as seen in the tremendous rise in the number of Cuban plantations within a relatively short time. In 1800, only 60 coffee plantations were reported in Havana jurisdiction (which included Matanzas at the time), and by 1817 that number had risen to 779, according to the 1817 census (von Humboldt [1856]1969:282). Approximately 75 of the total number were within the 1817 boundaries of Matanzas jurisdiction (Bergad 1990:32). Sometime during this 17-year period of exponential growth of coffee plantations, Cafetal Biajacas was established, and in 1822 it produced 52 tons of coffee. The date for the founding of Cafetal Biajacas is unknown, but to produce 52 tons of coffee in 1822, coffee trees must have been planted five to seven years previously, possibly around 1815 or earlier to produce that much coffee.

Cuban Coffee Planters

Throughout the Caribbean, coffee attracted planters of diverse economic and social scales because land requirements for the successful production of coffee were small and investments in expensive machinery were unnecessary (Trouillot 1993; Shepard and Monteith 2002; S. D. Smith 2002). Sugarcane, on the other hand, required large amounts of land, laborers, and machinery to be profitable, and consequently sugar production was always restricted to the wealthy. This characterization of coffee versus sugar plantations was equally true for Cuba. To establish and operate a coffee plantation was generally less than half the cost of a sugar plantation with comparable profitability (Bergad 1990:34, 57; Pérez 2000:42).

John Turnbull ([1840] 1969:263–64), a British traveler to Cuba in 1838, observed that the start-up costs for a sugar plantation of 30 caballerías (approximately 1,000 acres) independent of the land were $67,850. Establishing a coffee farm, even one that would ultimately become a sizable plantation, usually began with planting coffee on two caballerías (64 acres). If, and when, additional trees were planted, it was done incrementally over four to five years—the amount of time needed for coffee shrubs to reach full productivity to generate income (Bergad 1990:57). Turnbull ([1840] 1969:311–12) estimated the first year's investment in planting 40,000 trees was about $6,400, and by the end of five years on a plantation with a maximum of 200,000 trees, the total cost was $30,888.

The size of Cuban slaveholdings indicates small cafetales outnumbered larger ones, but most slave workers engaged in coffee production resided on larger plantations. In 1834, Cuban authorities reported 39,835 worked on 1,024 coffee plantations in western and central Cuba (García 2003b:18). Of these, 604 cafetales operated with 30 or fewer slave workers comprising 8,941 slave laborers with an average of 15 laborers per farm. A total of 30,894 slave laborers worked on the remaining 420 plantations with an average of 74 slave laborers. In Matanzas jurisdiction, Doria González Fernández (1991:170) estimated an average number of 67 slave workers for each coffee plantation based upon her study of the partidos of Ceiba Moche and Camarioca.

Most of our understanding of Cuban coffee plantations comes from larger plantations described in traveler accounts, planter essays, or nineteenth-century fiction. Little is known about the operation of small Cuban coffee farms or their owners. A number of North Americans with modest incomes who established coffee plantations initially came to Cuba as employees for commercial companies or agricultural managers for wealthy North Americans. Joseph Goodwin, a native of Hudson, New York, is an example of a North American who rose from the rank of plantation manager to become a small coffee planter. Goodwin (Diary 1821–27) came to Cuba in 1821 to work as the *mayordomo* [head overseer] on two coffee plantations, Buena Esperanza and Arca de Noe, belonging to George DeWolf, whose family of slave traders was based in Bristol, Rhode Island (DeWolf 2008).[2]

While working for DeWolf, Goodwin kept a diary detailing the operation of the two large coffee plantations each with over 100 slave workers. On February 5, 1826, after five years under DeWolf's employ, Goodwin, with his brother Lewis, set out with 24 enslaved persons to establish a coffee plantation that they later named Cornucopia. Goodwin continued to manage DeWolf's plantations for at least another year, then his diary abruptly ends with the last entry dated March 16, 1827.[3] What happened to the plantation Goodwin owned jointly with his brother and another investor? According to Laird Bergad (1990:58), coffee plantations in Matanzas underwent a fair degree of turnover. The small initial investment in a coffee plantation made it possible to suffer only minor losses, as well as profits from the sale of slave workers when owners decided to sell for whatever reasons. Bergad also found that most U.S. planters invested in coffee on a short-term basis and remained in Cuba for only a brief time.

Coffee planting also attracted affluent entrepreneurs and sugar planters, like Ignacio O'Farrill, the owner of Cafetal Biajacas, who desired not only to profit from its commercial success but also to establish palatial country estates. Cafetales developed into "showplace plantations" designed to impress peers and visitors through displays of opulence that highlighted the dominant role these planters held within the society (Vlach 1993:4–5). The term "showplace plantation," coined for the study of plantations in the southern United States, is equally applicable to many nineteenth-century Cuban plantations. Studies of Cuban architecture have shown the planter elite built lavish houses on their plantations and in nearby cities and towns (Carley and Brizzi 1997:82–84; cf. Llanes 1999:158–61).[4] Cuban architectural historian Alicia García Santana (1999:19) asserts that during Cuba's economic proliferation, the *criollo* class [Cuban-born elite] consolidated their power and projected their newly established status through "una continua ostentación de sus riquezas" [constant ostentation of their wealth]. Because cafetales functioned as year-round residences more often than sugar plantations, wealthy coffee planters, both criollos and recent immigrants, made their cafetales objects of opulent display.

Many of these cafetales also generated lucrative incomes during Cuban's coffee boom. Cafetal Carlota in the Matanzas partido of Ceiba Moche near Madruga yielded a harvest in one year worth more than $100,000 from 300,000 trees worked by 157 slave laborers (Wurdemann [1844] 1971:105). The owner of Carlota, James Drake, an immigrant from Ash, England, owned Drake Hermanos, the largest commercial house in Havana (Bergad 1990:35). With such sizable incomes gained from coffee farming, it is not surprising that an individual identified only as W. C. Gibbs offered James DeWolf, the uncle of George DeWolf, $150,000 for his coffee plantation, Marianne (figure 3.1), located west of Havana near the town of Artemisa on August 1, 1819 (JDWSFP, vol. 1). Apparently, DeWolf did not sell to Gibbs, and later he either gave or sold Marianne (known as

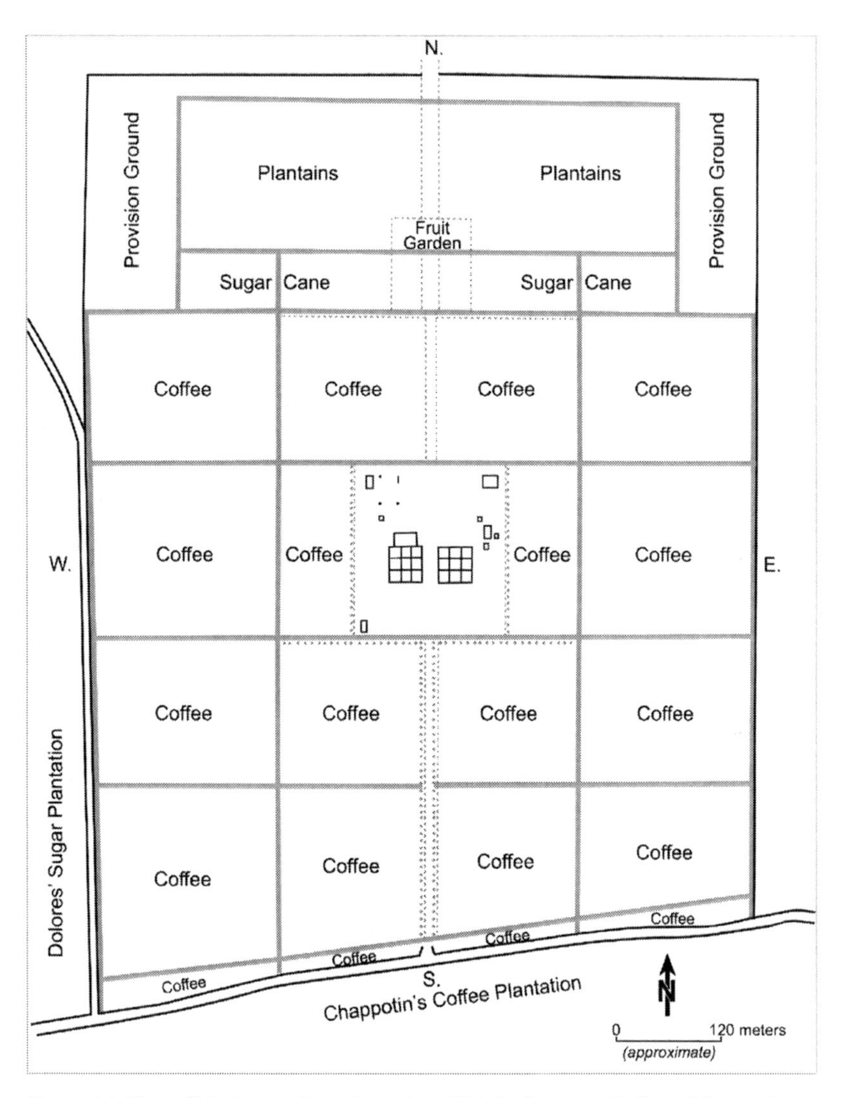

Figure 3.1. Plan of Marianne plantation, circa 1820. Redrawn and adapted from photograph of original in DeWolf Papers, MSS 382, Rhode Island Historical Society, Providence. Drawn by Syracuse University Cartographic Laboratory.

MaryAnne in the United States) to his son Mark Anthony, as he indicated in a letter, May 11, 1831, to the company Drake & Coit (JDWSFP, vol. 3). He kept his other cafetal, Mount Hope, with 129 slave laborers near Madruga for himself (ANC GSC leg. 871, no. 29460).

Cafetal Biajacas, located in close proximity to both Drake's Carlota and DeWolf's Mount Hope coffee plantations (shown in figure 2.1), fits within this definition of a country estate and showplace plantation. Ignacio O'Farrill's most valuable property at the time of his death was his sugar plantation San Juan de Nepomuceno, but his most impressive and valuable *casa vivienda* [dwelling house] and gardens were located at Cafetal Biajacas. In 1822, a report on the state of the region's wealth for Madruga pueblo described Cafetal Biajacas as consisting of six caballerías [approximately 200 acres] of cultivated land and seven caballerías of mountainous land with 102 slave laborers and 62 animals. The amount of land planted in coffee or the number of coffee trees is not given, but Cafetal Biajacas produced 1,050 *quintales* or 105,000 lbs of coffee that year. Given that the average cost per pound in the U.S. market was $0.20 in 1822 (Marrero 1985:11:116), the coffee harvest that year possibly earned at least $21,000.

By the 1820s, the Madruga area as well as other nearby districts held great promise for coffee cultivation. Coffee planters with both large and small slaveholdings coexisted alongside sugar plantations, numerous potreros [stock-raising farms], and sitios [subsistence farms]. The owners of these cafetales were both criollos and recent immigrants. Cafetal Biajacas, while not the largest coffee plantation in the area, was certainly among those with over 100 slave laborers. In 1834, only 100 of the 1,024 coffee plantations in western Cuba had more than 91 slave laborers (Garcia 2003b:18), making Cafetal Biajacas in the top 10 percent of coffee plantations with the largest slaveholdings.

Brief Coffee Boom

The Cuban coffee sector flourished during its golden age from about 1817 to 1830, when the unprecedented growth of coffee plantations made Cuba the world's leading producer (Ramírez Pérez and Paredes Pupo 2004:40–47). Near the end of this period, however, a series of economic issues and political conflicts between Spain and the United States emerged that negatively impacted Cuban coffee. These conditions contributed to a downward spiral from which many coffee producers, particularly in western Cuba, never recovered. During the decade from 1821 to 1830, the United States was the principal market for coffee produced in western Cuba. Eastern Cuba exported more of its coffee to Europe than to the United States and therefore was better able to survive the crises that befell Cuban coffee (Ramírez Pérez and Paredes Pupo 2004:42).

The first major crisis was a worldwide drop in coffee prices to less than half of previous levels. Expansion of coffee production in Cuba and the rise of new coffee producers, Brazil and the Dutch colonies of present-day Indonesia, resulted in an overproduction of coffee that exceeded projected consumption (Marrero 1985:11:116). In 1821, the average price per pound of Cuban coffee in the United States sold for $0.21, and by 1830 it was $0.08. Prices had steadily decreased in the United State while the amount of coffee Cuba exported to the United States increased, but after 1828, the amount of coffee exported to the United States also significantly declined. The United States imported 42 percent of its coffee from Cuba in 1821 and as much as 49 percent in 1826, but imports dropped to 29 percent in 1830. Although Cuba retained its role as the principal supplier of coffee to the United States from 1821 to 1830, Cuba was losing its share of the U.S. market to Brazil. Over the same decade, Brazilian coffee exports to the United States substantially increased, from less than 1 million pounds in 1821 to 14.6 million in 1830. Cuba exported 16 million pounds to the United States in 1830, only about 1.5 million pounds more than Brazil (Marrero 1985:11:111–12).

Spain added to Cuba's declining role in the U.S. coffee market by increasing the fees on North American ships entering and leaving Cuban ports in order to take control of Cuban maritime trade. Shortly thereafter, Spain imposed a high tariff on wheat from the United States to Cuba to protect Spanish wheat exported to Cuba (F. Pérez de la Riva 1944:72–73). Cuban scholars have criticized these actions as Spain's way of tightening its control on its few remaining colonies in the Americas. Francisco Pérez de la Riva (1944:72) claimed Spain had little interest in preserving markets for which there was not a direct benefit to Spain, while Levi Marrero (1985:11:116) referred to the tariff on wheat as an absurd fiscal policy.

The United States retaliated in 1834, imposing a tariff on Cuban coffee and tobacco and further reducing the importance of the U.S. market to

Cuban coffee. Because Brazil was able to produce large amounts of coffee and still profit from low prices, Brazil supplanted Cuba as the major supplier of coffee to the United States. By 1843, Brazil had become the world's largest coffee producer, followed by Java and Sumatra, with Cuba in third place (Marrero 1985:11:120).

Internal factors in Cuba also played a role in the declining importance of Cuban coffee. In his study of Matanzas jurisdiction, Laird Bergad (1990:34) found the coffee sector utilized larger numbers of slave workers per farm than on sugar plantations in partidos, such as Ceiba Moche during the formative years of coffee farming. This intensive use of slave labor on Cuban coffee plantations not only refutes the general assumption that sugar necessitated greater labor demands than coffee; it also suggests coffee production in western Cuba required more labor than in other plantation settings. But this intensive, perhaps excessive, use of slave labor proved costly when coffee prices decreased. By 1827, the number of enslaved laborers engaged in coffee production was equal to the number engaged in sugar production (Marrero 1985:11:114), but each slave worker on a sugar plantation generated more than three times the gross income of a slave worker on a coffee plantation (Bergad 1990:39–40).

Concerned with the effects of low coffee prices on Cuban agriculture, members of the Sociedad Económica discussed whether or not coffee production should be continued or abandoned. Francisco de Paula Serrano wrote an essay, *Memoria sobre el cultivo y beneficio del café*, published in 1829 by the Sociedad Económica urging coffee planters to simplify their use of labor by distributing some of the land to *colonos* [tenant farmers] who could produce coffee on small plots of land more cheaply than with slave labor. Serrano's position, viewed as progressive by later agricultural reformers and implemented in the late nineteenth and early twentieth centuries, received little support.[5] Instead, the Sociedad Económica decided to discourage further development of new cafetales, abandon small ones, and encourage large ones to make modifications geared toward improving coffee production (F. Pérez de la Riva 1944:57).

Whether or not coffee planters followed the recommendations of the Sociedad Económica is unclear, but massive abandonment of coffee farming and conversion to sugar plantations in western Cuba occurred in the 1830s and 1840s. Bergad (1990:40) believes the income difference between coffee and sugar per slave worker explains the transformation from coffee to sugar in Matanzas. Other planters, particularly foreigners, abandoned plantation agriculture altogether and sold their slave laborers to sugar planters. Slave laborers brought high prices due to the growing demand for labor on sugar plantations. By 1846, one-third of all enslaved laborers worked on sugar plantations (Bergad, García, and Barcia 1995:31). With the decline of coffee planting, Havana and Matanzas jurisdictions rapidly were transformed into a monocrop plantation society based on sugar.

The downturn in coffee farming captured the attention of astute travelers to the Matanzas region who commented on the changing social and economic landscapes. While visiting plantations owned primarily by North Americans in the partido of Camarioca in 1831, Mary Gardiner Lowell (2003:84), of the Lowell family dynasty based in Massachusetts, observed that a Mr. Smith was "erecting a mill for grinding sugar cane and has thought of turning his coffee estate into a sugar plantation." A few days later, she wrote that most of the foreign men in this part of the country were "addicted to the bottle and almost every individual is in debt. I never heard in any other place of so many bankrupts" (Lowell 2003:86). Peter S. Townsend, a physician from New York, equated low coffee prices with the brutal treatment of enslaved people. He observed an enslaved person subjected to *el grillete*, a form of shackling in which an iron ring attached to chains was placed very tightly around the ankle of an enslaved person who was forced to perform agricultural labor while carrying the heavy chains. After he described how the individual was shackled, Townsend wrote in his diary on August 28: "the low prices of coffee and the necessity of entailing as much labor as possible from the slaves ought not by any means to be considered a sufficient [justification] of this offensive and unconscionable treatment [of slaves]" (Townsend Diaries series 3, vol. 2). Later in the 1840s, Thomas Amory of Massachusetts and John Wurdemann of South Carolina, both of whom stayed at the Drake coffee plantation Carlota in successive years, noted that Carlota (Wurdemann [1844] 1971:105) and a cafetal next to it, San Rafael (Thomas Amory Diary 1843:3) were both once highly productive and valuable coffee plantations. By the time of their visits, however, these plantations only yielded enough income to maintain the enslaved people.

After the decline of coffee, some wealthy planters continued to operate their cafetales as country estates while earning money from other investments, namely sugar. Traveling to Cuba in the 1850s, Henry Hurlbert (1854:142) remarked that "although Brazil had broken down the coffee trade, coffee estates were still numerous in Vuelta Arriba [western upper district of Havana jurisdiction], where they are kept on the French models chiefly as ornaments to the sugar estates, vegetable farms, and homes for the younger or decrepit negroes." Ignacio O'Farrill followed a similar path with Cafetal Biajacas. In 1829, he began directing most of his resources to improving his sugar plantations, keeping Cafetal Biajacas as his country home where he resided during his final years. In time, however, he neglected Cafetal Biajacas, and shortly after his death in 1838, the cafetal was described to be in a "ruinous state" (ANC Galletti leg. 240, no. 1).

The final blow to coffee plantations in western Cuba developed not from economic or political causes but from hurricanes in 1844 and 1846. Historian Louis Pérez Jr. (2000:59–108) examines the economic and social impact of these devastating storms, showing how they were especially destructive to coffee. Unlike sugar or tobacco, coffee never rebounded. Coffee plantations particularly suffered because both hurricanes hit Cuba in October when most of the crop was nearing maturity for harvest. The crop was lost for those seasons, and millions of coffee trees were ruined, thus crippling the prospects of future crops for several years. Harvested coffee also fared poorly in coffee dryers, millhouses, and warehouses that were destroyed. With low coffee prices and increased competition from other producers, many planters sold their land and slave workers.

Both hurricanes hit Cafetal Biajacas. The one in 1844 destroyed the coffee works, and the one in 1846 destroyed all the trees (ANC Cotés leg. 227, no. 7). The property value of Cafetal Biajacas greatly depreciated. In 1841, the cafetal was valued at 68,910 pesos (ANC Galletti leg. 934, no. 6), and after the hurricanes, it was only worth 26,607 pesos, but the administrators of the estate decided to put the estate up for sale for 16,207 pesos. Coffee planting, however, was never restored at Cafetal Biajacas (ANC Cotés leg. 227, no. 7). Instead, the property was subdivided into subsistence farms.

Producing Coffee

Planters experimented with coffee culture throughout Cuba, but production predominated in three regions during the first half of the nineteenth century: the Sierra Maestra in eastern Cuba, Sierra del Rosarios in present-day Pinar del Río, and the *llanos* [flatlands] of Habana-Matanzas jurisdictions. Differences in rainfall, soil, topography, and water resources influenced the development of coffee culture in each of these regions. Coffee culture in Sierra Maestra and, to a lesser extent, Sierra del Rosarios more closely resembled coffee culture in former Saint-Domingue and Jamaica because these cafetales were located in hilly and mountainous terrains geographically separate from and therefore not in competition with lands suitable for sugar. In the llanos, however, coffee and sugar plantations coexisted side by side. Of the three areas, the llanos possessed the least favorable growing conditions for coffee, but when the Cuban coffee market collapsed, these lowlands were easily converted to sugar culture. The following discussion focuses on coffee production in the llanos, but comparisons and contrasts are made with the other regions when appropriate.

Establishing a Coffee Plantation

With the exception of expatriate French planters from the former colony of Saint-Domingue, most Cuban planters engaged in coffee production were initially unfamiliar with coffee cultivation. They usually learned about it from experienced administrators or managers they hired or indirectly by consulting published manuals or papers. Travelers sometimes noted that coffee planters had French administrators or mayordomos who were presumably knowledgeable in coffee planting (Wurdemann [1844] 1971:104). These managers, in turn, trained other employees and perhaps future planters. James DeWolf, for example, wrote to Joseph Catalogne, the administrator of his coffee plantations, on January 26, 1817, "I hope my son Francis will spend a considerable part of his time with you and get some idea of Coffee planting" (JDWSFP, vol. 2). Most coffee planters undoubtedly learned about coffee planting directly from those already familiar with it.

Coffee planters also consulted published essays written by planters who had experimented with different aspects of coffee planting. Papers on coffee planting circulated among members of the Sociedad Económica as early as 1797, and with the establishment of the annual *Memorias de la Sociedad Económica de Amigos del Pais* in the 1800s, several papers were published. By far the most influential publication on coffee was Pierre Joseph Laborie's *The Coffee Planter of Santo Domingo*. Laborie, a planter and lawyer from Saint-Domingue (Haiti), fled during the Haitian Revolution to Jamaica, where he completed his treatise and published it in 1798 (Delle 1998:108). Pablo Boloix, an early promoter of coffee cultivation in the Havana jurisdiction, translated *The Coffee Planter* into a Spanish version titled *Cultivo del cafeto o árbol que produce el café*, published in 1809.

Laborie's manual, however, was more comprehensive than many of the short essays published in the *Memorias*, as it covered everything from finding the proper site, planting, harvesting, and processing coffee, to managing enslaved workers. It possibly served as an overview to coffee planting prior to making the initial investment in land and laborers as well as a detailed guide once a cafetal was established. Cuban planters obviously followed his advice on many topics until they developed their own practices adapted to their local areas.

During Laborie's time as well as today, the optimal location for planting coffee in the Caribbean was in hilly areas at elevations approximately 500 to 1,000 m (1,640 to 3,261 ft) above sea level.[6] The advantages of the high elevations included a cooler climate, deeper and firmer soil, more frequent rain, a longer crop season, and longer-lasting coffee trees. Light, shallow soils at lower elevations caused coffee trees to be short-lived, necessitating frequent planting of new trees to maintain high yields of coffee beans. The growing season was also shorter at lower elevations, which required more laborers and drying platforms for the harvest. Low elevations did have two advantages over higher ones: (1) easy access to the fields for planting and harvesting and (2) because trees did not reach their full size as in higher elevations, more trees could be planted closer together in the same amount of space. Laborie (1798:6–7) estimated that in a square containing 2,500 trees at high elevations, 8,000 trees could be planted at low elevations that would yield as much coffee as in the better soils of higher elevations.

These differences between coffee culture at high and low elevations partially explain a number of features characteristic of cafetales in the llanos of Habana-Matanzas jurisdictions such as the large numbers of coffee trees planted on many plantations, continuous planting of thousands of new trees, and the large numbers of slave laborers on many coffee plantations in western Cuba.

After the site for a cafetal was selected, clearing the land and laying out the plantation took place. On the relatively flat lands of Matanzas, land designated for the plantation was usually cleared to form a symmetrical shape where the batey—the location for all domestic housing and structures for coffee processing—was placed at or near the center of the agricultural fields proportionally located on the front and sides of it (González Fernández 1991:167). James DeWolf's Marianne depicted in figure 3.1 followed this basic plan. The spatial organization of the plantation as a whole and within the batey was directly tied to the production of the crop.

Laborie (1798:35) highly recommended a symmetrical arrangement of the building site that included the batey, pastures, provision grounds, and agricultural fields. But he lamented that implementing such an arrangement was rare because it required a site with little downward slope. Typically on Cuban cafetales, a caballería (approximately 33 acres or 13.35 hectares) was subdivided into four equal *cuadros* [blocks or squares] and within each cuadro, 10,000 coffee trees were planted. The number of trees planted in a cuadro, however, varied according to the spacing between coffee plants and the other crops planted in the same fields with the coffee—two aspects of coffee culture debated among Cuban planters. Some planters experimented with subdividing a caballería into smaller cuadros. Alejandro Dumont ([1823]1833:33) proposed subdividing a caballería into 8 or 10 cuadros that would permit planting more trees in shorter rows, if only coffee, and no other crops were planted within a cuadro.

Once the agricultural fields and the roads or pathways between fields—known as guardarrayas in Cuba—were established, planting began. As a general rule, the coffee trees sprouted from saplings raised in a plantation nursery rather than from sowing seeds. Planting coffee from seeds was risky due to the high probability that wind or rain could move the seeds away from the desired location. In addition, planting from seeds increased the time it took for the coffee trees to bear fruit and produce income. Preparing the soil and digging holes to plant saplings preceded planting, and digging was usually a distinct activity that began several weeks before planting. At George DeWolf's plantations, Joseph Goodwin wrote, "commenced digging holes for coffee at Buena Esperanza," March 26, 1823, but "setting out the coffee" began June 7. At the end of the planting season, Goodwin estimated a total of 23,900 coffee saplings were planted (Goodwin Diary).

Coffee, a shade-loving plant, needs to be grown under a canopy of trees and plants in order to thrive. The original varieties of coffee brought to the Americas were intolerant of direct sunlight; therefore, it was necessary to provide shade for coffee grown in sun-drenched open fields. Shade was usually generated from plantains planted among the rows of coffee and fruit trees and other hardwoods planted between the edges of coffee fields and the guardarrayas. Trees along the guardarrayas not only provided shade and beauty but also protected coffee plants from wind and excessive rain. Many Cuban planters apparently used both sources of shade. For example, plantation inventories for Cafetal Biajacas indicate 10,000 plantain trees were intermixed within 40,000 coffee trees planted in five cuadros, and about 1,000 fruit trees, including coconut, oranges, *caimitos* [star apple], mamoncillos [Spanish Lime], avocados, mangos, and Spanish blackberry were planted along the guardarrayas (ANC Galetti leg. 934, no. 6).

Authors of coffee planting essays, however, debated the utility of planting plantain for shade. Laborie (1798:122) recommended using plantain for shade and coolness in "hot situations," but warned not to place the plantain too close to the coffee so that the *cafetos* [coffee trees] did not become entangled with it. Dumont ([1823] 1833:27) declared, "no he colocado entre mis cafetos, ni plátanos ni maíz, i que no apruebo semejante intercalación." [I do not place either plantain or corn between my cafetos, and do not approve of such interspersing.] He believed plantain should only be used on dry or inferior soils. In good soils, Dumont ([1823] 1833:13) argued that the plantain attracted harmful humidity to the ground's surface and required regular cleaning of its debris—fallen leaves, stems, and fruit—that could damage the cafetos. In his method of planting coffee, shade was obtained by placing mature coffee trees and saplings together within small cuadros of one-eighth caballería (about four acres) rather than the standard eight-acre squares and from fruit trees along the guardarrayas.

Nevertheless, travelers to western Cuba frequently described the planting of coffee with plantain. During his trip to Cuba in 1811–12, J. B. Dunlop visited the Cafetal Catalina in the Cusco district about 40 miles west of Havana and noted, "This article [coffee] together with Negro provisions such as Bananas, which are planted between the coffee fields when young, Maize & Yams are the prevailing articles of this Culture in this fertile district" (Mohl 1972:242). Over thirty years later, when John Wurdemann ([1844] 1971:104) observed "cane and coffee, interspersed with rows of plantains" at Cafetal Carlota and at Cafetal San Patricio, also in Matanzas jurisdiction, he stated: "amid the [coffee] shrubs rows of plantains are formed eighteen feet apart, and corn freely sown wherever the foliage permits the sun's rays to reach the ground; so that a coffee square produces also a crop of these two valuable bread stuffs" ([1844] 1971:142). Despite debates concerning the use of plantains for shade, coffee planters continued the practice, and even today it has been revived on organically, shade-grown coffee farms in areas of the Caribbean and Central America.[7]

Cafetos began to bear fruit three to five years after planting. Harvesting the bright red cherries, processing them into coffee beans, and preparing them for market were the busiest activities on the cafetal and often involved all of the field laborers. Although there were two basic methods for processing the harvested cherries, coffee planters in western Cuba universally employed the in-cherry or dry method in which coffee berries were placed in coffee dryers immediately after they were picked from the trees for a period of at least 21 days. Afterward, the dried outer casing and pulp were separated from the seed (the coffee bean) using an animal-driven mill known as a *molino de pilar* or *tahona*—a circular trough with a large wooden wheel (figure 3.2). Dried cherries were placed between the wheel and sides of the trough, which crushed the casing of the beans by pressing them forcibly against each other. Removal of the dried outer casing and pulp from the seed yielded coffee beans within an inner membrane known as *pergamino* [parchment].

In the wet method, coffee was dried within its parchment. Some type of de-pulping mill known as a *molino de descerezar* separated the soft outer casing and pulp from the bean. The beans were thoroughly washed in several successive washings to remove all residue of the pulp, and then the coffee was dried in parchment for six or seven days (Laborie 1798:49–54).

Laborie (1798:47) highly endorsed the parchment method because the in-cherry method required more labor and more coffee dryers, and it made the separation of the dried outer casing and pulp from the coffee beans more difficult. Additionally, the in-cherry method exposed the coffee to the elements for a much longer time at a critical stage of coffee processing. While in the dryers, the coffee needed careful monitoring of its exposure to moisture; consequently, it was turned periodically to make sure the beans dried evenly. Every night, slave laborers raked the coffee into heaps and placed them under a thin tentlike structure called a *basicol,* usually made from palm leaves to keep moisture out, but it was probably ineffective during a deluge. On the other hand, if the coffee stayed in the dryers too long, the sun could scorch it.

Despite its drawbacks, the in-cherry method persisted in western Cuba. There are several possible reasons for its widespread adoption. First, in-cherry processing produced coffee beans that weighed 3 percent more than those produced with the wet method, and coffee was sold by weight (Abbot 1828:52). Second, the beans produced by in-cherry processing had a distinctive taste that many people found pleasant (Laborie 1798:47). Finally, and most important, collecting the large amounts of water needed in the wet method for washing beans was difficult in western Cuba, particularly during the dry season when a significant portion of the coffee was harvested and processed (Ramírez Pérez and Paredes Pupo 2004:62–63).

Figure 3.2. A *tahona* or *molino de pilar* for milling coffee beans dried by the in-cherry method. Buena Vista Plantation, Las Terrazas, Artemisa, Cuba. Photograph by author.

Figure 3.3. "Coffee Sorters," Cuba, circa 1866. From Samuel Hazard, *Cuba with Pen and Pencil*, 1871, 488. Image LCP-02 as shown on http://www.slaveryimages.org, compiled by Jerome Handler and Michael Tuite and sponsored by the Virginia Foundation of the Humanities and the University of Virginia Library.

Water was often a scarce resource in western Cuba as noted by travelers (Abbot 1829:49, 96; Wurdemann [1844]1971:142–43). Coffee planters in eastern Cuba, on the other hand, employed the wet method and built elaborate systems of canals, dams, and reservoirs to control and hold water when it was needed for coffee processing (Ramírez Pérez and Paredes Pupo 2004:63).[8] The geography of western Cuba was less conducive for building this type of infrastructure because the small rivers and streams often dry up during the dry season.

Some planters, however, may have experimented with the wet method, building large structures for the collection of rainwater, like those preserved in ruins at Angerona, or using a *noria* [a waterwheel used to extract well water] and an adjacent structure to hold water at La Dionisia in Matanzas province (Hernández de Lara 2010:69, 74). Jorge F. Ramírez Pérez and Fernando A. Paredes Pupo (2004:69) suggest the enormous structures at Angerona were used to collect water for domestic use during the dry season. It is also possible that these containers stored water for the application of wet method processing at some point in their histories. Given the fact that Angerona was the largest coffee plantation in all of Cuba, the owners may have attempted to use the more expeditious wet method rather than the dry method, but later abandoned it.

Once dried, the parchment or husk needed to be removed from the bean. This was accomplished with a *molino de aventar* or *aventadora*—a fanning mill that winnowed the husk away from the coffee bean. From there coffee beans were sorted by hand into different qualities, an undertaking often reserved for women (figure 3.3), packed in bags or boxes, and sent to market. Coffee beans with a greenish-colored hue also known as *café oro* [golden coffee] brought the highest prices. James DeWolf expressed his disappointment to one of his managers on October 20, 1817, when he discovered that "part of the coffee in casks is very dark. . . . I hope the next crop will be more green & less of the black grains among it" (JDSFP, vol. 2). An abundance of green coffee beans confirmed that processing the crop was highly successful.

Labor Organization

Anthropologist Michel-Rolph Trouillot (1993:136–37) posited slave life was profoundly different on coffee plantations than on sugar plantations due to the simpler and less exhausting labor organization and work regimen of coffee culture. Trouillot credited the widespread use of task labor rather than gang labor in the production of coffee as a significant factor contributing to this difference. In task labor, slave laborers were assigned a specific amount of work to be completed within a specific time frame. Upon completion of the assigned task, laborers could undertake additional work for which planters offered rewards, or they could work for themselves. Under gang labor, a system originating from sugar culture, slave laborers worked the fields from early morning to sunset in groups or gangs under the supervision of overseers or slave drivers, known in Cuba as *contramayorales*. Trouillot (1993:135–36) found that as coffee cultivation expanded in the Caribbean, many planters adopted the task labor using gang labor only for the initial clearing of the land and possibly for digging thousands of holes for planting coffee saplings.

The extent to which Cuban coffee planters utilized task labor is unknown, as documentary evidence on this aspect of coffee culture is very fragmentary, but some sources suggest that gang labor prevailed. In the previously mentioned Joseph Goodwin daybook—the only known plantation journal of a Cuban coffee plantation—entries such as "one party trimming coffee," "another weeding," or "one cutting manure" are found throughout it and indicate slave labor was organized around gangs at George DeWolf's plantations.

David Turnbull's travel account provides additional support for the prevalence of gang labor when he criticizes Cuban coffee planters for failing to employ task labor in harvesting coffee:

> It is usual with the mayoral to insist on labourers bringing home a large basket [of coffee cherries], heaped on each of the three occasions that the gang returns to the works [the batey]—at the breakfast hour, the dinner hour, and at nightfall; and although this must be a most unequal measure of the labourer's diligence, since at one period of the season, or in one part of the plantation the difficulty of gathering a basketful may be much greater than at another, yet the practice is still persisted in. Thus imperfectly begun, it ought to have point the way to the system of task-work so successfully pursued in the British colonies, more especially at Demarara, and even some well-managed estates in the French island of Martinique and Guadaloupe; where it is found that the negro in a state of slavery works more assiduously, more efficiently, and more profitably for his master, when he has only a given amount of labour to perform in a given time, and when that being accomplished he knows that the remainder of the day will be his own, and that for a brief space before retiring to rest, he will in some sort be FREE! ([1840] 1970:308–9)

A staunch abolitionist, Turnbull possibly exaggerated the absence of task labor on Cuban coffee plantations. But Abiel Abbot (1829:39), sympathetic to slaveholders, made a similar observation to Turnbull when he contrasted slave labor in Cuba with that of South Carolina: "In Cuba, they have no measured task on coffee or sugar estates." Abbot noted enslaved Cubans rose at daybreak, began their work with short intervals to take their food, and labored until the light was gone. He also believed that slave workers in Cuba accomplished a third more work than the "tasked slaves" of Carolina (1829:40).

Cuban coffee planters may have combined gang labor with some aspects of the task system. On some large coffee plantations in Jamaica, field laborers were subdivided into gangs based upon age and gender, but work was allocated to complete a task within a specified time frame (S. D. Smith 2002:105). A few scattered references suggest slave labor may have been organized in a similar manner on Cuban coffee plantations. Thomas Amory recorded in his diary on March 24, 1843, that the owner of a coffee plantation near the Drake Cafetal Carlota told him "an able slave can pick 5 *arrobas* of coffee [125 lb] in 12 hours." Amory also noted, "We saw women so engaged [in picking coffee]" (Amory Diary 1843). His statements suggest that gangs may have been based upon gender, and a daily quota for picking coffee was set at 125 pounds for the average worker.

Turnbull estimated a similar average daily quota at 30 pounds of coffee beans prepared for the market ([1840] 1970:310). This was about 150 pounds of harvested cherries, as only about 20 percent of the cherry consists of coffee bean. Goodwin did not mention quotas in his daybook, but gangs were apparently ranked according to age and their capacity to do work. He occasionally referred to "prime hands" engaged in specific activities, and once noted "small fry weeding the potraro [potrero]," on February 9, 1824 (Goodwin Diary), indicating gangs of enslaved children were assigned specific tasks. Given the available evidence, it appears that enslaved Cubans on coffee plantations labored primarily under the gang system with perhaps some elements of task labor. Their workday averaged between 12 and 16 hours, depending upon the kind of work they were doing (Madden 1853:172–75).[9] While task labor offered certain advantages to slave laborers, it also ran the risk of becoming abusive should the planter or the overseers expect an unrealistic daily quota of work.

Annual Cycle

The labor of coffee planting was tied to an annual cycle of crop production. Planter essays like Laborie's describe a hypothetical annual cycle of coffee culture, but the Joseph Goodwin daybook provides insights into the actual cycle as he lived it at George DeWolf's plantations. The daybook is also very useful because it provides information on the work routine for five consecutive years on coffee culture as well as other kinds of labor that enslaved workers undertook.

A new growing season usually began in February or early March with digging holes for new trees, pruning and weeding existing trees, and collecting manure. Pruning and weeding took place most of the year as part of the ongoing maintenance of coffee trees. Harvesting coffee sometimes extended into February, and consequently some processing was also conducted, but all harvesting and processing were completed by the end of February. From early March to mid-May, varied activities took place. Digging holes for new coffee plants and collecting manure continued, but substantial time was devoted to activities unrelated to coffee culture: the collecting of stone, the building of structures, the cutting of timber, and on one occasion the manufacturing of arrow root. This was apparently a "dead period" in the annual cycle of coffee culture.

Coffee plants usually began blooming in March, sometimes as early as February, and continued blooming through April reaching peak bloom by the end of March. Trees full of white blossoms forecast a good crop. The pleasing fragrance of the coffee blossoms captivated visitors, some of whom drew comparisons between the full flowering of coffee trees and freshly fallen snow (Bremer 1853:2:344; Emerson Diary 1846). Planting coffee and a variety of provision crops such as corn, sugarcane for cattle and domestic consumption, rice, and *malangas* [cocoyam] began in May and continued through early August. Harvest started in late August but intensified in October through December.

In September, the first full month of the coffee-picking season, coffee and other crops, such as corn, were also harvested. Slave laborers worked on Sundays picking coffee and processing it well into the night during the intense harvest period. On November 29, 1823, Goodwin noted, "All driers full, finished work ½ past 11 all hands turned in at 12." Even in December, slave laborers obtained little respite from a grueling work schedule except on Christmas Day, and it was the only official holiday that enslaved laborers at George DeWolf's plantations could expect to be liberated from plantation work. In several diary entries, Goodwin acknowledged when a day was a "feast day" (a holy day and an official holiday), but he still required all hands to work, including on the beloved holiday of enslaved Cubans, the sixth of January, the Epiphany, known as el Día de Reyes [the Day of the Kings].[10]

January usually marked the end of the season, and most of the workers focused on the completion of any remaining picking, drying, and pounding (removal of the dry outer shell and pulp). Harvested cherries needed to be dried immediately to prevent fermentation, but once it was in the parchment stage, the winnowing, sorting, and packing could be deferred to a later time if necessary (S. D. Smith 2002:108–9). Although Goodwin's journal does not indicate that this was practiced at DeWolf's plantation, this may have occurred at Cafetal Biajacas. In the 1841 inventory, 70 barrels of coffee *en cascaras* (ANC Galletti leg. 934, no. 6) meant that the coffee had been dried but the outer casing and dried pulp had not been removed or that the coffee was in parchment.

Production of coffee in western Cuba shared similarities with coffee culture elsewhere in the Caribbean, except for two striking differences: the widespread application of the in-cherry or dry method of coffee processing and the use of gang labor as opposed to task labor. When Cuba emerged as a major producer and coffee prices were high, these labor-intensive practices possibly had little effect on profits, but when coffee prices drastically declined, both practices potentially contributed to Cuba losing its competitive edge in the world market.

Reliance upon the dry method, the short but intense growing seasons, and the need for more frequent replacement of coffee trees required more laborers in lowlands than at higher elevations. These requirements of coffee culture in lowlands may explain the need for more slave laborers on coffee plantations than sugar plantations in the Matanzas jurisdiction, as Laird Bergad observed. These circumstances no doubt led to the demise of many coffee plantations and hastened the transformation of Matanzas from a mixed agricultural economy to one based solely on sugar.

4

Built Landscapes of Cuban Coffee Plantations

Ebenezer William Sage, a merchant from Middletown, Connecticut, owned two coffee plantations with Ephron William Webster, his brother-in law, in Matanzas jurisdiction.[1] On May 2, 1825, Sage wrote to the new administrator of these plantations with detailed instructions for a major renovation of his Cafetal Santa Ana near the town of Sumidero. His list of landscaping and construction projects included building a wall embankment in front of the house; planting as many trees and shrubs around the house as possible; covering the banks with dirt and Bermuda grass; extending the avenues of trees and replacing older plantings with palms; tearing down an old house and reusing the bricks, timbers, and doors for a building to be located behind the house; elevating the front avenue with stone up to a sandbox tree; constructing a fence on the perimeter of the property; and installing a gate in front of a tree avenue leading to the potrero (Sage Letterbooks).

Sage's planned renovation of the non-income-producing spaces of his cafetal came as a surprise when in earlier correspondence he complained about the low market prices for coffee. Three years earlier in 1822, he attempted to sell Santa Ana to a William Savage for $117,000, but was unsuccessful, and on November 25, 1823, he complained to Thomas Page, a business associate in Boston, "I know not how I am to get on particularly if no offer is made for Santa Ana or the Ontario estates" (Sage Letterbooks). Sage either overcame his financial woes or, in spite of them, proceeded with the implementation of his desired renovations.

In 1832, a visitor, Mary Gardner Lowell, wrote a description of Santa Ana in her diary indicating that Sage's intended improvements were not only executed but resulted in a stunning finished product.

> The Santa Ana is a most beautiful plantation in [S] Lumidero. The whole place is in high state of cultivation and here I have seen the handsomest palms which have yet greeted my sight in the island. Mr. Sage's house is beautifully located upon a hill commanding a very picturesque view of the estate & surrounding country. On one side at the base are his secederos [secaderos] or coffee dryers; his out-buildings of various description, & the boheas [bohíos]. In front, the slope is finely wooded, but not so as to interfere with the view, & a large sand box tree faces the house standing on an elevation of stone work which has a very pretty effect; the garden is kept in good order, and here one sees every species of tree plant & shrub that Cuba produces; both Mr. and Mrs. Sage are fond of cultivating them. (Lowell 2003:76)

Lowell's description of Santa Ana is consistent with other traveler accounts of Cuban coffee plantations.

Planters and visitors regarded the Cuban cafetal as a paradise with its beautiful gardens, orchards, guardarrayas lined with fruit and other flowering trees, and commanding vistas of the surrounding area (Singleton 2005b). Owners of these so-called paradisiacal cafetales were associated with grace, civility, and prestige; therefore, these coffee plantations became status symbols for the well-to-do and for aspiring social climbers (Pérez 2000:43). Perhaps this explains Sage's motivation to embellish his cafetal even when doing so may not have been a sound financial decision.

This chapter examines the built landscapes of coffee plantations from the perspectives of planters and visitors and, to a lesser extent, slave laborers. Architectural and landscape historians use the term "built landscape" to refer to the buildings, yards, streets, fields, trails, fences, tree lines, and all other elements of our surroundings that are products of human intervention (Ellis and Ginsburg 2010:2). Planters owned and directed the creation of coffee landscapes, visitors described them in their travelogues, and slave laborers performed the labor to produce them. Analysis of slaveholder geographies of containment—practices used to check slave mobility—begins in this chapter focusing on the spatial organization of Cafetal Biajacas and other Cuban coffee plantations. As part of the built landscape of slavery, the wall enclosure is examined here as a way of "othering" enslaved people by concealing their living spaces in order to create and maintain distance between the enslaver and the enslaved.

The Plantation Batey

The batey—the site for all the domestic buildings and structures for coffee processing and storage—was the centerpiece of the cafetal and the focus of most archaeological studies of plantations. Laborie (1798:13) advised planters to carefully plan where to place this settlement and urged that it be placed in the center of the property, but the location needed to be easily accessible and close to water, timber, and stone. He also stressed that all the buildings within this settlement, including the slave quarters, should be "arranged, as much as possible, within sight and reach of the mansion house" (1798:36). To accomplish this, Laborie (1798:37–38) recommended a symmetrical order to the arrangement of the buildings, dryers, and houses as he believed this served the dual purpose of an orderly and expeditious production of the crop as well as surveillance of the slave laborers.

Laborie's repeated emphasis on symmetry, possibly derived from the classical Roman architecture of Vitruvius, became an important attribute stressed in the layout of Cuban plantations for the next 50 years (Burroughs 2013:127). Another source for the concern with symmetry emanated from the Italian Renaissance through Andrea Palladio and his contemporaries. Palladio drew upon classical Roman principles of symmetry, order, and proportion in his designs of Italian agricultural villas built between 1540 and 1600 (Bentmann and Müller [1970] 1992:2–3). In the Palladian villa, the main dwelling was elevated, placing the owner at the center of an earthly paradise demanding attention from afar.

According to Reinhard Bentmann and Michael Müller ([1970] 1992: 101–2), social theorists of the Frankfurt School, the agricultural villa represented a new architectural format and lifestyle in the Italian countryside that expressed the ideals of an elite merchant class who prospered from capital gained in the burgeoning international trade. The villa replaced the feudal castle, but its presence, unlike the feudal castle, was not justified on the basis of a military or strategic need; therefore, the presence of the villa marked the emergence of a new hegemony that changed the character of social relations in the Italian countryside from feudalism to capitalism.

They also argue that the Palladian villa architecture became the model for villas of subsequent architectural styles (including plantations) from late baroque through neoclassicism up to the late Victorian period. And they further posit "at particular moments and in specific societies, Palladio's forms were reverted to . . . when a society with colonial, imperial, and capitalist tendencies has had to legitimate itself through artistic production, thus seeking to articulate its claim to hegemony by architectural means" ([1970] 1992:93). While Bentmann and Müller overstate the sociopolitical use of Palladian villa architecture, their point is that Palladian architecture was utilized to impose a worldview that naturalized the power and authority of a privileged few.

Archaeologist Mark Leone (2005:63–99) has offered similar interpretations regarding the use of baroque architecture and landscapes in mainland North America. Baroque was the other major architectural tradition originating from the Renaissance characterized by a rich ornamental style that utilized elements such as gilded wood, stucco, or marble, illusory effects such as trompe l'oeil, and a proliferation of geometric forms. Palladian architecture, on the other hand, emphasized the use of mathematical proportions based on classical Roman architecture with minimal use of ornamentation. These opposing architectural styles were deployed to achieve similar goals, but they were imbued with different meanings. Leone (2005:82), following the analysis of Fernand Braudel (1979:488–93), asserts that the ostentatious baroque style demonstrated the desire for power or position rather than power already achieved. Bentmann and Müller ([1970] 1992:31, 105–6) contend that the classical temple architecture of Palladianism and its later revivals expressed the central position that owners perceived of themselves within a social order modeled after the hierarchical relationships of the ancient temple gods.

Palladian elements found in plantation landscapes include elevated great houses, symmetric layout of outbuildings and grounds, concealment of workers' quarters from the formal plantation landscape, and tree-lined avenues leading to the grand entrance of the great house. Through Palladio's *Four Books of Architecture*, first published in 1570, Palladian architecture spread throughout Europe and the Americas and became a standard source in art and architecture curricula at the Royal Academy of San Fernando in Madrid, for example, and myriad drawing schools (García Melero 1992:18–19). Palladio's work was also used in the training of military engineers (Paul Niell, pers. comm. 2009) presumably responsible for surveying and laying out many Cuban plantations. Although true Palladianism had declined by the late eighteenth century, many of its concepts were revived and applied in new ways through the spread of neoclassicism.

Neoclassicism—a term coined only about 100 years ago and not used historically—broadly refers to artistic manifestations from 1750 to 1830 that drew upon classical art and architecture as well as the filtering of the antique tradition through the Renaissance and the seventeenth century for inspiration (Irwin 1997:8). Archaeological rediscovery of the ancient Roman cities Herculaneum and Pompeii in the first half of the eighteenth century generated neoclassicism, which emphasized the use of simple symmetrical compositions, geometrical spatial organization, motifs drawn from the ancient world, the triumphal arch, temple-like forms, and minimal ornamentation, among other characteristics (Irwin 1997).

As part of the Bourbon reforms, Carlos III, who financed excavations at Pompeii and Herculaneum, introduced neoclassical architecture throughout Spanish America for public buildings and monuments (Niell 2013a:xviii). Neoclassicism, however, was multivalent, as it held various meanings and values throughout the Spanish Empire. Latin Americans may have associated neoclassicism not with the authority of the Spanish Crown but with the revolutionary spirit of France and the United States (Niell 2013a:xxii). As countries in mainland Latin America gained their independence during the first quarter of the nineteenth century, they increasingly turned to the architecture of France and Italy to transform the layout and architecture of their cities and towns (J. F. Scott 1999:184–86, 193; 2012).

In Cuba, the criollo elite adopted many aspects of neoclassicism and attributed certain elements of their domestic architecture to French sources. For example, several Cuban authors have claimed that the H-shaped floor plan, similar to the one found in the great house at Cafetal Biajacas, came to Cuba by way of French immigrants (Villaverde [1882] 1977:2:20; F. Pérez de la Riva 1952:372; Álvarez Estévez 2001:60). While French expatriates in Cuba made numerous contributions to Cuban art and architecture, the

H-shaped floor plan has erroneously led some to believe that the owner of Cafetal Biajacas was French (Álvarez Estévez 2001:60). Documentary sources, however, do not support this assertion.

Many Cubans embraced neoclassicism, but they did so selectively and for different purposes, as suggested by its diverse usage in Havana. When José Ricardo O'Farrill, a brigadier of the royal armies and a founding member of the Sociedad Económica, built his neoclassical house at the beginning of the nineteenth century (figure 2.3), he reinforced his allegiance to Spanish colonial authority. At the same time, he helped pave the way for what became the growing acceptance of "classicism to represent things Cuban" that flourished in subsequent decades (Niell 2010:352). Other aristocratic Cubans incorporated baroque features such as ornamental plastered or gilded decoration into the interior décor of neoclassical houses, thereby combining the ostentatious display of baroque with the symmetrical floor plans and unadorned exteriors of neoclassicism (García Santana 1999:19). Still others simply added neoclassical touches to update houses built in the *mudéjar*, the Spanish Moorish style, with unroofed central patios (Llanes 1999:178). The term *buen gusto* [good taste] often referred to neoclassicism in Spain and many parts of Spanish America, but in Havana it sometimes became a referent for reconciling various architectural styles of the past and present (Niell 2013b:444). For some Cubans, buen gusto symbolized a newfound Cuban identity, distinct from Spain (Carley and Brizzi 1997:83).

Like the built landscape of Havana, Cuban plantations, particularly cafetales, contained a mixture of architectural styles. Neoclassical concepts in plantation layouts and temple-like great houses were combined with medieval forms—towers, walls, gateways. Together, these different architectural traditions coalesced in landscapes that showcased the power of the planter elite and hierarchical social order on the plantation. Such displays of affluence and power had their critics among the Cuban intelligentsia. In his treatise on Cuban agriculture, Francisco de Paula Serrano (1837:48) questioned the wisdom for the large expenditures of money and labor allocated to the building of great houses on coffee plantations when many of the same owners economized on purchases of clothing and food for enslaved laborers. He particularly criticized the use of elevated towers and arches, embankments, gates, and high walls, as these reminded him of "aquellos palacios del feudalismo revestidos con el aparto y magnificencia como para anunciar el señorío, deslumbrar, intimidar á sus vasallos y ponerles más manifiesta la distancia enorme que media de la humilde y apacible choza al palacio imponente y bullicioso" [those feudal palaces cloaked with ceremony and magnificence as to announce the lordship to his vassals, to dazzle, intimidate, and to make very clear to them the huge distance between the humble and calm hut and the imposing and bold palace] (1837:48). Serrano's statement provides evidentiary support for a major argument of this chapter: *Cuban coffee planters deployed architectural forms, like the wall enclosure at Biajacas, or landscaping elements to distance themselves from their enslaved workers and to highlight their privileged status and power*. Moreover, Serrano's critique demonstrates that this interpretation is not simply a present-day reading imposed upon the past but also the perspective of a nineteenth-century observer and fellow Cuban coffee planter.

Many Palladian elements during the neoclassical fervor found their way to Cuban plantations, but the hierarchical order and symmetrical layout of the buildings and spaces are most frequently described in nineteenth-century travel accounts. While these descriptions are often skewed by stylistic adherence to the "picturesque"—the period's romanticized, aestheticized way of describing landscape (Irwin 1997:186–200)—they nonetheless enable us to envision the spatial organization of many Cuban coffee plantations. Few drawn plantation plans, and none for Cafetal Biajacas, have survived to the present. Examination of several accounts suggests that the spatial arrangement of the buildings followed a hierarchical order with the great house elevated on the highest point in the batey and all other buildings placed below it in succession according to their importance.

On plantations lacking elevated areas, embankments faced with stone or grand avenues lined with royal palms leading to great houses made them appear to be the most imposing buildings upon entering the cafetales. Houses with trilevel floor plans, another characteristic of Palladian villas, with the lower level for service quarters and pantries, a second floor with parlors, and a third floor with bedrooms, stood out even more prominently than the typical single-story dwellings found on most Cuban plantations. North American travelers referred to these trilevel houses as built in the "American style," which hints at a potential North American influence on

Cuban neoclassical architecture.[2] The elevated house provided stunning views of the countryside, but also possibly served as a subtle panopticon—a surveillance device used to force self-discipline on those being watched through the threat of being constantly observed (Foucault 1979:200–205). Slave houses, coffee dryers, and the warehouses were generally located below the great house and in close proximity to the mayoral residence. In some cases coffee dryers were arranged vertically, forming a stairlike pattern that rose above all the other buildings where it was also possible to obtain a view of the surrounding countryside (Lowell 2003:95). At the very end of the batey, enslaved workers sometimes kept their livestock (Wurdemann [1844] 1971:105).

The plan of the batey for James DeWolf's Marianne plantation (figure 4.1) represents the hierarchical sequence described above within a symmetric plan. The succession of buildings and other landscape features began with the great house (A) and the detached kitchen (B). Opposite the great house, the well (L), the formal garden (M), a horse stable (N), and a building for carts and wagons (O) formed a complex centered on the planter household. A grove of orange trees separated the planter-centered area from the coffee works and other activity areas of the plantation. Behind the orange grove several outbuildings stood on one side of the square, including structures and pens for pigeons (E), fowl (F), and ducks (G); a hospital (H); a cookhouse or kitchen for the hospital (I); and a crib (J) presumably for the storage of corn or other food crops. Directly across from these buildings, on the opposite side of the square, the mayoral house (Q) was placed strategically for the observation of activities in and around these buildings, in the slave quarters (R), and within the coffee-processing complex with its warehouse (C), coffee dryers (D), and circular coffee mill, most likely a tahona (K).

One slave quarter is considerably larger than the others, which may be related to the different ways in which slave workers were housed according to gender, marital status, or other factors. Next door to the mayoral house was the sapo or stocks (P), possibly a plantation prison where enslaved people were confined. *Sapo* appears to a misspelling of *cepo*—a device very much like a stocks made from wood planks carved with foot, hand, and head holes for locking those parts of the body down into one position for punishment (Ortiz [1916] 1988:236). Fredrika Bremer (1853:2:337) de-

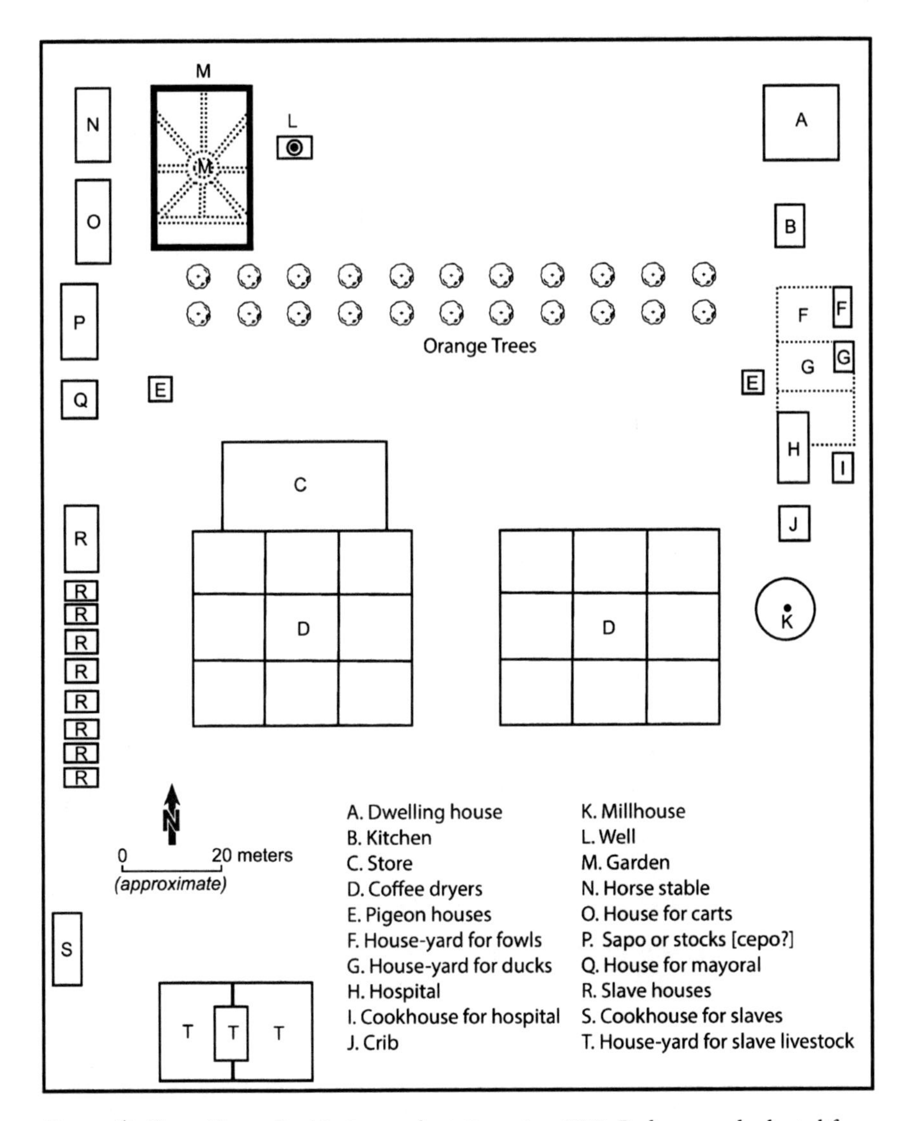

Figure 4.1. Plan of batey for Marianne plantation, circa 1820. Redrawn and adapted from photograph of original in DeWolf Papers, MSS 382, Rhode Island Historical Society, Providence. Drawn by Syracuse University Cartographic Laboratory.

scribed such a device located within a prison cell at a sugar plantation she visited, and Abiel Abbot (1829:143) referred to the plantation prison at a coffee plantation as the "stocks." A potential prison cell was identified at Cafetal Biajacas, and these so-called plantation prisons are discussed later. The central kitchen for the slave laborers (S) and the pens for the livestock belonging to slave workers (T) are located at the very end of the batey.

The plan of Marianne, if executed, incorporated many aspects of the spatial planning Laborie recommended and illustrated in his book, but with one notable difference—the pronounced segregation of the planter residence and its dependencies from the rest of the batey. Laborie's designs combined the planter house and coffee warehouse in the same building, making the planter residence part of the coffee works—a practice rarely implemented on the coffee plantations of elite owners in western Cuba. At Cafetal Biajacas, however, the coffee warehouse and the mayoral residence were housed in the same building (ANC Galletti leg. 936, no. 6).

The orange grove spatially separated the planter residence from the rest of the batey at Marianne, and other planters in Cuba apparently used trees and shrubs for a similar purpose. Ebenezer Sage instructed his administrator to plant shrubs around the great house at his coffee plantation Santa Ana. Similarly, Benjamin Norman (1845:53) observed a "village of thatched huts laid out in a perfect square and buried in overshadowing trees" on a coffee plantation in Güines jurisdiction, which included the partido of Madruga (shown in figure 2.2). The description suggests that the trees partially separated and screened the slave quarters from the great house, although the houses were apparently still visible.

Social segregation of plantation spaces emerged in slaveholding societies throughout the Americas as part of a broad process found in the European world beginning with the rise of modernity (Chappell 2010:75). Renaissance artists visually excluded the quarters of farm workers and servants in their fresco art painted on the walls of agricultural villas. This type of picture, which Bentmann and Müeller ([1970] 1992:85–87) refer to as "villa within a villa," depicted the grand house and the leisurely life of the villa owner as an expression of his or her self-image and social position without any reference to the people who made that life possible. Concealment of the living quarters for laborers was a fundamental principle of the Palladian villa architecture. Architectural historian and classicist Charles Burroughs

(2013:116) contends Palladio likened the living spaces for laborers to parts of the human body that are necessary to the functioning of the organism but are kept hidden from the view of outsiders. Excluding the people who performed all the labor was a way of othering them—subordinating them to an inferior position.

In plantation settings, othering manifested itself in various ways from subtle differences in building facades to distinguish between black- and white-occupied dwellings (Ellis 2010:151–52) to devising passageways to hide slave work from slaveholders' view (Chappell 2010:86–88). Terrence Epperson (1990:32) was one of the first archaeologists to explore the othering of slave laborers in plantation spaces. He found planters manipulated plantation spaces to keep enslaved laborers under surveillance but, at the same time, made them invisible from a direct gaze of the great house on mid-eighteenth-century plantations in Virginia. Later in the nineteenth century, new attitudes toward hygiene and international trends toward the improvement of worker housing spurred the relocation of slave laborers from the damp, dark basements within planter houses to well-built, detached kitchens and slave quarters (Chappell 2010:76). Detached kitchens protected the great house from potential fire and provided better ventilation and light and a healthier environment for enslaved domestics to live and work. Such buildings also moved the sounds, smells, and the people away from the planter house.

The long tradition of excluding and segregating workers' quarters from perspectives of great houses forms the basis for my argument that one potential use of the wall enclosure at Cafetal Biajacas was to hide or screen slave activities from the view of the casa vivienda. Located on a *meseta* [small plateau], the irregularly shaped batey of Cafetal Biajacas is relatively flat, and at eye level, all the buildings appear to be at the same elevation (although the casa vivienda is actually about 1 m higher than all the other buildings). Placing the casa vivienda on the northeastern most point of the plateau visually elevated it, particularly when looking up from downhill on the northern and eastern sides of the house (figure 4.2). The rear wall of the casa is only about 65 m from the slave village; if it were not for the wall enclosure concealing the slave quarters, the rear windows of the great house could look onto the slave village. Walls divide space into parts, and the enclosure effectively separated the slave village from the nearby casa vivienda

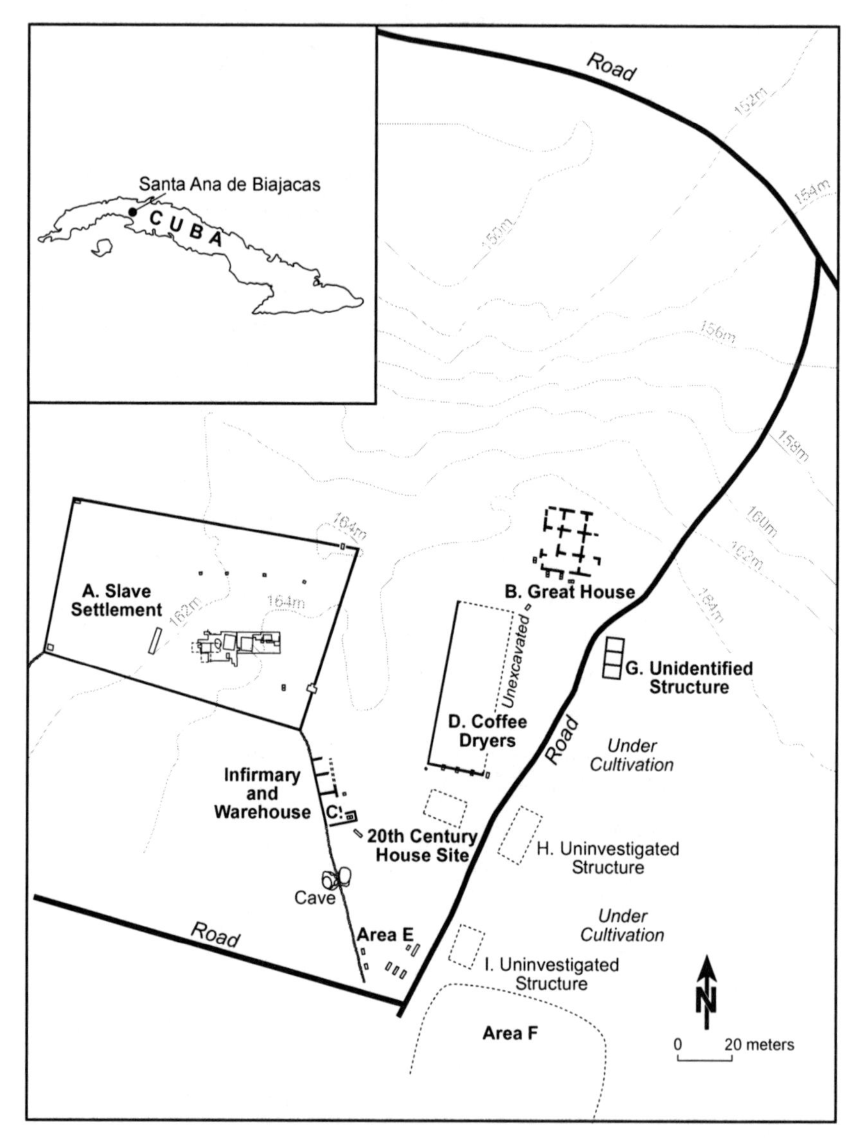

Figure 4.2. Plan of archaeological investigations of the batey for Cafetal Biajacas showing three extant ruins (A, B, and C) and all other loci identified from archaeological investigations. Drawn by Syracuse University Cartographic Laboratory.

as well as from the other plantation buildings. Trees and shrubs could have produced a similar effect as in the plan of Marianne, but the wall enclosure offered the added benefit, from the slaveholder's viewpoint, of constraining slave movement.

Concealing the slave village within the enclosure showcased the masonry casa vivienda built in the fashionable neoclassical style, while excluding enslaved people and their slave quarters from the formal landscape as Renaissance painters had done in their fresco art following the Palladian principle of concealment. This exclusion reinforced the subordinate role that enslaved people held in Cuban society. Serrano's previously mentioned comments suggest that Cuban coffee planters intentionally used architecture for othering their enslaved laborers and for flaunting their money and power.

Cafetal Biajacas is presently the only known plantation in Cuba with slave houses contained within a standing wall enclosure. But slave quarters enclosed in a similar fashion and built around the same time, the first quarter of the nineteenth century, have been identified elsewhere in the Caribbean. On St. Croix, U.S. Virgin Islands, William Chapman ([1991] 2010:108) describes three plantations: East Clifton Hill, Castle Coakley, and Estate the Williams, all large plantations with over 100 slave laborers and owned by British expatriots living on the island when it was a Danish colony. The slave quarters at each plantation consisted of masonry row houses containing multiple living units enclosed within masonry walls forming settlements that Chapman ([1991] 2010:108) termed "slave compounds." The height of the enclosure walls is not given, but at the Estate the Williams, the outer walls of some of the houses were incorporated into the enclosure walls indicating some enclosures rose as high as the height of the houses. Chapman believes these well-built houses along with other new types of slave quarters found on St. Croix arose from the influence of architectural literature and increased experimentation directed toward improving worker housing in Great Britain beginning in the late eighteenth century.

In another study, Kenneth Kelly (2008:395) reported masonry slave dwellings enclosed within a masonry wall at Grande Pointe plantation in Guadeloupe, in the French Antilles. As was the case in St. Croix, the houses were well built and laid out in orderly rows. The wall enclosure stands at 1.5 m today, but the original height was probably in excess of 2.0 m. Kelly suggests the wall may have served to confine enslaved laborers to their dwellings during turbulent times, noting the occurrence of a nearby slave revolt in 1793. He also proposes the possibility that the enclosure was used for both aesthetic and practical purposes. Land available for the slave village at Grande Point was limited, requiring the planter residence to be located very close to the quarters. In an earlier study Kelly conducted with Douglas Armstrong (2000) on slave houses, they found planters wanted to distance themselves from slave villages because they associated them with filth and illness. Many planters in the southern United States regarded slave quarters in a similar way (Vlach 1993:36). At Grande Pointe, the wall separated the planter residence from the slave village, but it also obscured the slave village from the planter's views of the sea and surrounding area.

At the plantations in St. Croix and in Guadeloupe, the slave quarters were built of masonry and arranged in gridlike layouts. In both places, the houses reflect efforts to improve or build more permanent slave dwellings than earlier slave houses and, at Grande Point, perhaps to control slave movement as well. The houses within the wall enclosure at Cafetal Biajacas, however, were not of masonry but were lightly framed structures, bohíos, presumably with mud walls. Additionally, limited excavations within the settlement suggest the houses were not arranged following a grid, and the houses appear to have been oriented in varied directions. These findings may be an indication that the slave inhabitants were able to build their housing to their own liking. The height of wall enclosure of 3.35 m (11 ft) and the earthen slave dwellings within it at Cafetal Biajacas add further support to the interpretation that the wall was intended to visually conceal, distance, and separate the slave quarters from the nearby planter residence. No efforts were directed toward building slave quarters of masonry like the buildings outside the enclosure at Cafetal Biajacas as was the case for the sites in St. Croix and Guadeloupe. O'Farrill apparently was unconcerned about how the slave houses were constructed or how they were arranged within the wall enclosure, but he wanted them contained and concealed from the rest of the plantation.

Whatever his reasons for constructing the wall enclosure, Ignacio O'Farrill did not enclose the slave houses within a wall at either of his sugar plantations. The reason for this remains unclear, but he frequently resided and later died at Cafetal Biajacas. At San Juan Nepomuceno, just a few kilometers from Cafetal Biajacas, the large slave population numbering 185 in 1822 resided in 60 bohíos constructed of the same *embarrado y guano* [earthen walls with palm-thatched roofs] as those of the coffee plantation. The absence of references to bohíos in the inventory descriptions of La Concordia, O'Farrill's sugar plantation in Tapaste, suggests the enslaved people were housed in a barracón—a building used for housing a large number of slave laborers. None of the inventories mentions a *cercado de los bohíos* [wall enclosure] for the bohíos at San Juan Nepomuceno, an item always listed in the inventories for Cafetal Biajacas.

O'Farrill considered Cafetal Biajacas his country home (he also owned a townhouse in Havana), whereas San Juan de Nepomuceno was his moneymaker. An administrator or mayordomo for the plantation most likely lived in the small, nondescript casa vivienda listed on the inventory for San Juan de Nepomuceno (ANC Galletti leg. 934, no. 6). The lack of wall enclosures at O'Farrill's sugar plantations points to the strong possibility that construction of the wall enclosure was directly related to the frequent presence of a resident owner.

O'Farrill's reasons for constructing the wall will never be completely understood but may have included several possible interrelated objectives: to block the view of the slave quarters from the planter residence because he perceived them to be unhealthy and/or untidy; to distance the planter residence from the slave quarters following the Palladian principle of concealing the living spaces of laborers; and to constrain slave movement, first, in order to keep enslaved people from leaving the plantation and, second, in order to confine disruptive behavior to the plantation, protecting the planter and overseer in the event of a *levantamiento* [uprising]. Based upon multiple sources, including reports made to the captain-generals, these small-scale rebellions, usually involving a single plantation, occurred regularly, and slaveholders took precautions that they thought would prevent them.

Envisioning the Batey at Cafetal Biajacas

Interpretation of the built landscape at Cafetal Biajacas derived from research efforts to envision the aboveground appearance and the spatial organization of its batey from present-day remains of the site. Lack of a drawn plan, comparable to that of the DeWolf Marianne plantation, combined with the goal of undertaking archaeological investigations to learn about the lives of the former inhabitants of the plantation required developing a site map (figure 4.2). The initial map captured the topography of the site and the floor plans of the extant ruins for the wall enclosure surrounding the slave settlement (A), the casa vivienda or great house (B), and the infirmary and warehouse (C). The map was expanded and updated as more of the batey was investigated through archaeological survey, excavations, and geophysical prospecting.

Details contained in the plantation inventories aided in the identification of all masonry buildings and structures, particularly for the infirmary/warehouse, which matches the dimensions and description of a building in the inventory identified as the *enfermería y almacenes del maiz* [infirmary and corn storage]. Site visits to other Cuban cafetales, nineteenth-century illustrations, descriptions in travel accounts, and consultation with local residents familiar with the site of Cafetal Biajacas also contributed to identifying, locating, and interpreting the plantation spaces at Biajacas.

Locating and Identifying Plantation Spaces

Extant ruins usually indicate that a site is well preserved, but at Cafetal Biajacas, particularly outside the enclosure, this was not the case. Agricultural activities, road construction, subsequent occupation, and the possible use of earth-moving equipment have significantly altered the site and compromised the archaeological resources associated with the coffee plantation era circa 1815–46.[3] Despite these drawbacks, archaeological investigations yielded the remains of several slave bohíos within the enclosed slave settlement, as well as a foundation for a set of coffee dryers (D), a plantation-era building of unknown function (G), and 17,487 artifacts, most of which date to the time of the coffee plantation era. Field research from 1999 to 2002 focused on finding evidence of the slave bohíos within the wall enclosure and from 2003 to 2006 on rediscovering the layout of the cafetal outside the wall enclosure.

The loci designated F, G, H, and I became evident for the first time in 2006 when the project was drawing to a close due to dwindling funds. Until that time, all the area east of the road running north-south was always planted in sugarcane 8 to 10 ft high and obstructed our view of these archaeological resources. Curtailment of sugarcane cultivation at the site in 2006 and the planting of low-growing crops enhanced the visibility of the site to east of the north-south road. Area F was a portion of an agricultural field planted in *maní* [peanuts] with artifacts visible on the ground surface among the rows of peanut plants. The project team collected these artifacts, all of which dated to the first half of the nineteenth century and corresponded to styles and patterns with artifacts recovered from within the enclosed slave settlement. Unfortunately, it could not be determined if these objects were associated with razed plantation buildings once located nearby or if they have been originally deposited elsewhere on the cafetal and brought to that location through plowing or other earth-moving activities.

Locus G, a masonry foundation measuring approximately 6.40 m × 14.35 m, was unearthed in my absence after the removal of thick vegetation and minimally excavated to reveal its floor plan in 2008. Its floor plan and size correspond to the description in the inventories of the detached kitchen that serviced the great house, but its location in front of the casa vivienda seems a bit odd. Detached kitchens on other Cuban plantations are usually located to the rear of the great house. The construction and orientation of G suggest that it is contemporaneous with the great house, coffee dryers, and the wall enclosure, but determining its function must await additional research. Designating it as a kitchen would require locating remains of some type of *fogón* [hearth] in or near that location. It is very likely that this structure, although originally built during the era of the cafetal, was reoccupied at a later date. A local resident in his 70s at the time, and now deceased, told the project team that he remembered an elderly woman named Gollita living in that location when he was a child.

Loci H and I have not been investigated; therefore, it is not known if they are intact foundations of former buildings or dense concentrations of stone debris. Limestone is ubiquitous throughout the site, occurring both naturally in the soil and in the debris of razed masonry walls and buildings as limestone was the primary material used for making *mampostería*—a masonry product used in the construction of all the masonry buildings at Cafetal Biajacas. The location of H and I appear ideally situated for structures comprising the coffee warehouse-mill complex along with the twentieth-century house site which may have been built over a plantation-era foundation.

The early twentieth-century house site, however, was also not investigated. This is the location where Patricio Pérez—the patriarch of the local residents (one of whom worked with the field crew) that live only about 200 m south of the batey—built his house when he moved to the area in the 1890s. According to his descendants, his wooden frame house was still standing as recent as 30–40 years ago. During the field research, it was only identifiable by a slightly raised area, a scatter of stones, and a narrow footpath alongside the raised area. Many of the early-twentieth-century artifacts recovered from the excavations of coffee dryers possibly once belonged to this household.

With several of the loci outside the enclosure located, and the northern and western boundaries of the batey defined, it was still unknown how much of the batey extended to the south and east. To address this concern, in June 2009, I conducted a pedestrian survey through the agricultural fields to the south and east after these fields had been plowed but before major planting had begun. I looked for artifact scatters, foundations, or nonstructural features (wells, privies, trash pits) appearing on the ground surface. I was particularly interested in seeking evidence of the formal entrance to the plantation such as foundations for stone fencing or a stone gatepost as I had observed at La Dionesia, a coffee plantation near the city of Matanzas (Hernández de Lara 2010). Because ruins of the front stairway leading to the front entrance of the great house faced eastward, I assumed that the entryway to the plantation would be located toward the east. Most entrances to Cuban plantations lead directly toward the front entrance of great houses. Although I did not find any evidence of an entrance or other structures, I was struck by the large number of fruit and palm trees located rather haphazardly within these fields. These randomly located trees may well be offshoots of the 1,000 fruit trees and numerous royal palms that once graced the plantation, including some planted in the avenues leading up to the great house. Long-term agricultural activities to the south and east of the batey, however, have obliterated any aboveground structural remains of the entrance. The extant trees may be the only remnants of the former avenues and gardens that once fronted the batey.

Analyzing Excavated Spaces

The vast majority of the field research geared toward rediscovering the built landscape of the batey at Cafetal Biajacas concentrated on the loci west of the north-south road and outside the enclosure A in figure 4.2. Our investigations began with excavating test units near exterior walls of B, the great house, and C, the infirmary/warehouse. These tests were intended initially to aid in determining possible dates of construction for the two buildings, but no definitive date could be established for either building from either archaeological or documentary sources.

The great house was most likely completed around the early 1820s when the plantation was prospering. Yet only two decades later, after O'Farrill's death, Francisco Galarraga, the administrator of his estate, stated the house was in "complete ruin," showing signs of a crumbling foundation that could collapse at any time (ANC Galetti leg. 240, no. 1, pieza 8). Minimal excavation was also conducted within the interior of the house, but this activity posed a hazardous situation because many of the large fallen stones utilized in the house construction weighed well over 100 lbs each and needed to be removed to thoroughly study the building. Some stones were ultimately removed to expose the floor level of the house and to record traces of the fresco wall paintings found in every room.

The most spectacular of the paintings, found in the *sala* or main living room in the center of the house, depicted a floral motif reconstructed and illustrated in figure 4.3. According to Rachel Carley and Andrea Brizzi (1997:126–27), wall painting in the sala was typically used to create the effect of wainscoting, and floral motifs, like this one, emerged in Cuban wall art by the nineteenth century when classically inspired patterns discovered at ancient Italian cities became popular. The floral pattern in figure 4.3 seems to drape a keystone motif that is suggestive of classical Roman design (Paul Neill, pers. comm. 2013). All of the wall art identified on the ruins of the great house was in the neoclassical style and not in the so-called primitive style found in many Cuban houses that are attributed to black Cuban artisans (Fischer 2004:57–76). It is also possible, however, that black artisans produced wall art in the neoclassical tradition as well. Both the symmetrical, H-shaped floor plan and the motifs of the wall painting

Figure 4.3. Reconstruction of mural art in the *sala* of the great house at Cafetal Biajacas. The floral pattern is suggestive of classical Roman features. Reconstruction of wall pattern and illustration by Claudia Roessger.

indicate the casa vivienda were designed in the neoclassical style fashionable in Cuba from the late eighteenth to the mid-nineteenth century.

Built in a perfect square, the one-story casa vivienda measured 26 *varas* on each side (approximately 21.73 m or 71.3 ft), an area of 676 sq varas (484.6 sq m or 5,216 sq ft) with an *azotea* [rooftop terrace], a sala, five rooms, and an *oratoria* [a chapel], 10 doors and nine windows, and a stairway with a small closet attached to it (ANC Galletti leg. 941, no. 6). An exterior stairway, the imprint of which can still be seen on the south facing wall of the casa, provided access to the rooftop terrace (Singleton 2001:107, plate 2). Houses designed similarly in the cities of Havana and Matanzas also had rooftop terraces. Fredrika Bremer spent her evenings in Havana on "the roof of the house which is flat . . . [it] is the principal place of assembly for Cuban families when in the evening they wish to enjoy *la brise* [the breeze] (Bremer 1853:2:264–67). Such houses were less common in the countryside, but at the Wilsons' plantation house in Matanzas jurisdiction, Mary Lowell stated, "We went on the roof of the house which has a pretty view of Camarioca river" (2003:85). At Cafetal Biajacas, the rooftop terrace or the second floor of the coffee warehouse/residence for the mayoral were the only structures tall enough to observe activities within the open areas of the slave enclosure unless there was a bell tower as is suggested from the description of the bells found in the inventory. Cafetal Biajacas apparently had three bells, one enclosed in a stone platform, and the other two mounted on wooden posts; two were located in the fields and pastures, and the third was on the batey where it faced both the cafetal and potrero (ANC Galletti leg. 245, no. 1, pieza 1).

Household furnishings and personal possessions listed in the inventory were in keeping with those of the planter elite. Such objects are displayed in various Cuban house museums and showcased in publications depicting the historical interiors of Cuban houses.[4] O'Farrill's possessions were perhaps not as elaborate as the wealthiest planters,' and several items—vestments, gold and silver-trimmed patens, and prayer books—were indicative of his role as a Catholic priest. Several pieces of furniture were made of mahogany, including four small and two large tables, a large bed with a damask headboard, a marble-top chest of drawers, a display cabinet, and a trunk. Other wooden furniture included a bed, three cedar tables, 20 chairs, and 12 red-colored stools or benches. The house also contained two crystal chandeliers, four marble floor lamps, numerous paintings and prints, two gold-trimmed mirrors, a silver spittoon, several fine pieces of needlework and other textiles, and 50 to 70 books (ANC Galletti leg. 245, no. 1, pieza 1).

Unfortunately, there is no mention of ceramic and glass tableware, a void that artifacts recovered from archaeological investigations could have filled, but our efforts to locate trash deposits exclusively associated with the great house were unsuccessful. Even when excavation units were placed some distance away from the great house, cafetal-era artifacts were always mixed with much later materials, making it impossible to attribute these artifacts specifically to the great house. A small number of artifacts (n=233) uncovered from units placed near the house contained only coffee plantation–era artifacts. One Spanish lead-glazed earthenware bowl (El Morro), five English-made tableware vessels, a green-glazed ointment jar (also called a rouge jar [Dawdy and Weyhing 2008:372–75]), and two glass bottles were recovered.

Although it is difficult to offer interpretations from such a small number of recovered objects, together with the household furnishings described in the inventory, some tentative observations on the material life of Ignacio O'Farrill can be offered. The decorations and furnishings appear to be comparable to homes of other wealthy families accustomed to entertaining (Llanes 1999:154). O'Farrill could accommodate numerous visitors with the large number of chairs and stools, and perhaps most visitors came to his house seeking spiritual guidance or he may have performed mass for a small group in the chapel. With an extra bed, he possibly hosted overnight guests occasionally like the owners of neighboring plantations.

Investigations at C, the presumed infirmary/warehouse, were primarily intended to determine the building's function. The project team initially designated this building the *almacén* [warehouse], based on the curious use of *tejas* [roof tiles] to line holes punched into the exterior wall of the small wing making the building L-shaped (figure 4.4). A large portion of a *horma de azúcar* [sugar mold] was inserted into the top of the exterior wall of the building closest to the slave settlement. We assumed that these holes indicated the building served a specialized purpose rather than a domestic living space. Possibly they were used to ventilate an area lacking windows. The inventories confirmed that the building was not a domestic quarter, but the function of the small wing was still unclear. The 1838 inventory indicated that it was a small kitchen that serviced the infirmary (ANC Galletti leg. 245, no. 1), but the 1841 inventory only gave its dimensions of 4 varas × 4 varas (approximately 3.34 m × 3.34 m or 10.97 ft × 10.97 ft) with no indication of its function.

In a 2002 field trip to a former cafetal, also named Santa Ana, near Tapaste, we found a kitchen still in use contained similar holes near the roof. The holes in the kitchen building, however, appear to have been made during the original construction of the wall with the holes arranged in a uniform pattern, whereas those in C appear like an afterthought—knocked out of the wall after a solid wall had been built. Perhaps the small room was originally intended for storage or some other purpose that did not require ventilation.

Figure 4.4. Ruins of wall with holes on small wing of C, the infirmary/warehouse at Cafetal Biajacas. Photograph by author.

Similar air holes are described in other Cuban plantation buildings. Lourdes Domínguez (1986:276) identified "air holes with ceramic tubes" on the front wall of an interior latrine at the barracón of the sugar plantation Taoro. Abiel Abbot (1829:143) observed a more sinister use for the air holes in rooms where enslaved people were confined at the Angerona coffee plantation. He described the infirmary as "the building intended for those who are morally infirm, as well as physically. At each end of the infirmary, therefore, in the basement story, is an apartment called the stocks, the one for male criminals, and the other for female. They are spacious arched rooms, and well ventilated with spiracles." Richard Dana ([1859] 1966:63) referred to the stone building used for the solitary confinement of enslaved people as a "penitentiary" on a sugar plantation he visited in which each room was "dark, but well ventilated." According to Dana, Cuban slaveholders believed enslaved people feared darkness and solitude and used solitary confinement for extreme punishment. In the plan of the batey at the Marianne plantation, the building identified as the "sapo or stocks" (figure 4.1, letter P) indicates that a building separate from the plantation hospital was solely dedicated to the purpose of confining enslaved people for punishment.

Excavations within the small wing yielded artifacts at the floor level of the building below the fallen wall and roof debris suggesting enslaved people once inhabited the small room.[5] These artifacts are not only similar to artifacts recovered from the slave settlement but three of these in particular are common finds at nineteenth-century slave sites found elsewhere in the Americas: a gaming piece refashioned from a fragment of a factory-made slipped ware; a mass-produced, five-hole bone button; and a blue-faceted glass bead. The artifacts, by themselves, do not necessarily mean that enslaved people occupied this room, but they do strongly suggest the possibility. The archaeological evidence does not support a conclusion that the room functioned as a kitchen: it lacked a hearth, and the recovered artifacts are related not to food preparation (as would be iron kettles or clay pots) but rather to food consumption, including ceramic tableware and a few bottles.

Given that the room was part of the infirmary, it could have served as a place of isolation for infirm individuals thought to have contagious diseases or for punishment. Confinement in plantation jails and subjection to vari-

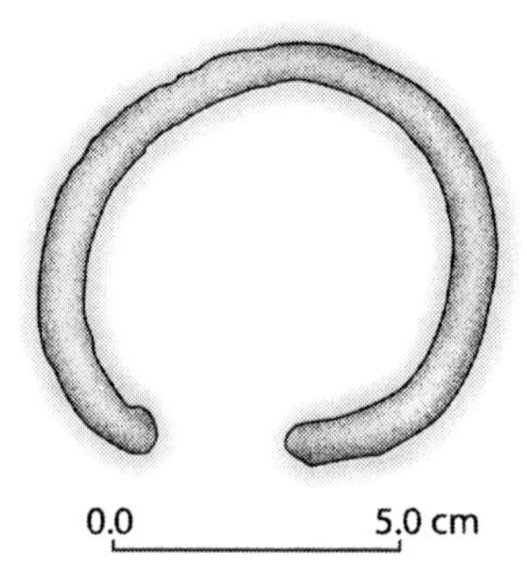

Figure 4.5. Iron leg shackle found in excavations of coffee dryers at Cafetal Biajacas. Drawn from photograph of artifact by Syracuse University Cartographic Laboratory.

ous forms of bodily restraint were common forms of violent treatment of enslaved people on Cuban plantations. A fragment of a grillete [shackle] (figure 4.5) recovered from excavations of the coffee dryers and a cepo, previously defined, listed among the tools and equipment on an inventory at Cafetal Biajacas (ANC Galletti leg. 940, no. 6), document that these cruel treatments were meted out at Ignacio O'Farrill's coffee plantation.

The vast majority of artifacts recovered from C consisted of roof tile fragments, a finding that concurs with the inventory description that the infirmary was roofed with tejas. All the other artifacts could be found at any domestic site, and only one recovered artifact—a fragment of an ointment jar—is suggestive of medical practices. The inventory indicated that the infirmary was sparsely furnished with only three beds, a cauldron, and an empty medicine cabinet. The mayoral possibly kept the medicines, as administering medicine to infirmed slave laborers was a responsibility Joseph Goodwin noted, July 21, 1821, as the mayordomo for the George DeWolf plantations (Goodwin Diary). Medicines may also have been stored in the great house. The infirmary at Cafetal Biajacas was evidently a multipurpose building that housed infirm slave workers, stored provisions such as corn, and perhaps functioned as the plantation jail. Because the building fulfilled multiple purposes, it is not surprising that artifacts do not indicate a specific usage.

Our most ambitious undertaking in rediscovering structures outside the enclosure has involved uncovering the coffee dryers. The lack of aboveground evidence for coffee dryers and thick vegetation throughout the site required developing a subsurface testing strategy that would indicate the probable location of the coffee dryers. The project team opted for geophysical prospecting—a suite of noninvasive techniques used for detecting buried deposits of potential archaeological interest—rather than a field strategy utilizing shovel test pits (STP) typically used in North American archaeology.[6]

In 2003, and again in 2006, the Departamento de Geociencias, Instituto Superior Politécnico José Antonio Echeverría (ISPJAE) in Havana conducted geophysical testing in a large area bounded by the standing ruins on three sides and the north-south road on the fourth side (see figure 4.2). The primary method used is known as *microgravimetría,* a geophysical prospecting method based upon the study of contrasts in the density of geological materials found occurring together, independently of where the materials originated (Carraz Hernández and González Caraballo 2004). Microgravimetría has been successfully employed to locate foundations, latrines, and concentrations of artifacts in Cuban archaeological projects. The application of this method at Cafetal Biajacas was designed to locate evidence of the coffee dryers and a slave cemetery. Several geophysical anomalies—areas of potential archaeological interest—were identified. Test excavations exposed a masonry foundation and floor, later designated as Locus D, the foundation for a set of coffee dryers. None of the test excavations yielded evidence of a cemetery.

After test excavations revealed the intact foundation of D, one side was completely excavated to determine its length and the possible function. We designated Locus D, the coffee dryers, based on its size and dimensions, approximately 60 m long and 18 m wide, and on a local resident telling us he remembered seeing a standing platform of the coffee dryers many years ago in that approximate location. Recovery of a white powdery substance, presumably residue from the cement-like mixture poured over the stone foundation to form the platforms, provided additional support that this structure was the coffee dryers. This substance was only found in the excavation of D and not in any of the other masonry construction.

Excavations of 132 units, each measuring 1 m × 1 m, yielded 3,782 artifacts from Structure D. The artifacts span the late eighteenth century to the present day and reflect two kinds of depositions: (1) items discarded after the coffee dryers were no longer in use until they were razed and (2) coffee plantation–era items initially discarded elsewhere on the plantation, but redeposited in and around Structure D as a consequence of some other kind of disturbance. Despite the disturbed provenience of these artifacts, some interesting finds include the previously mentioned leg iron and iron chain links possibly associated with it, ceramics stamped with French maker's marks, a fragment of a measuring scale in pounds and ounces, and fragments of a millstone most likely used to grind corn.

Locating a foundation for the coffee dryers was an important find for reconstructing the spatial organization of the batey, but it is unlikely that Locus D contained all the coffee dryers once used on the plantation. Based on the dimensions given for each coffee platform from other Cuban plantations, Locus D possibly accommodated only four contiguous coffee dryers, each measuring approximately 18 m × 15 m. While there was no standard size for coffee dryers, the suggested size for each coffee platform at Cafetal Biajacas is consistent with measurements found in other sources. Serrano (1837:50) recommended that each platform measure 16 varas × 20 varas [approximately 13.37 m × 16.72 m]), and John Wurdemann ([1844] 1971:142) recorded a measurement of 50 ft × 60 ft, approximately 15.24 m × 18.29 m. The total number of coffee dryers was proportional to the harvest, and Serrano (1837:51) advised 16 coffee dryers for plantations that produced 4,000 *arrobas* [100,000 lbs] of coffee, whereas Wurdemann observed that an estate of 400,000 trees had about 25 ([1844] 1971:142).

Plantation inventories for Cafetal Biajacas indicate there were 22 coffee dryers. Assuming this number was accurate, most of the dryers are unaccounted for. A large part of the batey outside the enclosure and between the other buildings was most likely covered with coffee dryers as suggested in the conjectural reconstruction of Cafetal Biajacas (figure 4.6). The effect of so many dryers obviously restricted movement within the batey. Recovery of additional evidence of dryers is possible but may be difficult because this portion of the batey has been subjected to considerable agricultural reuse and occupation since the abandonment of the plantation in 1846.

Geophysical anomalies were also indicated in the location designated Area E. The project team investigated this area to determine the nature of the archaeological remains and to find evidence to substantiate the local claim that it was the site of a cemetery.[7] No evidence of a cemetery, however, was uncovered, and the small number of artifacts (104 fragments) recovered from 20 1 m × 1 m units did not provide any indications of

Figure 4.6. Proposed reconstruction of batey at Cafetal Biajacas based on archaeological and documentary sources. Drawn by Syracuse University Cartographic Laboratory.

the former use of Area E. Most Cuban plantations had cemeteries, and they were located either on or close to the batey. These cemeteries usually contained burials of both the planter family and enslaved laborers. Eulalia Keating described the plantation cemetery where her aunt was buried on a plantation in Matanzas jurisdiction "as neatly enclosed and has handsome trees in it" in her diary January 9, 1839 (Bauduy Family Papers). Two of three extant plantation cemeteries that the project team visited in the vicinity of Cafetal Biajacas were also enclosed within low masonry walls about 1.5 m [5 ft] high or lower than that. The third may have been enclosed at one time, but this is no longer the case.

Envisioning the batey of Cafetal Biajacas entailed a process that utilized the layering of data obtained from diverse archaeological and historical resources culminating in the proposed reconstruction of the batey (figure 4.6). Several aspects of this reconstruction are conjectural (bell tower, coffee mill and coffee warehouse, and placement of additional coffee dryers), but these are based upon historical descriptions and site visits to other Cuban cafetales. Because the site of Cafetal Biajacas has been subjected to considerable reuse and disturbance, it may be impossible to document the former location of these conjectural elements through archaeology. The irregular-shaped batey at Cafetal Biajacas, though smaller than the plan of the Marianne plantation, was very similar to many other Cuban coffee plantations with the notable exception of the enclosed slave settlement.

Creating Paradise or Hell?

This chapter has focused on the description and analysis of the built landscape of Cuban coffee plantations from the perspectives of planters and visitors. Cuban coffee planters directed their efforts toward creating earthly paradises for the enjoyment of themselves and their guests. Visitors—consumers of these landscapes—reveled in the beauty of the cafetal, and through their travelogues they reinforced the metaphor of the cafetal as paradise. In addition, Enrique Sosa Rodríguez (1978:99–103) found in his study of nineteenth-century Cuban fiction the *cafetal-paraíso* [paradisiacal cafetal] provided a literary motif that veiled the "hell" to which enslaved laborers were subjected. His analysis shows the paradisiacal cafetal diminished its association with the labor (like the villa art of Italian Renaissance painters) involved in creating it and the inhumanity that enslaved laborers endured. To conclude this chapter, a slave narrative and an account of a slave uprising from a travel diary are briefly discussed to consider how enslaved Cubans perceived these plantation spaces and how their views contrasted with those of planters and visitors.

Perhaps the most poignant contrast between a visitor perspective of the built landscape of a Cuban coffee plantation and that of an enslaved Cuban is found in reference to the coffee dryers. Widespread use of the in-cherry or dry method for processing coffee beans in western Cuba required numerous coffee dryers to accommodate the longer drying time for each day's harvest. Consequently coffee dryers often dominated much of the space within the batey from 1,000 to 6,000 sq m (Ramírez Pérez and Paredes Pupo 2004:70). With coffee dryers occupying so much space, it restricted movement within the batey. Mary Gardner Lowell complained about the encroachment of the coffee dryers on one plantation: "the secadéros come quite up to the piazza" (2003:92). But at another, she wrote, "we dine between three & four consequently there is no time after our return except to stroll a little upon the secadéros or coffee dryers in front of the house" (2003:81).

The coffee dryers are also emphasized in the only known slave narrative written by an enslaved Cuban during the time of slavery. Juan Manzano, an accomplished poet manumitted (freed from slavery) with funds raised by his patrons, was enslaved for 30 years and spent most of his time as a house servant in the city of Havana. As a teenager, Manzano spent about five years on a plantation in Matanzas that he called El Molino [the mill], where his parents and siblings also lived and worked, and he performed domestic work (Schulman 1996). His references to the *tendal*—another term for coffee dryer—as he moves through the plantation indicates El Molino was a coffee plantation.

Manzano does not describe the coffee dryers or any part of the plantation, but the coffee dryers become a point of reference in his narrating two horrific events in his life. The first is the brutal whipping of his mother: "When the watchmen arrived from the yard where the coffee is dried, they led us away and I saw my mother put in the sacrificial place for the first time in her life. . . . Bewildered, seeing my mother in this position, I could neither cry nor flee. I was trembling as the four blacks shamelessly overpowered her and threw her on the ground to whip her" ([1840] 1996:73). The second is Manzano's memory of being passed off to various servants for removal to a sugar mill where he was to receive a beating: "[Santiago, a house servant] tied me up and led me to the yard where the coffee is dried, where he handed me over to a black who was waiting for me. We took the road to San Miguel sugar mill" ([1840] 1996:81).

In both descriptions, it appears that it was necessary to pass through the coffee yard in order to move to other locations of the plantation. In this way, the coffee dryers served as an impediment that restricted movement through the space. This secondary function of the coffee dryers was presumably an unintentional consequence of utilizing the dry method of coffee processing, though bateys were often organized, as Ramiro Guerra Sánchez ([1948] 1974:51) found at Jesús Nazareno, to control the traffic flow within it so that each person entering or leaving followed a designated path.

Another way in which enslaved people perceived the built environment differently from owners or visitors was in the appropriation of plantation buildings and spaces. John Vlach (1993:17) provides suggestions of how enslaved persons claimed various spaces as their own such as a slave cook claimed the kitchen or a slave weaver claimed the loom house in the southern United States. Eulalia Keating recorded in her diary on March 15, 1839, an example of enslaved Cubans appropriating and reinterpreting plantation spaces during a slave uprising at a sugar plantation. According to Keating, when the plantation bell rang for the Ave Maria (a prayer asking for the intercession of the Virgin Mary), 30 enslaved workers of the Lucumí nation [an ethnic designation] attacked the white managers at the Montalvo estate, a nearby sugar plantation. By using the bell chime for their own purposes, the enslaved workers transformed the meaning and usage of the plantation bell from a regulating device intended to keep them in line to one that allowed them to wield power.

Although the small group of slave rebels controlled the plantation for only a few hours, during that time they forced the planter family to stay within the confines of the great house, defeated the local patrol, and persuaded all the remaining enslaved persons—young, old, and infirm—to flee with them to the woods. By the time the army arrived at the plantation, all the slave workers had fled. Without a labor force, Rafael Montalvo, the owner of the plantation, extended a pardon to all of those who had run away if they surrendered. But the leaders of the revolt continued to resist, and several were mortally wounded by the army, while six others apparently took their own lives before they could be captured (Bauduy Family Papers).[8]

The brief account of a slave uprising at the Montalvo plantation and Juan Manzano's memories of plantation spaces at El Molino offer insights, though miniscule, into slave perspectives of plantation landscapes. Unfortunately, such perspectives leave no material traces, but nonetheless contribute to interpretations of plantation space. Not only were slaveholders' views of their plantations at odds with those of enslaved people, but slaveholders never completely controlled their plantations (Upton [1985] 2010) and "often found themselves constricted by the very environments they so diligently arranged and commanded" (Ellis and Ginsburg 2010:4).

On March 24, 1843, Thomas Amory described a young coffee planter named Jiménez who found himself in this predicament. Jiménez owned a beautifully designed, highly productive coffee plantation with 70 adult slave workers near Cafetal Carlota in the partido of Ceiba Mocha. He complained to Amory that his life in the countryside was "a great deprivation" in which he felt "banished from the city" because his "coffee estate requires his constant attention" (Thomas Amory Diary). Jiménez obviously felt the need to be present on the plantation as much as possible to maintain the discipline and order he demanded, even though he found doing so to be a personal burden. While Jiménez's self-imposed exile from the city can never be compared to the geographies of containment forced upon slave laborers, his attitude shows that creating a planter's paradise could have had undesirable ramifications for some slaveholders. Enslaved people were well aware of the limitations to slaveholders' control over their plantation landscapes and used this knowledge to their advantage. They tactically chose when to leave the plantation for nocturnal gatherings, to run away, or to incite rebellions.

The power dynamic between enslavers and the enslaved was always unequal, but enslaved people seized control of plantation spaces occasionally in plantation uprisings and on a more frequent basis through negotiations with their enslavers. Some Cuban planters acknowledged and accepted that certain plantation spaces, namely, slave living quarters, belonged to enslaved people; therefore, they did not care to regulate these designated slave areas even when pressured to do so by their peers and colonial authorities. Perhaps Ignacio O'Farrill was of this opinion as well and chose not to intervene in either the construction of slave houses or in the activities that took place within them. Instead, he had the wall built around the slave houses so he could visually conceal and separate the slave houses from the rest of the plantation, creating his ideal of paradise.

5

Housing Enslaved Cubans

On October 22, 1825, Cecilio Ayllon, governor of Matanzas jurisdiction, issued Reglamento Policia Rural [regulations for rural policing] four months after a major slave rebellion in the partido of Guamacaro. During this uprising, approximately 200 enslaved persons primarily from coffee plantations attacked 24 plantations and farms. Fifteen whites and 43 blacks lost their lives in the struggle (Barcia 2012:132, 160). According to Gloria García (2003a:84), this rebellion differed from those before and after it in the amount of bloodshed and in the destruction of property and crops.

The rebellion set in motion new policies and practices for the social control of enslaved peoples, including safeguarding slave quarters to contain slave movement. In Ayllon's *reglamento* under the section titled "Medidas de Seguridad" [security measures], article 14 required the following:

> De esta fecha en tres años se habrá construido en toda finca, cuya dotación esceda [exceda] de treinta negros un edificio apropósito para que se recojan estos y reúnan bajo una llave, teniendo este los convenientes alojamientos á fin que estén divididos los estados y los sexos. En las fincas de menor dotación podrán reconcentrarse lo más posible los bojios [bohíos], poniéndose bajo una estacada espesa de cuatro á cinco varas de alto con su puerta y llave segura.
> [Within a period of three years from today on every farm whose workforce exceeds 30 slaves a building must be constructed for the purpose of bringing them together and locking them up, it is advised accommodations should aim to divide them according to marital status and sex. On farms with less than 30 workers, put the (slave) bohíos together as much as possible, placing them behind a thick

> palisade 4 or 5 *varas* (approximately 3.34 m or 11 ft or 4.18 m or 13.71 ft) high with a door and secured with a key.] (ANC GSC, leg. 1469, no. 57999)

Prior to this mandate, the 1789 *real cédula* [royal decree] on slavery contained few specifications for slave housing.[1] It only stipulated that slaveholders provide separate rooms or buildings protected from inclement weather and to designate separate rooms or buildings for unmarried and infirm slave men and women (García 2003b:57). The new policy of keeping workers under lock and key would be reiterated in later slave codes and proposed in planter essays.

Slaveholders in Cuba, like those throughout the Americas, notoriously ignored ordinances regulating slavery, particularly when they perceived such laws as infringements upon their efforts to maximize profits. Building new quarters or a palisade around existing houses was a capital expenditure many coffee planters could ill afford particularly when coffee prices drastically declined in the late 1820s. Moreover, lax enforcement of the 1825 ordinances (García 2003a:91) provided little incentive for coffee planters to invest in costly new slave housing.

Some planters, however, apparently did comply with the new regulation. Roura Álvarez and Angelbello Izquierdo (2012:75) cite Abiel Abbot's (1829:12–13) description of a slave quarter nearing completion at W. Taylor's Carolina sugar plantation in 1828 as an example that not only met the regulation but also was an early prototype of what became known as the *barracón de patio*. In a similar vein, both archaeological evidence and written description of the enclosed slave quarter settlement at Cafetal Biajacas indicate that it met all the criteria of Ayllon's mandate for plantations with bohíos. Ayllon, however, specified the construction of a palisade around slave houses on farms with fewer than 30 slave men and women, whereas the slave population at Cafetal Biajacas was over three times that number in 1822 (ANC GSC leg. 871, no. 29460).

The fact that the enclosed slave settlement so closely resembled the criteria of the 1825 ordinance raises the question of whether it was built following the 1825 rebellion or before that time. I have shown that the enclosure concealed, separated, and distanced the nearby planter residence from the slave quarters while keeping the slave houses hidden and removed from the idyllic view of the plantation. Here I examine how the enclosed slave settlement fit within the broader planter discourse on slave housing in Cuba that began with Ayllon's reglamento in 1825 and continued through the early 1860s. An examination of the two main categories of slave housing, ordinances pertaining to slave housing, planter recommendations, and the housing practices for enslaved laborers as observed from written, visual, and archaeological sources are used to analyze and interpret the archaeological data of slave houses recovered from the enclosed slave settlement.

Object Biographies of Slave House Forms

An object biography addresses questions concerning the origins, cultural influences, and transformation of an object in order to highlight its significance or to reveal characteristics that might otherwise remain obscure (Kopytoff [1986] 2000:379). This discussion briefly traces how the two broad categories of buildings became the dominant forms of Cuban slave quarters. First, the bohío was a detached house (comparable to the slave cabin of Anglophone America) usually with a thatched gable roof, sometimes a hipped roof, with walls made of reeds, *yaguas* [inner bark usually of the royal palm], mud, or wooden planks. Floors were either earthen or made of wooden planks raised on timber or stone piers. Second, the barracón was a single building used to house a large number of slaves, sometimes the entire slave population on a plantation. Some barracones consisted of long rows of adjoining, contiguous rooms that shared common walls, like rowhouses; others were large buildings subdivided internally into rooms or cells. Prior to the 1830s, barracones were constructed from various kinds of materials, but after that time, they were primarily masonry.

Both types of slave housing were used throughout the nineteenth century in Cuba, but some writers used the term *bohío* to refer to the individual rooms or cells of barracones, whereas others consider a row of adjoining, contiguous rooms *bohíos conjuntos* [attached bohíos], not a barracón (Ortiz [1916] 1988:200). Additionally, because of its association with slavery, the word *barracón* was sometimes used, and it is still used today in Cuba, to refer to any type of slave quarter. These differences in the usage of the terms make it unclear what kind of slave housing existed on a particular plantation when only the terms *bohío* or *barracón* are used without additional description. Despite this problem, bohíos were more commonplace than barracones for housing enslaved people throughout Cuba (R. Scott [1985] 2000:17; Roura Álvarez and Angelbello Izquierdo 2007:137; 2012:24). Unlike the barracón created solely for slave housing, the bohío has had a long presence in the Americas, becoming part of the vernacular architectural traditions of Latin America as a whole, particularly on the Spanish Antilles—Cuba, the Dominican Republic, and Puerto Rico—where Europeans first encountered it.

El Bohío Cubano within the Circum-Caribbean

The word *bohío* derived from the presumed Taino [an Arawak-speaking people] term *buhio*, meaning "house" (Jopling 1988:5), which entered into Spanish language and culture with the voyages of Christopher Columbus. Bartolomé de Las Casas wrote in his *Historia de las Indias* Columbus's description of the Taino dwellings: "[They] make their houses of wood and straw in the form of a bell. These are very high and spacious, such that ten or more persons lived in each one." Las Casas goes on to say that the main posts were driven into the ground in the form of a circle and the roofs were covered with a sweet-smelling straw (Deagan and Cruxent 2002:33). Gonzalo Fernández de Oviedo y Valdés, another sixteenth-century observer of aboriginal life in the Caribbean, in *La historia general y natural de las Indias* provides further details of aboriginal dwellings in illustrations that show two forms: one circular or polygonal, known as a *caney* and occupied by caciques [chiefs], and the other a four-sided structure (Jopling 1988:8–9) that resembles the bohío of the last five centuries.

Early Spaniards in the Americas quickly appropriated and modified the bohío to suit their own tastes. At La Isabela, the first European town in the Americas (1493–98) founded on the north coast of present-day Dominican Republic, most colonists lived in bohíos of wood and thatch. But they built them in sizes comparable to modest housing of late fifteenth-century Spain (Deagan and Cruxent 2002:129). Bohíos initially served as dwellings for the first Spanish settlers in Cuba, but affluent inhabitants of sixteenth-century Havana replaced the walls of yaguas with wooden boards or mud construction and earthen floors with *hormigón*—a cementlike substance. Owners of wood-plank bohíos referred to them as "casas de tabla y guano" [wooden planked houses with palm roofs] and often used them as rental property in Havana (F. Pérez de la Riva 1952:333). As houses of stone, *mampostería* [a masonry product combining rough stone, lime, and other materials] and *tapias* [earthen construction] became more plentiful, the bohío was relegated to housing for the poorer classes of people. But the basic floor plan of the bohío was sometimes incorporated into the larger houses of wealthy classes of people in wings running lengthwise to the main structure built during the early centuries of colonial settlement (García Santana 1999:33).

In Havana, efforts began in the late sixteenth century to remove the bohío from the city limits because the thatch roof posed a fire hazard. The *cabildo* [town council] of Havana petitioned higher authorities in 1576 to prohibit building roofs with guano or straw (F. Pérez de la Riva 1952; García Santana 1999:15). Other towns eventually followed Havana's lead, but the disappearance of thatched-roofed bohíos from Cuban cities and towns was a long, slow process during which time several fires caused considerable damage. As late as the nineteenth century, fires in the towns of Batabanó in Mayabeque province and San Antonio de los Baños, Artemisa province in 1821, and in the city of Matanzas in 1845 were all attributed to fires initiated in bohíos (F. Pérez de la Riva 1952:336).

By the time large numbers of enslaved Africans arrived in Cuba to labor on plantations in the nineteenth century, the thatch-roof bohío had been banished to the countryside and primarily identified with white non-slaveholding subsistence farmers, pejoratively referred to as *monteros* or *guajiros*. Planters most likely utilized the bohío for slave quarters because it could be built quickly with inexpensive, readily available materials. But bohíos also carried the stigma of being associated with the lowest rungs of a hierarchical society and perhaps became another way of othering enslaved laborers.

The stereotypical slave bohío described and popularized in nineteenth-century Cuban fiction and other writings consisted of building materials similar to the aboriginal bohío framed with *cujes* [twigs, sticks, or similar plant materials comparable to wattle] and the walls filled in with yaguas rather than wooden boards or earthen construction.[2] Anselmo Suárez y

Romero (1859:202–3), a Cuban writer known for his detailed descriptions of slave living conditions, wrote this rare account of enslaved Cubans building a *yagua bohío*:

> Los días de fiesta son los que se conceden a los negros para hacer sus bohíos, porque en los de trabajo sólo tienen lugar para comer al mediodía la ración, y para acostarse a dormir por la noche en cuanto llegan del campo. De suerte que hoy abren los hoyos y clavan los horcones, de allí a ocho días cruzan los cujes, y al cabo de otros tantos cubren con yaguas y con guano las paredes y echan la cobija; . . . La figura de los bohíos es por lo regular un cuadrilongo, sí bien perfectamente trazado con el techo de dos aguas, que es el que más se usa en todas las casas del campo. . . . Después que entierran los horcones y entrelazan los cujes, sean derechos o torcidos, lisos o nudosos, y unos más largos y más gruesos que los otros, desaliño en que poco se diferencian los guajiros, y después que arman el esqueleto de arriba, comienzan a cobijar y a tapar las paredes.
>
> [Holidays are given to the slaves to make their bohíos because during work they only return to the places where they live for their noon meal and to sleep for the night as soon as they arrive from the field. They opened the holes today in order to drive the posts, afterward they intertwine the cujes up to eight days, and in the end with many others they cover the walls with yaguas and palm and put up the palm roof; . . . The shape of the bohíos is an average oblong; if good, it is perfectly aligned with the gable roof, which is used most often on rural houses. . . . After setting the posts in the ground and intertwining the cujes, some of which are straight or bent, smooth or knotty, some longer and thicker than others, this untidiness slightly distinguishes these (slave bohíos) from those of white countrymen, and after they assemble the top frame, they begin to thatch the roof and fill in the walls].

Suárez y Romero described the basic construction of bohíos (also illustrated in figure 5.1), which was similar for those made with wooden planks or mud walls, but these materials involved more costs, labor, or time. Wooden planks needed to be cut and smoothed before they could be used for building, and nails, an additional expense, were needed to put the boards

Figure 5.1. Cutout of a bohío illustrating the light, timber-frame construction. The stones around the structure observed on photographs of bohíos in the Dominican Republic were used to provide added support to the foundation. Drawn by Syracuse University Cartographic Laboratory.

together to form the structure. Earthen walls were low cost, but plastering a wattle-framed bohío with a mud or lime mixture added additional steps to the building process. From the planter's perspective, the yagua bohío offered monetary and time-saving advantages over other materials. It is also possible that enslaved Cubans preferred the yagua bohío because they were familiar with houses using similar construction techniques and materials in Africa. When given the opportunity to build their own housing in various places in the Americas, Africans chose to build houses similar to the yagua or mud-wall bohío.[3]

Enslaved Cubans' knowledge of construction similar to the yagua-walled bohío raises the question of how Africans contributed to the bohío's modification and transformation. Cuban writers often refer to the bohío as a product of *transculturación*—a newly created or transformed artifact or practice resulting from interaction and exchanges of diverse people (Ortiz [1947] 1995a:97–98). While the African role is acknowledged in the transformational process of the bohío (García Santana 2000:15; Roura Álvarez and Angelbello Izquierdo 2007:137), specific African contributions to this house form have not received systematic study in Cuba as elsewhere in the Caribbean. It may be difficult to identify specific African influences in bohío construction and use because dwellings similar to the yagua-walled bohío are found among indigenous peoples living in tropical areas all around the world. Differences in construction techniques or materials were at best subtle, and therefore African innovations to the construction of the bohío most likely went unnoticed and, unfortunately, unrecorded.

More than 60 years ago, however, Cuban historian Francisco Pérez de la Riva (1952:337–38) offered insightful, though pejorative, comments on how Africans changed various elements of the bohío and the use of space within them (he viewed African modifications to the bohío negatively). He noted several ways they transformed the bohío: bringing kitchens indoors, eliminating windows, reducing the number of doors to one small one in the front, and sharing their dwellings with pigs, chickens, goats, and lambs that could enter, leave, and stay inside like in their lands in Africa.

In her study of the Puerto Rican bohío, architectural historian Arleen Pabón (2003:20–21) refers to the elimination of windows and reduction of doors as a transformation from the open character of the aboriginal bohío to one with a more introverted character. She interprets the introverted bohío as an Africanism that permitted enslaved people to shut out the oppressive world outdoors in order to obtain a sense of privacy and definition of their own spaces indoors. Through historic photographs, Pabón further demonstrates that the characteristic features of the introverted bohío persisted in Puerto Rico well into the first half of the twentieth century. The absence of windows is also a common feature on the bohíos pictured in Elpidio Ortega's (2000) survey of housing in the southwestern region of the Dominican Republic. The widespread absence of windows and secondary doors on nineteenth- and twentieth-century bohíos may well have been an African innovation.

Despite its cost savings and the possibility that some slave laborers may have preferred it to other kinds of construction, the yagua-walled bohío had its drawbacks. Because it was made of highly perishable materials, it needed frequent maintenance and was highly vulnerable to wind, rain, and fire. Many slaveholders used the yagua bohío only for temporary housing while awaiting the construction of more permanent slave quarters of wood or earth. According to Roura Álvarez and Angelbello Izquierdo

(2007:140), wooden bohíos were used more frequently for slave houses than earthen ones, but written records indicate that slave bohíos at Cafetal Biajacas were made of earth. Earthen construction, when it was used, had several advantages over wood, including lower cost, greater longevity, and better resistance to fire (Van Beek 2008:19–38).

The Spanish tradition of building in mud dates back to the invasion and occupation of Spain by the Moors—an Arabic-speaking North African people—in the eighth century (Van Beek 2008:3). In Cuba, Spaniards possibly began building in mud as early as the first half of the sixteenth century. In 1534, the Spanish Crown issued a cédula to *encomendadores* [the grantees of encomiendas] to build all houses and other structures of stone or earth (García Santana 1999:14) in order to preserve the forests for shipbuilding and the maritime trade. Earthen construction varied from region to region in Cuba, but tapia (rammed-earth construction) was commonly used. Building with tapia involves constructing walls from earth compacted by pounding or ramming it usually into metal or wooden forms. The forms help to prevent the walls from collapsing and keep the thickness of the wall a uniform size (Van Beck 2008:3).

Earthen slave houses are typically identified in nineteenth-century documents as *embarrado y guano, embarrado cuje* [wattle-and-daub], or simply *embarrado*. Embarrado, a general term for plasterlike mixtures, consists primarily of earth or clay, but plant materials were often added as a tempering agent to make the clay more workable (figure 5.2). It was used to plaster exterior walls, interior walls, or both, and García Santana (1999:36) classifies embarrado as a variety of tapia, but used in rammed construction without forms or to plaster wattle frames for wattle-and-daub construction. Diverse forms of housing were built from embarrado both in towns and rural areas, and some plantation great houses were constructed of it. Houses made of this material are still found today in historic neighborhoods of towns and rural districts such as in Trinidad in the province of Sancti Spíritus in central Cuba.

The plantation inventories for Cafetal Biajacas indicate that the slave bohíos were constructed of guano and embarrado, but excavations within the enclosure did not yield any preserved fragments of embarrado to complement or support the written description. This lack of archaeological evidence of embarrado, however, is not surprising because the natural con-

Figure 5.2. Example of *embarrado*, a construction material made primarily from earth and used historically in Cuba. The slave quarters at Cafetal Biajacas were made from it according to the plantation inventories and were similar to this extant historical structure in Trinidad de Cuba, Sancti Spíritus Province. Note the inclusion of plant fibers for temper to make the material workable and traces of paint on the exterior surface. Photograph by author.

tents of embarrado (clay, plant material, and sometimes lime) could have easily been plowed into soil or hauled to another location after the slave houses were razed.

Bohíos built with wooden boards and thatched palm roofs were the most common type used for slave housing, and they are still the most prevalent type seen today in Cuba. Present-day bohíos reflect modifications that late nineteenth- and early twentieth-century Spanish immigrants to Cuba made to them. One of the most significant transformations resulted in doubling the floor space by placing two bohíos together in an L-shape arrangement (García Santana 1999:33, 43 figure 9).

The Cuban bohío through time has provided housing for diverse groups of people, each putting their own stamp on it. Housing slave workers was only one of the many roles in the long and varied history of the bohío.

Figure 5.3. Popular poster of bohío with Cuban flag, sold in bookstores. This supports the claim that the bohío is now an important symbol of Cuban nationhood. Photograph by David Broda, Syracuse University Photo and Imaging Center.

Over the years, the meaning of the bohío changed from housing associated with poor people to a symbol of Cuban nationhood that many artists and writers celebrate (figure 5.3). In revolutionary Cuba (post-1959), it also epitomizes the process of transculturation in an architectural form because it combines elements belonging to aborigines, Africans, and Spaniards (García Santana 2000:12; 2012:xxii).

El Barracón

Honorato Bernard de Chateausalins is often credited with introducing the term *barracón* to Cuban slaveholders through his book *El Vademecum de los hacendados cubanos o guía práctica para curar la mayor parte de las enfermedades; obra adecuada a la zona tórrida, y muy útil para aliviar los males de los esclavos* [The medical handbook for Cuban plantation owners or practical guide to cure most diseases; work suitable in the torrid zone, and very useful to alleviate slave illnesses], first published in 1831. In his often-quoted passage, Chateausalins (1854:35–36) advised that slave quarters

> se fabriquen en forma de barracón con una sola puerta, cuidando el administrador o mayoral de recoger la llave por la noches. Cada cuarto que se fabrique no tendrá otra entrada que una sola puertecita y al lado una ventanilla cerrada con balaústres para que el negro no pueda de noche comunicarse con los otros.
> [be constructed in the form of a barracón with only one door, kept locked at night under the care of the administrator or overseer. Each room should be built with only one entrance through a small door, and on the opposite side a small window closed with balusters so that the slave cannot communicate with the others.]

Born in France in 1791, Chateausalins graduated from medical school in Paris in 1817 and came to Cuba in 1818. As a physician, he treated the slave laborers belonging to the Drake family (Moreno Fraginals 1978:3:198), whose coffee plantation Carlota was near Cafetal Biajacas. Later he became a professor at the University of Havana and an influential member of the Sociedad Económica (J. Pérez de la Riva 1975:26).

Chateausalins (1854:91) believed housing enslaved people in barracones would accomplish two important goals: first, protect them from disease and, second, prevent them from engaging in unauthorized activities at night that deprived enslaved people of their rest and created an atmosphere for slave rebellions. He found most slave bohíos to be poorly maintained—full of holes, cold, and drafty—conditions that caused illnesses, particularly in children. In addition, he believed bohíos were difficult to safeguard and therefore facilitated nocturnal slave activities such as visiting neighboring plantations for romantic partners, searching for alcoholic beverages, and robbing slaveholders of sugar, coffee, or other crops that they gave to tavern owners in exchange for alcoholic beverages. Finally, Chateausalins (1854:36) justified locking up enslaved people at night as a security measure to prevent clandestine activities, running away, and rebellions.

Prior to Chateausalins's publication in 1831, barracones existed in Cuba, but they were rarely referred to as such, and they were generally not built of masonry (J. Pérez de la Riva 1975:26). Zoe Cremé Ramos and Rafael Duharte Jiménez (1994:3) conducted a survey of inventories for coffee plantations dating from 1809 to 1848 in the Grand Piedra region in eastern Cuba to determine if barracones were used for slave quarters on coffee plantations. Juan Pérez de la Riva (1975:400–401) claimed French slaveholders, the predominant planters of that region, did not quarter their slave laborers in barracones but in bohíos. Their study revealed that many coffee plantations housed enslaved people in buildings meeting the definition of a barracón, but they were simply called *casas de negros* [slave houses]. The dimensions of these buildings and the number of enslaved persons on these plantations indicate that these slave quarters were not bohíos but large buildings housing numerous workers. These barracones, however, were constructed of the same kinds of materials as those in the bohíos, including wood, embarrado, and embarrado cuje often with thatched roofs. Later in the 1840s, barracones of mampostería are described with increased frequency (Cremé Ramos and Duharte Jiménez 1994:7).

In western Cuba, the word *barracón* also appears to be absent from most pre-1830s inventories and ordinances.[4] For example, Ebenezer Sage housed 31 men, 9 women, and 16 children in a building he listed on an inventory and included in a letter written January 22, 1822, as a "long building" containing five large rooms and several small ones at his plantation Santa Ana (Sage letterbooks). Similarly, Aylłon's description of "un edificio apropósito" [a building for the purpose] of housing 30 or more workers in the 1825 reglamento met the definition of a barracón several years before the word *barracón* came into common parlance in Cuba as a type of slave quarter.

The word *barracón* became associated with slavery on both sides of the Atlantic. According to Moreno Fraginals (1978:2:74), slave traders coined the term in the sixteenth and seventeenth centuries to refer to the factories or lodges used for housing African victims sold into the slave trade while awaiting the horrific Middle Passage to the Americas. Barracones on the West Coast of Africa were normally constructed from wooden planks and roofed with thatch. The victims were chained within the barracones to prevent them from running away (Law 1998:102). The term *barracón* was later used to describe slave barracks in Brazil as well as in some Spanish colonies prior to the introduction of the term to Cuba.

Cuban barracones are generally grouped into two types: the nave (a Brazilian term), a long, narrow building usually with a gable roof (Roura Álvarez and Angelbello Izquierdo 2012:28) and the barracón de patio, a square or parallelogram-shaped floor plan with an open space or courtyard in the center. The sizes and floor plans for barracones varied, but the nave was usually consistent with Sage's English name for it as the "long building." Floor plans of naves indicate that some naves met Fernando Ortiz's description of bohíos conjuntos—a row of attached, contiguous rooms sharing a common wall, but with each room having its own entrance (figure 5.4). Other naves, however, consisted of open interior spaces with only one or two entrances that were sometimes subdivided into smaller rooms with wooden or yagua partitions. When Fredrika Bremer referred to the slave quarters she visited at the coffee plantation La Concordia as "lying open which reminds me of the large barns in our own country" (Bremer 1853:2:410), she most likely was describing an undivided or minimally subdivided nave similar to the two examples illustrated in figure 5.4.

Most large naves, however, were subdivided into smaller rooms. Juan Pérez de la Riva described a large nave at the sugar plantation Santa Barbara in the jurisdiction of Güines belonging to a member of the O'Farrill family measuring 55 × 14 varas [46 m × 11.7 m or 150.8 ft × 38.4 ft] where the exterior walls were of mampostería, but pine boards were used to subdivide the interior space into 40 rooms (1975:24). The nave at Santa Barbara housed 38 men, 62 women, and 36 children. Naves of this type

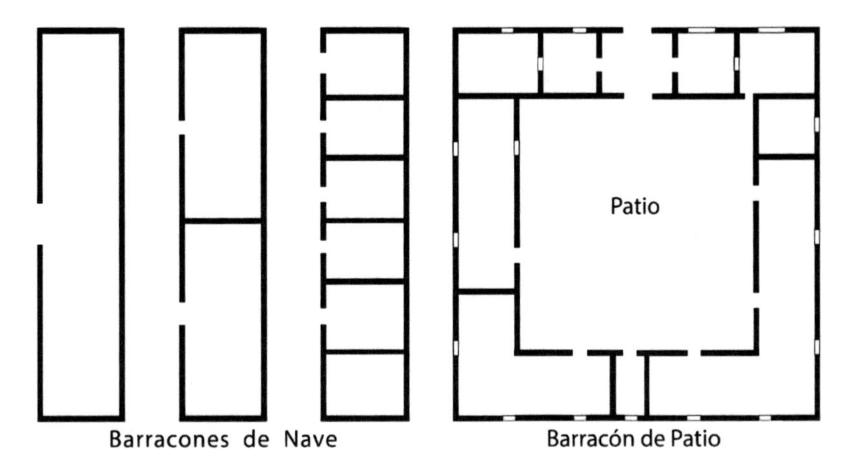

Figure 5.4. Floor plans of Cuban barracones. Adapted from illustration in Lisette Roura Álvarez and Teresa Angelbello Izquierdo (2007:137). Drawn by Syracuse University Cartographic Laboratory.

could be locked at night because they usually contained only one door to the outside.

The barracón de patio, on the other hand, was usually a square building with numerous rooms or cells, each opening onto a yard area where a central kitchen and other dependencies were located (figure 5.4). Although Chateausalins's writings are believed to have inspired this type of barracón, early prototypes of this form began appearing in the late 1820s such as the previously mentioned one at W. Taylor's Carolina plantation. Another early example described in the travel diary of Peter Townsend on September 4 consisted of a three-sided, presumably U-shaped building that housed 60 at the Eloise plantation near the city of Matanzas (Townsend Diary). Barracones de patios, for the most part, did not have a significant presence in Cuba until the 1840s. Some scholars suggested increased slave uprisings during the 1830s, and the alleged slave conspiracy known as La Escalera in 1844 (Paquette 1988) motivated sugar planters with large slaveholdings to build barracones de patio (J. Pérez de la Riva 1975:28; Moreno Fraginals 1978:2:74).

Generally constructed from mampostería with tejas, the barracón de patio could be quite large, with some measuring 80 varas × 120 varas [66 m × 103 m or 219.4 ft × 329.1 ft], sometimes with two floors, and housing as many as 300–500 people. These buildings could also contain separate living areas for indentured Chinese laborers who began arriving in Cuba in 1847 (Yun 2008:16) to supplement slave labor or for contramayorales [foremen], as well as infirmaries, a central kitchen, and even confinement cells for those subjected to solitary punishment. Some published floor plans of barracones de patio indicate that turnstiles were installed at the main entries to monitor who was coming in or going out one by one.

Lourdes Domínguez (1986:275) found a turnstile in her archaeological study of the barracón de patio at the Taoro sugar plantation. This finding documents that these surveillance devices were installed in some Cuban slave quarters. She also discovered a second entrance she referred to as "el trasiego de carros," a type of service door large enough for small carts or wagons. She speculated this second entrance was used by slave drivers, Chinese workers, kitchen workers, and other nonslave personnel who lived and worked in the barracón. Juan Pérez de la Riva (1975:31), however, using plantation inventories as his primary source, believed a second entrance of this type was an uncommon addition. Guards stationed at the entrances of barracones and at watchtowers or bell towers provided additional oversight. The practice of using elevated structures for surveillance may have predated the rise of the barracón de patio.

The barracón de patio generated both praise and criticism. Supporters endorsed it as a marvel to agricultural progress for creating hygienic living conditions and thereby increasing efficiency at plantations (Cantero [1857] 2005:245; Burroughs 2013:122–23). Contemporary detractors condemned it for making the living quarters of plantation laborers like a prison (Serrano 1837:45). By the mid-1850s, a U-shaped variation emerged with one side of the patio left open instead of being completely surrounded on all four sides (similar in concept, but on a much grander scale, to the one Townsend described) (J. Pérez de la Riva 1975:44). Perhaps the goal of the U-shape construction was to make it feel less like a prison; however, surveillance was not spared. In the layout of the sugar plantation La Ponina, the bell tower was positioned close to the open side of the barracón, providing a guard stationed in the tower with a clear view of who was entering and exiting (Cantero [1857] 2005:223).

High construction costs in addition to a design intended for large workforces rendered the barracón de patio unfeasible for most coffee plantations. Coffee plantations with barracones usually had some form of nave and not a barracón de patio, with two possible exceptions: Angerona, originally one of the great coffee plantations in San Marcos de Artemisa located in the province of Artemisa, and La Manuela near the south coast of Mayabeque Province. Angerona was most likely the largest Cuban coffee plantation, reputed to have had as many as 450 enslaved workers (Isidro Méndez 1952). Some authors assumed that Angerona had a barracón de patio, based on the size of the workforce and the extant ruins of the slave settlement (F. Pérez de la Riva 1952:362; Van Norman 2005:170). Using archival and archaeological data, Gabino La Rosa Corzo's (2012:20) study of the plantation indicates the slave settlement underwent three phases of construction, but during the lifetime of Cornelio Souchay, the founder of Angerona, the slave laborers lived in bohíos. Sometime after Souchay's death in 1837, his heirs built a barracón de patio, evident in the present-day ruins.

In 1828, Abiel Abbot visited Angerona and described the first construction phase of the slave settlement consisting of bohíos: "The bohea, or square of negro huts, is judiciously arranged on a hill. . . . Two families are accommodated under one roof, and a space of a few yards is left between each two buildings fenced by an open picket. In this manner, the negro huts enclose a large square, which is entered by an iron gate" (1829:144). Abbott's description suggests that bohíos were arranged in a manner that surrounded an open area or a patio. Such an arrangement is very similar to Moreno Fraginals's (1978:2:68–71) description of the "nueva planta" [new plan]—bohíos laid out in a U-shaped pattern or closed on all four sides forming a square—which he suggested served as precursors to the barracón de patio.

The inventory taken after Souchay's death described the slave quarters as "un barracón que se compone de veintisiete casas encerrades en su mismo recinto por trozos de reja entre cada casa, un torreón a una esquina y una gran puerta de fierro en la entrada" [a barracón composed of 27 houses contained in the same area with a small piece of ground between each house, with a tower in the corner and an iron gate at the entrance] (La Rosa Corzo 2012:20). This description is very similar to Abbot's except for the addition of the tower, which La Rosa Corzo identified as the second construction phase. Without the tower, the slave settlement seems to resemble, at least in concept, the enclosed settlement at Cafetal Biajacas. It is curious, however, that it is referred to as a barracón and not as 27 bohíos within an enclosure (the way the slave houses are described on the inventories of Cafetal Biajacas).

La Rosa Corzo (2012:21) determined that the third phase of construction was a barracón de patio through detailed measurement of the extant ruins. He discerned 14 houses built into the wall that he identified as housing for the mayorales and other service buildings, and 39 rooms that housed the workers. The transformation from bohíos to a barracón de patio, however, appears to have been implemented when the plantation had begun producing sizable yields of both coffee and sugar in the mid-1840s. By 1859, the plantation only produced sugar (La Rosa Corzo 2012:25).

The ruins of La Manuela, on the other hand, present a convincing case of a slave quarter that was initially constructed as a barracón de patio to house slave workers on a coffee plantation. Through an investigation of standing ruins, Luciano Bernard Bosch, Victor Blanco Conde, and Alexis Rives Pantoja (1985:67–70) found that the slave quarter at La Manuela met the criteria of a barracón de patio. They identified approximately 40 cells, each measuring about 6 m sq that housed 160 workers who once lived on the plantation. Their study of the standing ruins complemented a description of the slave quarters in an inventory taken in 1835, and they concluded that the structure was a barracón de patio because it displayed aspects of a fortified jail, a characteristic typically attributed to this type of barracón. Jail-like qualities of Cuban slave housing, however, were not restricted to the barracón de patio. Barracones-nave often had only one or two doors that were locked at night, and the massive wall enclosing the slave bohíos at Cafetal Biajacas also resembles a jail, with only one door for entry and exit. But the slave settlement at Cafetal Biajacas was not a barracón, although it probably functioned as one, and it was referred to as a barracón on at least one occasion (AHPM GPC leg. 12, no. 50 [1837]).

For most of the nineteenth century, barracones apparently coexisted with bohíos, but they were not generally referred to as barracones until the 1830s. With the exception of La Manuela and possibly Angerona, few coffee planters constructed barracones de patio. Given currently available archaeological and written evidence, Fredrika Bremer's 1853 observation accurately describes the use of barracones in western Cuba: "[I]t seems as if the coffee plantations were distinguished from sugar plantations by the style of the bohea [barracón]" (1853:2:410). Today extant barracones of both types have been converted into houses and other buildings, and the ruins of others are seen throughout the Cuban countryside. The ubiquitous presence of barracones and the invisibility of slave bohíos led some present-day observers to incorrectly suggest that barracones completely replaced bohíos (Singleton 2006:269). This, however, was not the case. Because bohíos are impermanent structures, they leave few aboveground traces once they are razed. For this reason, archaeological research is necessary to document their former presence at a particular site.

Bohíos versus Barracones

Benito García y Santos, a slaveholder in the Matanzas partido of Macuriges, complained to Governor-General Gerónimo Valdés on May 12, 1843, regarding the need for security on slave houses in his vicinity. In his letter, García y Santos claimed only 6 of the 40 or more coffee plantations in Macuriges had barracones with sufficient security, and on the remaining plantations enslaved people "viven y duermen en bohíos de malísima construcción que les facilitan el entrar y salir cuando y a las horas que se les antoja, por con siguiente acudir y visitar a reuniones robas asesinatos, formar conspiraciones, y más desordenes de cualquier clase y tamaños" [live and sleep in very poorly constructed bohíos that facilitate the entry and exit at hours whenever they crave to go and travel to gatherings, rob, murder, and plan conspiracies, and many other disturbances of whatever sort or size] (ANC GSC leg. 942, no. 33246). Gerónimo Valdés responded to the complaint by issuing a *bando* [proclamation] to the Slave Code of 1842, dated July 20, 1843, requiring slaveholders to proceed quickly with the construction of slave dwellings in a building or location in which "debiendo quedar todos en las noche bajo de llave" [all (enslaved persons) must be locked up at night] by the end of four months (ANC GSC, leg. 942, no. 33246).

Macuriges had been the site of an uprising in 1835 involving 130 enslaved persons (ANC GSC leg. 997, no. 33070), and that situation may have added to Valdés's desire for urgent action. Valdés also restated the conditions of the 1842 slave code requiring slave owners to house single men and women separately in quarters secured with keys at night and, if possible, put married couples in separate dwellings. Although the 1842 ordinance did not specify housing slave workers in barracones, colonial officials and many slaveholders equated secured slave quarters with barracones, not bohíos. Whether persuaded by their own experiences or by Chateausalins's writings denouncing bohíos, proponents of the barracón pointed to the difficulty of guarding bohíos. Bohíos, they felt, enabled slaves to engage in both on- and off-site clandestine activities. No doubt reports of enslaved people gambling, buying, selling, drinking alcoholic beverages, or hoarding pilfered items reinforced fears that slave bohíos posed a threat to the security of all people living in the countryside.[5] Clearly, Benito García y Santos espoused this view.

The housing situation in Macuriges indicates that a significant number of Matanzas slaveholders, particularly coffee planters, apparently had not complied with the Ayllon 1825 ordinance or with the more recent 1842 slave code regarding housing. Macuriges not only provides an example that shows most Cuban slaveholders did not comply with these ordinances, but more important, it points to a divide among slaveholders regarding slave housing: some wanted to continue the system of bohíos; others preferred to adopt barracones. Cost and security of slave housing were significant issues that have been emphasized in the historiography of Cuban slavery, but as the following discussion indicates, there were additional considerations that influenced planter decisions on slave housing. The split among slaveholders on housing seems less about cost and more about contrasting approaches to control slave laborers in the realm of slave housing. Proponents for bohíos seem to have envisioned an enslaved peasantry quartered in detached houses that would encourage family formation and independent production that would ultimately reduce incidents of rebelliousness. Advocates for barracones, on the other hand, appear to have likened slavery to convict labor, quartering the slaves in housing that checked their movement and suppressed rebellious behavior. Of course, some slaveholders belonged to neither camp but quartered enslaved workers in ways that best suited their plantation operations.

A slaveholder's decision concerning the type of slave housing to build depended on a number of factors: cost, durability, notions of hygiene, surveillance of slave activities, slave access to their provision gardens, and the formation and maintenance of families. Undoubtedly, cost impacted planter decisions. The difference in costs between a masonry barracón and a settlement of earthen or wooden bohíos was quite substantial. Juan Pérez de la Riva (1975:24–25) estimated a barracón-nave cost between 4,000 and 10,000 pesos and a barracón de patio cost over 20,000 pesos. Bohíos, on the other hand, were usually valued on plantation inventories between 25 and 50 pesos each (see, for example, Oficina del Gobierno Constitucional [OGC] 1821). Assessed values on inventories are not equivalent to construction costs, but they provide some indication of minimal replacement costs. Given these values, to house 200 laborers in 50–70 bohíos would have been considerably cheaper than the construction cost for the least expensive masonry barracón.

Cost most certainly played a role in the persistence of the slave bohío, but some wealthy planters preferred bohíos for other reasons. Several months preceding the promulgation of his notorious 1842 Cuban slave code on November 14, Gerónimo Valdés wrote a letter dated February 23, 1842, on reforming the hygiene, morals, and provisions for enslaved people, and circulated it to 13 slaveholders of the planter aristocracy. With regard to slave housing, Valdés posed the following question: "¿Cuál sea un sistema más conveniente para regularizar las costumbres y moralidad de los negros casados: si hacerlos vivir por familias en bohíos separadas; hace algún prejuicio a los intereses del dueño?" [Which system is more convenient to regulate the customs and morality of married slaves; if slaves are housed as families in detached bohíos, does this harm the owner's interest?] (ANC GSC leg. 941, no. 33186; García 2003b:81). The reasons for Valdes's concern are unclear, but he apparently believed enslaved people living in bohíos could somehow undermine the economic interests of slaveholders.

Several of the planters responded, including Jacinto González Larrinaga, Rafael O'Farrill, and Sebastián de Lasa, that bohíos were better for married workers because they preferred living in them and they encouraged family formation and reproduction. Some planters also saw the bohío as more advantageous than barracones in maintaining the practice of family *conucos* [slave provision gardens] and for raising slave-owned livestock. Other planters, for example, Domingo Aldama, the owner of several large sugar plantations with over 400 slave workers at Santa Rosa, housed them in barracones. But he emphasized in his response to Valdés that he believed housing slave families in either detached bohíos or on separate floors within barracones would not harm a planter's interest (ANC GSC leg. 940, no. 33158; Barcia Zequeira 2003:216). In the end, the planters agreed with Aldama that married workers could live in either bohíos or separate floors within barracones (Barcia Zequeira 2003:152). Valdés, however, demonstrated his preference for barracones when he issued the previously mentioned bando to the 1842 slave code in response to the complaint from Macuriges in July 1843.

Outraged advocates for the slave bohío retorted in a letter to Valdés, August 15, 1843, that locking up workers at night would only contribute to unrest and rebellion rather than provide security. José Montalvo y Castillo stated, "Un hombre forzado al trabajo diurno y encerrado de noche no puedo vivir contento" [A man forced to work daily and locked up at night cannot live contently] (García 2003b:35). The Marqués de Campo Florido agreed with Montalvo y Castillo and added that enslaved people cherished their bohíos as "una propiedad inviolable, en que reúnen todo cuanto lícitamente adquieren con el trabajo que hacen para así muy a gusto en las horas descanso" [sacred property in which they have gathered everything they legally acquired through the work they do for themselves on their own time] (García 2003b:36). Their responses help explain why some slaveholders chose not to adopt barracones or build walls around bohíos despite nocturnal departures or running away by enslaved laborers.

Valdés, however, did not relent, and a prison-like slave regime was legally sanctioned on paper but not necessarily implemented on most plantations. Valdés was recalled to Spain in September 1843, and his successor, Leopoldo O'Donnell, apparently did not enforce the bando because Benito García y Santos complained once again in 1845 to O'Donnell about the lack of security in slave housing at Macuriges (Barcia 2008:107–8). Furthermore, a study of the principal slaveholding districts in Matanzas conducted in 1850 indicated bohíos continued to be the predominant form of slave housing. In Cárdenas, a major sugar producing area with large slaveholdings, the governor reported of its 221 sugar plantations that 98 contained barracones, and of those only 73 were built of mampostería (García 2003a:36). The remaining plantations kept the bohío system, but reputedly with better security than those used in previous years (Moreno Fraginals 1978:2:75). Moreover, locking up workers at night did not yield the expected results. The practice reduced the frequency of slave nocturnal departures from plantations to nearby taverns where they were believed to have drunk alcoholic beverages or exchanged goods, but it did not eliminate such activities (García 2003b:36).

Elite planters led the discussion on slave dwellings, but the interests of planters with smaller slaveholdings were also taken into consideration. In 1837, Francisco de Paula Serrano offered recommendations for building barracones affordable to coffee planters of modest means in his general essay on Cuban agriculture. Serrano (1837:45) advised coffee planters to build barracones for the security, durability, and healthy conditions they provided but argued that they need not be like jails or army barracks. He gave detailed instructions for building a gable-roofed barracón constructed of mampostería and wood that he estimated would cost 2,000 pesos (half the cost of the lowest cost estimate given above). The building could contain as many as 16 rooms each measuring 3 varas × 3 varas (2.5 m × 2.5 m or 8.2 ft × 8.2 ft) for married couples and their children, and two wings, one for single men and the other for single women. Serrano (1837:45–47) also emphasized the importance of windows and proper ventilation. He was highly critical of Chateausalins's recommendation of using balusters on the windows, which added to the prisonlike atmosphere. Instead, he advised locating windows high near the roofline or using skylights.

Although it is very difficult to assess the impact of Serrano's essay or others on the average planter, standing ruins of masonry barracones-nave found on sites of former coffee plantations with small slaveholdings suggest that some small coffee planters were motivated to build barracones.[6] For some planters, the durability of masonry construction possibly outweighed other considerations. The thatched roofs of bohíos were not only fire hazards but also extremely vulnerable to high winds and storms. Joseph Goodwin wrote in his diary on two occasions (March 10, 1822, and August 29, 1823) that high winds damaged the palm roofs of the bohíos. In one of these incidences, the workers complained of sleeping in the cold, and Goodwin became concerned that they would become sick and need to spend time in the plantation infirmary. The two incidences Goodwin recorded caused minor damage compared with damages from a major storm or hurricane. Hurricanes completely wiped out bohíos on many plantations, forcing slave workers to take refuge in the great house or other plantation buildings still standing (Pérez 2000:63, 79). Few coffee plantations in western Cuba survived the hurricanes of 1844 and 1846, but those that did were restored apparently with masonry slave dwellings when these operations resumed. La Concordia succumbed to both hurricanes but had been partially restored with a barracón-nave by the time of Fredrika Bremer's visit in 1851 (1853:404–10).

In 1861, almost two decades after the passage of the 1842 reglamento and Geronimo Valdés's bando of 1843, Álvaro Reynoso (1861:328–29) proposed returning to the old system of bohíos because the barracón system had failed miserably. Instead of providing healthy living conditions, in many cases they became worse. Enslaved people often made alterations to their rooms to store their harvests, reducing the amount of living space, and cooked in their rooms without proper stoves, creating smoke and fires. He recommended following the practice of José Ricardo O'Farrill, Ignacio's older brother, for his sugar plantation Cayajabos (about 2 mi north of Santa Ana de Biajacas) as a model for Cuban plantation owners to emulate. According to Reynoso (1861:330), José Ricardo O'Farrill never adopted barracones but kept bohíos, making sure that they were neat and orderly, and O'Farrill did not need to exercise severe policing of his workforce. Reynoso further suggested to slaveholders still skeptical about returning to bohíos for security reasons that "se podría cercar todo el pueblo para mayor seguridad, con una gran muralla, aunque estamos convencido de que semejante precaución, no es necesaria" [one could encircle the entire village with a large wall, although I am convinced that such a precaution is unnecessary]. This final statement suggests that the practice of building a palisade or wall around slave bohíos was known, but perhaps not widely practiced at the time of Reynoso's publication.

In the discussion above, direct references to building a wall around detached slave dwellings are found in Ayllon's ordinance and in Reynoso's essay. Even Gerónimo Valdés's bando alludes to a similar practice of concentrating slave dwellings in a location or building. All these references suggest enclosing slave houses within a palisade was not an unusual practice in Cuba and may have been an expected or a desired way of securing slave dwellings. Yet presently available evidence from both archaeological and written sources indicates few slaveholders implemented this practice, or if they did, the physical evidence of these structures did not survive to the present.

Unlike the masonry wall at Cafetal Biajacas, some palisades were possibly of timber or of earthen construction that were later razed, and the practice of building such enclosures is long forgotten. For example, the lithograph of Manaca sugar plantation in Cantero's ([1857] 2005:224) *Los ingenios . . . de la isla de Cuba* depicts slave bohíos surrounded by a fence of vertical timbers or wooden pickets. Although it is doubtful that a picket fence would have prevented enslaved people from leaving plantation premises at night or provided the kind of security civil authorities and many Cuban residents wanted, it was a cheaper alternative to building a masonry wall. A timber wall would also have complied with the law, as none of the ordinances specified the kind of construction material to use to build these walls.

Fortunately, the well-preserved masonry enclosure at Cafetal Biajacas provides a unique opportunity to analyze the wall and buried evidence of the slave bohíos within the enclosure. The archaeological research undertaken within the wall enclosure is examined in the following section, which focuses on construction details of the wall and slave houses and how the slave houses compare with written and visual descriptions of slave bohíos.

Excavating a Poblado de Esclavo Amurallado

From the onset of the field research at Cafetal Biajacas, the archaeologists approached locus A (see figure 4.2) containing the slave dwellings as a *poblado de esclavo amurallado* [palisaded or walled slave settlement]. On our very first visit to the site of the cafetal, a local historian of the Madruga area told the project team that the plantation known as Santa Ana de Biajacas or El Padre had an unusual barracón. It contained detached bohíos surrounded by the present-standing wall of mampostería. Close inspection of the wall on a second visit to the site revealed it was built as a freestanding masonry structure and not attached to interior walls as in the case of a barracón de patio exemplified in La Rosa Corzo's (2012) study of Angerona. Later subsurface testing supported our field observation as well as references to the cercado de los bohíos [the enclosure for the bohíos] at Cafetal Biajacas in the probate inventories taken in 1838 (ANC Galletti leg. 240, no. 1, pieza 1; ANC Galletti 245, no. 1, pieza 1) and valuation of Ignacio O'Farrill's properties taken in 1841 (ANC Galletti leg. 934, no. 6).

Analyzing Wall Construction

The wall enclosure was built of mampostería—a stone masonry construction—made of *mampuestos* [rough stone] or stone rubble as opposed to *sillería* [dressed stone]. Mampostería can be constructed in numerous ways, from laying each stone one by one with or without mortar, to producing masonry resembling poured cement by uniting stones with a blend of lime, water, and other materials such as gravel or clay. Over the centuries, local variations to these construction techniques developed wherever Spaniards introduced this type of stone masonry. Consequently, a particular form of mampostería in one place may be called by a different name elsewhere. In the wall enclosure, stones of varying sizes were united with a mixture of gravel and mortar to fill in the gaps between the larger stones so that each stone has many points of contact with the lime-based mortar. According to an early twentieth-century manual of Spanish building techniques, this type of construction is referred to as *mampostería de careada* [face-to-face] (Rebelledo 1910:108).

Stones in the great house, on the other hand, are quite large but fairly uniform in size, and many appear to have been cut and shaped to create flat surfaces. This type is referred to as *mampostería de concertada* [harmonized] (Rebelledo 1910:108). Some cut stones are also found in the wall enclosure, particularly around the entrance and along the corners, but most of the stones in the enclosure do not appear to have been cut or shaped. Finishing the walls with plaster or stucco is customary in the construction of mampostería. In keeping with this practice, the exterior walls of the enclosure were finished with a lime-based plaster (figure 5.5), but either the interior walls were left unfinished or the plaster has completely eroded away.

Most of the wall enclosure is fully intact and measures 3.35 m [about 11 ft] in height precisely equivalent to 4 varas.[7] Most likely, the intended height for the wall was 4 varas. The wall thickness is 0.70 m, and construction of mampostería typically produces thick walls. The wall thickness of buildings at Cafetal Biajacas varied from a minimum of 0.64 m in the warehouse/infirmary to 0.87 m, slightly over one vara, in the walls of the

Figure 5.5. Exterior wall of western edge of enclosed slave settlement. Photograph by Lisette Roura Álvarez.

great house. Each side of the enclosure measures a different length with the following approximate measures rounded to the nearest whole number: the north facing is 104 m; south facing, 101 m; east facing, 71 m; and west facing, 60 m (figure 5.6).

The area within this irregular shape is huge, approximately 6,862 m^2 or 73,860 ft^2, and it is unclear how this large space was utilized. The archaeological evidence of bohíos was found on the higher end of the enclosure, and it is possible the lower end was used for grazing or to shelter animals in thatch huts, as John Wurdemann observed at the Drake family's Cafetal Carlota ([1844] 1971]:105). The irregular shape of the enclosure may be an artifact of the terrain and the use of fence lines to establish boundaries for separate plantation spaces. The north facing wall is positioned on the edge of a relatively flat area at the top of a steep incline, whereas the south and west facing walls form the outer boundaries of the plantation batey and separated it from other areas of the plantation.

Our surveys of the areas beyond the south and west walls suggest that there were no buildings in these areas during the coffee plantation era, though we did find what appeared to be the remains of lime kilns about 100 m or more behind the westernmost wall (figure 5.5). Additionally,

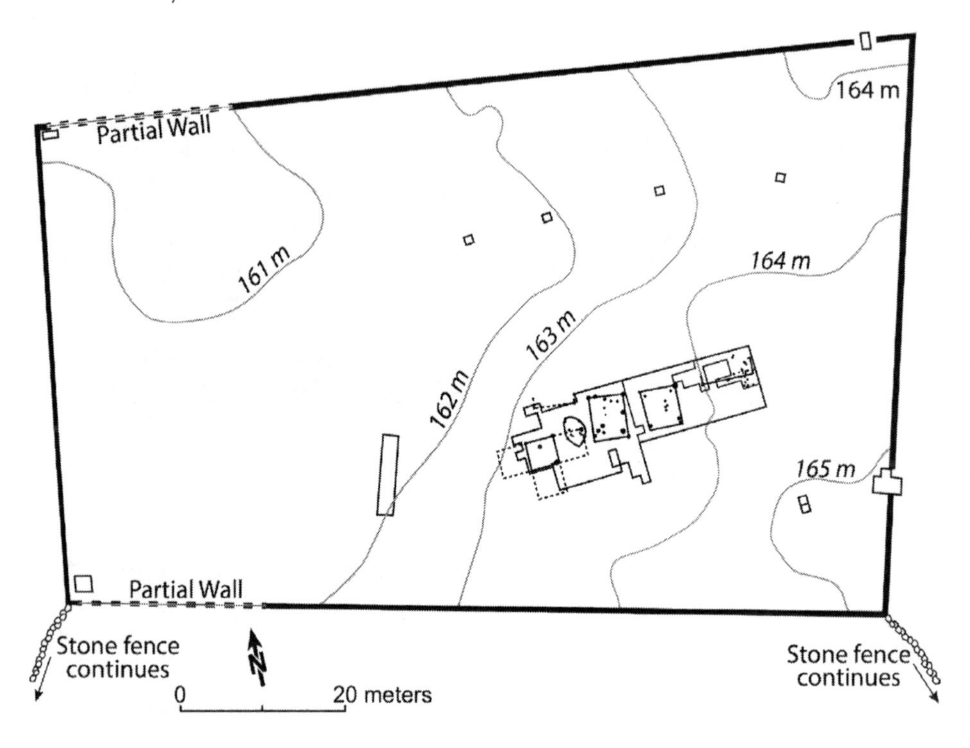

Figure 5.6. Plan of archaeological investigations within the enclosure. Drawn by Syracuse University Cartographic Laboratory.

extending from the southeastern and southwestern corners of the enclosure are stone fences measuring 1.25 m (4.1 ft or 1.5 varas) in height that further establish boundaries between spaces, possibly between properties. The stone fence on the southeast corner of the enclosure connects to the building designated as the *almacén/enfermería* [warehouse/infirmary] and continues eastward for about 88 meters. The fence originating from the southwest corner goes a rather long distance, at least a kilometer or more all the way to the Biajacas River. Although it is possible that some of this fencing postdates the period of cafetal, the plantation inventories indicate that there was extensive stone fencing at Cafetal Biajacas. The fencing may have separated the property belonging to the cafetal from the property belonging to the adjacent potrero.

At some unknown time, portions of the wall measuring 25–28 m on both the north and south facing walls were partially, but not completely, removed presumably after the abandonment of the site. Curiously, only stones from the upper two-thirds of the wall were removed, leaving the lowest courses of stone up to a meter in height intact. Stones were also removed from a small area on the northern wall measuring 2.25 m wide where it appears that a second entrance into the enclosure was made. Initially, this entrance appeared to be part of the original construction because it resembled an arc-shaped entryway, albeit with missing stones, comparable to those illustrated in floor plans of barracones de patio. Upon closer study, it was decided this entrance was not part of the original construction because it lacked the finished, flattened surfaces that were necessary to properly hang a door or gate and were found on the intended entrance to the enclosure on the wall facing east. The second entrance looks like a portion of stone wall was knocked out to create an opening without repairing or finishing the damaged stone that has since caused additional stones to fall out from the wall in subsequent years. Presumably this entrance was made after the coffee plantation was abandoned or when the enclosure was no longer functioning as a device to contain slave activities inside the enclosure. After O'Farrill's death, the workforce at Cafetal Biajacas was reduced to 17 elderly slave laborers, and it probably was unnecessary to lock them up at night. The original entrance measures 2.7 m (8.86 ft) wide, which roughly coincides with 3.35 varas. An entrance of this size was wide enough not only for people to enter and leave but also to bring in wagons or carts.

The enclosure is located on a subtle slope where the easternmost edge of the wall is about 4 m higher than the westernmost edge of the wall. Most of the excavation focused on the higher elevation where there was evidence of slave bohíos and scatters of artifacts. At the lower elevation, units within an exploratory trench were excavated to determine if structures or nonstructural features such as trash pits, privies, and fire pits were constructed at these lower levels, but none were found. Excavation units placed at the rear corners of the wall revealed that the wall was built upon a foundation of mamposteria similar to the wall construction extending 0.64 m (2.1 ft) below the ground surface.

Datable artifacts found at or below the base of a foundation usually can provide some indication of when a foundation was laid and the structure built. At the very lowest level of the excavation near the base of the wall only three artifacts were recovered: a fragment of a sugar mold, a machine-cut nail, and a machete blade. Unfortunately, these artifacts were produced and used for most of the nineteenth century, so they cannot provide a date range of a decade or two. However, the machete blade provides a potential clue for dating the wall. The blade appears to be from a *machete calabozo*, a locally made, hand-forged iron tool with a blunt edge that planters preferred for slave use because it lacked a sharp point (see figures of machetes in chapter 6). These machetes were used widely on Cuban plantations around 1820, but they proved to be too heavy and cumbersome for cutting sugar, and so their usage waned on sugar plantations (Ramos Zúñiga 1984:54) but endured somewhat longer on coffee plantations. Although it is unclear when these machetes were first produced, the 1820 date provides a tentative *terminus post quem*—a date after which the wall was built. In other words, the wall could have been built earlier or later, but given our current knowledge of these machetes, the earliest potential date is around 1820. An 1820 date corresponds to when the plantation was highly productive with 102 workers, and by that date the neoclassical great house was most likely completed.

Building the wall enclosure was a major capital expenditure requiring the labor of skilled stonemasons. In the appraisal of the buildings at the coffee plantation, the wall was valued at 5,270.7 pesos, the third most valuable structure of the plantation, with the great house valued the highest at 8,110.6½ pesos, and the coffee warehouse valued the second highest at 7,372.3½ pesos (ANC Galletti leg. 934, no. 6). This sizable allocation of resources for the wall points to its importance in the plantation operation. Although the wall conceivably served several purposes, containing the workers was a major reason for its construction, given slaveholders' concerns about the security of slave dwellings.

To build such an expansive wall required considerable labor. What role did slave laborers at Cafetal Biajacas play in constructing the wall that imprisoned them? Undoubtedly, some were engaged in activities related to construction, including gathering stones, making the lime for the mortar, hauling these materials to the worksite, and preparing the stones. The slave lists for Cafetal Biajacas provide no information on occupational skills of the residents; therefore, it is difficult to know for sure if there were masons among them.

Some coffee plantations did have slave workers who were skilled in masonry and carpentry (González Fernández 1991:173), whereas other planters hired white or free black artisans for skilled jobs. Ebenezer Sage, for example, contracted with a stonemason and carpenter to undertake the renovation of his coffee plantation Santa Ana, which included building a stone embankment in front of his great house. These free artisans possibly trained and supervised slave gangs to undertake some of the skilled aspects of these projects. Slave laborers most definitely performed many of the tasks related to the construction of the wall enclosure at Cafetal Biajacas, possibly including those requiring skilled stonemasons.

Rediscovering Slave Bohíos

Study of the imposing masonry wall enclosure with its permanent signature on the landscape contrasted sharply with locating and identifying lightly framed bohíos invisible from aboveground. The initial goal of the first season of excavation in June 1999 was to determine the preservation of the site. It was obvious that the land within the wall enclosure had been farmed for many years and perhaps served as a site for other agricultural and domestic activities after the slave settlement was abandoned. Our objective was to identify, if possible, archaeological deposits associated with the former slave residents, including any evidence of their houses.

Finding evidence of timber-framed buildings from archaeological investigation can be a tricky proposition because after a building is abandoned, the timbers are often removed, salvaged, and reused. If the timbers are left in place, they will eventually decompose. It is often possible to identify the holes dug for the purpose of driving wooden posts (postholes), and in the best of circumstances it is possible to identify traces of decayed timber posts that show up as stains or imprints in soil (postmolds).

In a karst terrain like that of Cafetal Biajacas, postholes are usually evident in holes dug through the limestone sediment to position timber posts. The project team discovered this to be the case at the slave settlement site even before beginning excavations. While clearing thick vegetation within the enclosure before laying out exploratory excavation units, we discovered a posthole (Singleton 2005a:189). We then designed a field strategy excavating areas extending from this posthole in all directions until we could identify a patterned arrangement of posts in four corners and four off-centered postholes near the middle of the area. This four-sided outline was designated Structure 1 (figure 5.7) and presumed to be a slave bohío because 95 percent of the recovered artifacts from the enclosure, including the few objects found in the postholes, date to the first half of the nineteenth century when the coffee plantation was in operation.

In subsequent field seasons from 2000 to 2002, we continued to find more postholes, but it became increasingly difficult to see clear patterns indicative of bohíos. We found 93 postholes in an area in which 281 contiguous, 1 sq m units were excavated. We eliminated postholes less than 10 cm (4 in) in both diameter and depth from final maps because at that size they were unlikely candidates for supporting the main framing posts for the structure (see figure 5.1). We also distinguished human-made holes from those occurring naturally by deep gouges observed on the walls of the postholes. These gouges resulted from the use of a chisel-like tool, most likely a *barreta*, a long-handled iron tool—to dig the postholes.

After considerable mapping and remapping of the postholes, thinking and rethinking about which postholes were most likely once parts of structures and which were not, and connecting and reconnecting the dots on paper that represent the mapped postholes, four, possibly five, additional structures were tentatively identified (figure 5.7).[8] The area designated for Structure 2 showed numerous small holes, many of which were probably unrelated to the construction of a slave bohío except for a possible wall connecting several postholes and on one side forming two possible corners of a building. The area designated for Structure 3 is approximately the same size as that for Structure 1, but it contained a great many more posts. Some of the other postholes possibly supported timber piers used to raise a wooden floor off the ground. The area for Structure 4 contained numerous postholes, indicating that the building was either a stand-alone structure of rounded rather than rectangular shape or that it may have been part of Structure 5. If the former, then it may not have been a dwelling but an outbuilding such as a *baracoa*—a small thatched-roof structure enslaved people used for storing food crops grown in their provision gardens (F. Pérez de la Riva 1952:338).

Early-twentieth-century images of Cuban rural settlements found on postcards, sketches, and other popular media depict outbuildings associ-

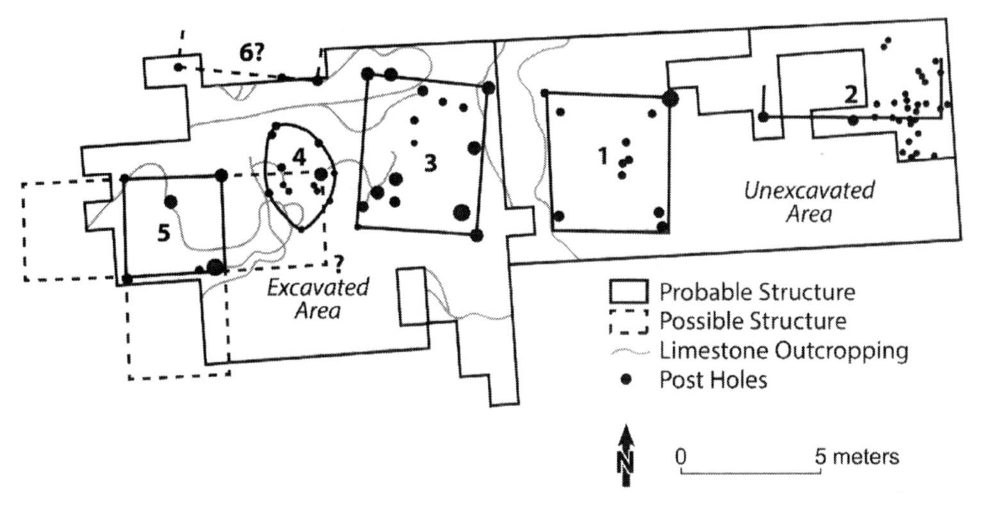

Figure 5.7. Plan of excavated postholes and proposed configurations of slave bohíos. Drawn by Syracuse University Cartographic Laboratory.

ated with bohíos in various sizes and shapes, so a rounded baracoa would not have been unusual for these makeshift sheds. If Structure 4, however, was part of Structure 5, then a post for the southeast corner of the structure is missing, making that configuration of postholes an unlikely prospect for a structure. Structure 5 consisted of four corner posts with one center post; it is either a small slave dwelling about half the size of Structures 1 and 3, or it is also an outbuilding like Structure 4, assuming the postholes represent a stand-alone building. If Structure 5 is found to be a larger building, it more likely extends to the west or possibly to the south in unexcavated areas.

The suggestion that Structures 4 and 5 may not have been slave dwellings is supported in the inventories for the plantation that indicate that at least one *gallinero* [chicken house] was also located within the enclosure. Moreover, discrepancies in the total number of slave bohíos found in the three inventories may reflect differences in what was being counted. Two inventories (ANC Galletti leg. 245, no. 1 and Galletti leg. 934, no. 6) indicate a total of 30 slave bohíos whereas a third inventory (ANC Galletti leg. 240, no. 1) indicates there were 45 slave bohíos. Thirty slave bohíos seem reasonable for a *dotación* [workforce] of 81 before O'Farrill's death, but 45 slave houses seem unlikely for 81 persons. The additional 15 bohíos, assuming that this was an accurate count, may well have included other outbuildings such as baracoas or storage sheds. Obviously additional excavations are necessary to better define Structures 2, 4, and 5 as well as structures associated with other postholes, like those appearing to form a wall for a possible sixth structure above Structures 4 and 5.

Visualizing the aboveground appearance of these structures from the irregular placement of the uncovered postholes presents a challenge particularly for those familiar with the well-aligned posts found in the post-in-hole or earth-fast building tradition of the Anglophone world. Bohíos, particularly those built by people of African descent, were constructed in an improvisational manner with whatever materials were available. In a free black village outside Limonar in Matanzas jurisdiction, Fredrika Bremer (1853:2:316) noted that the bark [yagua] and woven brushwood (wattle) houses with palm-leaf roofs "seemed built by guess, and with as little trouble as possible." Similarly, Africanist archaeologist Merrick Posnansky (1999:27) characterized most African village housing, as well as the housing of most preindustrial societies, as ad hoc structures built to meet an immediate end. This is not to say that African building was inferior to European building. But African domestic structures found in the countryside are often unplanned with little concern for precise measurements. Descriptions of bohío construction regardless of the builders' ethnicity, however, indicate these dwellings were largely improvised.

Recovered artifacts can also provide some indications of the building's appearance. Beyond the 232 machine-cut nails, very little identifiable building hardware was recovered, with the exception of a *gozne* [hinge] typical of those found on window shutters of Spanish colonial houses. A few fragments of window glass were recovered from excavations, but bohíos rarely had glassed windows even in the houses of the few affluent farmers who occupied them. Curtains, shutters, or iron gratings were generally used to cover windows rather than glass (Jopling 1988:22). The window glass may well have been deposited at the site after the slave village was abandoned.

Interpretations regarding the dimensions, spacing, or orientation of the structures must remain tentative until additional field research is undertaken. Yet a few observations on these aspects of the structures can be offered at this stage of research. The two completely excavated structures, 1 and 3, measure 5 m × 7 m (16.4 ft × 23 ft). This size is consistent with detached, single-pen slave houses excavated in the Caribbean and North America, as well as with the present-day single-galley Cuban bohíos, which are somewhat longer and narrower than these slave bohíos.[9] The absence of postholes in the area south of Structures 3 and 4 (figure 5.7) suggests it was a location of either yard areas or a street running between rows of houses. The close spacing between structures in the slave settlement is a documented feature of Cuban plantations depicted in lithographs (Cantero [1857] 2005:224) and observed in standing ruins of detached slave/wage laborer quarters in the Valley of Sugar Plantations where the bohíos are only about 1 m (3.28 ft) apart from each other (Roura Álvarez and Angelbello Izquierdo 2012:95, figure 15). The 1825 Ayllon ordinance mandated placing bohíos close together, presumably for better surveillance, and this practice possibly originated at that time.

The close placement of bohíos may partially explain references to slave activities, particularly clandestine ones, taking place within bohíos as opposed to outdoors. Archaeologists increasingly focus on the yard areas of slave quarters because yards were the most likely areas for many domestic and social activities. And excavation of yards usually yields greater densities of artifacts than inside slave houses (Wilkie and Farnsworth 2005:185–206). At Cafetal Biajacas, artifacts were found to be fairly evenly distributed throughout the site, presumably the result of long-term plowing; therefore, a comparison between indoors and outdoors was not possible. Limited yard spaces between houses may indicate that outdoor activities occurred in an open communal space within the settlement such as the western end of the settlement or some other unexcavated area. At the Eloise plantation, Peter Townsend noted in his diary on September 9, 1830, "little groups [of enslaved people] cooking in the open" within the vast enclosure of a three-sided barracón.

The varying orientations of buildings are a striking contrast to slave quarters laid out symmetrically in rows typically found on antebellum plantations in the southern United States and on some Caribbean plantations. In Structures 1 and 3, the long side of the rectangle runs north–south, whereas in the proposed outlines of Structure 2 and Structure 5, the long side of the rectangle appears to run east–west. Post-emancipation depictions of rural settlements with a predominance of Afro-Cuban occupants show bohíos of varying sizes and oriented in different directions. Both the improvisational construction and variable orientation suggest that the enslaved people at Cafetal Biajacas were able to build their houses to their own specifications, as observed elsewhere in the Caribbean (Armstrong 1999:179; Higman 1998:146-47). Ignacio O'Farrill, following other advocates of the bohío for housing enslaved laborers, apparently chose not to interfere with the construction of slave houses.

Despite limitations in the archaeological investigations of the slave poblado at Cafetal Biajacas, this research infuses new empirical data for analyzing the Cuban slaveholder discourse on slave housing. The concerns facing Cuban slaveholders were not simply a matter of the cost of slave housing versus secure or durable housing. Some slaveholders who continued to quarter slave workers in bohíos could afford to build barracones, but they chose not to because they saw advantages in bohíos. The dialogue between Gerónimo Valdés and the planter aristocracy is quite telling of the negotiations between enslavers and the enslaved on matters of slave domestic life. Housing enslaved Cubans in bohíos appears to have been one of those areas of negotiation.

Because the slave poblado at Cafetal Biajacas presents a departure from unwalled bohíos or barracones, Roura Álvarez and Angelbello Izquierdo (2012:30) suggest that the enclosed slave village represents a newly discovered third category of housing used in Cuba. Instead of thinking of the slave village at Cafetal Biajacas as a third type of housing, I prefer to interpret it as an alternative approach that incorporated from a slaveholder's perspective the advantages of both bohíos and barracones. The masonry wall functioned like a fortified barracón or a barracón de patio that facilitated locking up enslaved workers at night. But unlike a barracón where crop storage and private spaces were limited, enslaved people at Cafetal Biajacas could live in family units or with other single residents in bohíos they built for themselves to their own specifications. They also had access to small yard areas where they could erect baracoas for crop storage and raise backyard animals (chickens, pigs, goats, or lambs) nearby.

Finding a solution to the bohío versus barracón dilemma was certainly not unique to Ignacio O'Farrill. Francisco Aguirre, owner of Cafetal el Salvador near the town of Banes west of Havana, housed newly acquired slave workers in a barracón, but longer-term workers lived in bohíos (Van Norman 2005:171). Other slaveholders, perhaps in keeping with earlier slave codes, apparently housed single slave men and women in barracones and married couples in bohíos. Cuban slaveholders were trying to balance several issues—cost, compliance with the law, security concerns, and what they thought was most appropriate for their plantations—to resolve problems with slave housing. Additional research undertaken on Cuban plantations may disclose other ways planters chose to house their workers.

The practice of enclosing slave dwellings within a masonry wall has been identified on other Caribbean islands (Chapman [1991] 2010:108–9; Kelly 2008:294–96). But the wall enclosures at these plantations do not appear to have been as tall and imposing as the one at Cafetal Biajacas and may have served purposes other than containing enslaved people. These examples nonetheless challenge arguments that this practice was found only in Cuba.

To resolve the question of when the wall was built, I consider first whether it was built in response to the ordinance of 1825. The approximate 1820s date assigned to the wall is based upon the recovery of a presumed machete calabozo and coincides with the passage of the ordinance, but a precise date of construction may never be known. Ignacio O'Farrill was most likely motivated to build the wall for reasons other than complying with an ordinance. At the same time, there is little doubt that the containment of enslaved people was an important if not a primary function of the wall. Considering this sinister purpose, slave life behind the wall is carefully examined.

6

Enslaved Actors and Provisioning

Apolinar de la Gala, the Military Commission prosecutor, reported to Captain-General Miguel Tacón on December 2, 1837, that he had begun to monitor plantations at the request of the governor of Matanzas because he had heard of several incidents of slave mistreatment by overseers. At Lima, a sugar plantation in the partido of Santa Ana located between Ceiba Mocha and Guamacaro, Gala observed workers wearing little or no clothing and eating rotten meat and poorly prepared *funche*—a dish made from boiling dried ground corn in water.

Like many Cuban authorities as well as some slaveholders, Gala believed inadequate or poor quality food rations encouraged slave resistance, particularly running away and forming *palenques*—long-term communities of runaways. Gala ended his report by warning that the current situation could lead to a catastrophe on the island, "pues es sabido que el sufrimiento tiene sus limite" [for it is known that suffering has its limits] (ANC GSC leg. 998, no. 33105). Underfeeding was a frequent complaint brought to attention of the captain-generals, and some Cuban historians contend it often fueled slave resistance (Barcia 2008:10; La Rosa Corzo 2005:178).

Slaveholders throughout the Americas skimmed on rations. On some plantations, enslaved people were responsible for providing all or a major portion of their own food, and they either bartered or sold any surplus food they produced. One of the major contributions that archaeology brings to the study of slavery is the examination of how enslaved people supplemented plantation rations, not just food but also household and personal items that they made or acquired for themselves. This chapter examines how the enslaved residents of Cafetal Biajacas were provisioned. They most likely engaged in various forms of trade, but they possessed fewer objects than enslaved peoples elsewhere in the Caribbean and in North America where excavations have yielded considerably more artifacts. No doubt the wall enclosure impeded slave access to trade in Cuba. Other examples of slaveholder obstacles to slave self-provisioning and trade are examined in this chapter.

La Dotación at Biajacas

The enslaved people who lived within the enclosure formed the dotación, the workforce, of Cafetal Biajacas. They were the social actors whose agency, cultural practices, and living conditions are inferred from the archaeological findings examined in this study. These archaeological data provide the primary sources for uncovering the voices of the dotación at Biajacas, as no judicial records containing the oral testimony of the enslaved like those utilized in recent studies of Cuban slavery provide perspectives from enslaved persons at Cafetal Biajacas.[1] Archaeologists often argue that the materials recovered through their investigations consist of the unintentional remains of human action that can yield insights into the lives of past peoples from their own perspectives. The artifact interpretations presented in this study are premised on this assertion. Interpreting the lives of enslaved peoples from their own perspectives is an important objective of the archaeological study of slavery that is proposed here.

As is often the case in the study of a specific plantation, little information is recorded for the vast majority of the slave laborers beyond their names, gender, and age at the time an inventory or other legal transaction involving them was undertaken. In 1838, 77 enslaved men, women, and children were recorded on an inventory of Santa Ana de Biajacas with their names, ages, and *naciones* (ethnic designations or place of birth) as shown in table 6.1. This table also indicates the final destination of most of them, after approximately 60 were relocated to O'Farrill's sugar plantations. The inventory takers indicated the list excluded four runaways—all male—who had been missing for some time, but noted their names and naciones, making a dotacíon of 81 before Ignacio O'Farrill's death (ANC Galletti leg. 245, no. 1, pieza 1). A dotación of 77 in 1838 was 25 fewer enslaved persons than the 102 recorded in 1822 on a *padrón* [register] for Madruga Pueblo (ANC GSC leg. 871, no. 29460), a reduction of approximately 24 percent

Table 6.1. List of enslaved workers at Cafetal Biajacas, 1838

No.	Name	Sex	Age	Ethnic Designation	Final Location
1	Agustín	Male	60	Carabalí	San Juan
2	Angel	Male	30	Carabalí	San Juan
3	Demetrio	Male	40	Calabalí	San Juan
4	Isidro	Male	-	Calabalí	Ran away
5	José	Male	-	Calabalí	Ran away
6	Mariano	Male	30	Calabalí	San Juan
7	Sotero	Male	30	Calabalí	Concordia
8	Valentín	Male	70	Calabalí	Biajacas
9	Alejo	Male	25	Congo	Concordia
10	Caimito	Male	45	Congo	Biajacas
11	Carlos	Male	60	Congo	San Juan
12	Cosme	Male	45	Congo	San Juan
13	Dionisio	Male	50	Congo	Biajacas
14	Feliciano	Male	30	Congo	Concordia
15	Francisco	Male	35	Congo	Concordia
16	José Rosario	Male	30	Congo	San Juan
17	Julio	Male	45	Congo	Biajacas
18	Lorenzo	Male	25	Congo	San Juan
19	Lucrecio	Male	45	Congo	San Juan
20	Marcelo	Male	45	Congo	Concordia
21	Andrés	Male	60	Ganga	Concordia
22	Anastasio	Male	50	Ganga	Biajacas
23	Domingo	Male	40	Ganga	San Juan
24	Fulgencio	Male	35	Ganga	San Juan
25	Francisco	Male	35	Ganga	???
26	Juan Bautista	Male	-	Ganga	Ran away
27	Juan de Dios	Male	45	Ganga	San Juan
28	Pío	Male	40	Ganga	San Juan
29	Sebastián	Male	30	Ganga	San Juan
30	Sixto	Male	35	Ganga	San Juan
31	Trinidad	Male	35	Ganga	Concordia
32	Carlos	Male	70	Lucumí	Biajacas
33	José María	Male	35	Lucumí	Concordia
34	Marcos	Male	50	Lucumí	San Juan
35	Miguel	Male	30	Lucumí	Concordia
36	Pedro	Male	50	Lucumí	Biajacas
37	Rafael	Male	30	Lucumí	San Juan
38	Remigio	Male	25	Lucumí	Concordia
39	Santiago	Male	55	Lucumí	???
40	Sotero	Male	30	Lucumí	Concordia
41	Félix	Male	45	Maená	San Juan
42	Martín	Male	-	Maená	Ran away
43	Narciso	Male	65	Maená	San Juan
44	Pablo	Male	30	Maená	Concordia

45	Sixto	Male	30	Maená	San Juan
46	Valeriano	Male	45	Maená	Biajacas
47	Francisco	Male	45	Mina	San Juan
48	Gabriel	Male	60	Mina	San Juan
49	Julián	Male	50	Mina	San Juan
50	Lorenzo	Male	45	Mina	Biajacas
51	Carlos	Male	25	Criollo	San Juan
52	Félix	Male	25	Criollo	San Juan
53	Fermín	Male	2	Criollo	San Juan
54	Ignacio	Male	2	Criollo	San Juan
55	José	Male	25	Criollo	San Juan
56	José Lino	Male	30	Criollo	Biajacas
57	Simón	Male	18	Criollo	San Juan
58	Augustina	Female	30	Carabalí	Biajacas
59	Andrea	Female	45	Carabalí	Concordia
60	Dolores	Female	45	Carabalí	Concordia
61	Fortunata	Female	40	Carabalí	San Juan
62	Juana	Female	45	Carabalí	Concordia
63	Leonarda	Female	30	Carabalí	Biajacas
64	María del Carmen	Female	50	Carabalí	San Juan
65	Merced	Female	50	Carabalí	San Juan
66	Rosa	Female	35	Carabalí	San Juan
67	Rosalía	Female	40	Carabalí	Biajacas
68	Gabriela	Female	25	Conga	Concordia
69	Josefa	Female	35	Conga	San Juan
70	Luna	Female	30	Conga	San Juan
71	María Josefa	Female	30	Conga	Concordia
72	Martina	Female	40	Conga	San Juan
73	Inés	Female	35	Ganga	San Juan
74	Isabel	Female	35	Ganga	San Juan
75	Bernarda	Female	30	Lucumí	Biajacas
76	Isabel	Female	35	Lucumí	Biajacas
77	Mónica	Female	30	Lucumí	San Juan
78	Camila	Female	18	Criolla	San Juan
79	Cirila	Female	1	Criolla	Biajacas
80	Fermina	Female	2	Criolla	San Juan
81	Rosalía	Female	4	Criolla	San Juan

of the workforce. Of the 77, 53 were men and 24 were women. Enslaved men frequently predominated on Cuban plantations, but male to female ratios were usually less pronounced on coffee plantations, as some planters preferred women for harvesting coffee and for sorting dried beans into the market grades or qualities used in the coffee trade (Van Norman 2013:53).

The inventory takers apparently did not record the actual ages of those over 20, but rounded them to the nearest 5. Additionally, these age designations were apparently not based on chronological age but on physical appearance and, perhaps, market value because some of the assigned ages increased considerably between 1838 and 1841. The ages given in the table are those recorded shortly after Ignacio O'Farrill's death. Most were between 30 and 45. Only five children are listed, two boys and three girls, all under the age of 5 (ANC Galletti leg. 240, no. 1, pieza 1). The small number of children supports the fact that the slave population in Cuba, as was often the case in other parts of the Caribbean and mainland South America, did not reproduce itself. Only through continuous importation of Africans was the slave population maintained (Bergad, García, and Barcia 1995:36).

The term *nación* refers to the ethnic or cultural affiliation of the African-born captives. The origins of these terms and their relevance to African ethno-linguistic groups are debated and are problematical for interpreting the cultural origins of enslaved Cubans (Barcia 2014:297). Many of these terms were products of slave traders, who often used place-names along the coastal areas of West Africa to designate the departure points from which victims left Africa. For example, Minas may refer to Elmina, first a Portuguese and later a Dutch trading post on the former Gold Coast in present-day Ghana (DeCorse 2001a). Similarly, Calabalí refers to two of three ports—Old Calabar and New Calabar—found on the Bight of Biafra, the southeast coast of present-day Nigeria.

Gwendolyn Hall argues that trying to understand these ethnic designations through the eyes of Europeans has led to questionable results. Instead, she posits these specific ethnic designations in records found in the Americas were often self-identifications. Hall supports this thesis from her study of court proceedings, which indicate that when a slave witness was sworn in, he or she was asked, "What is your nation?" (Hall 2005:41). She also reasons that the civil authorities who took estate inventories would not have known the long list of ethnic designations found in many documents and similarly would have asked enslaved people their nation. It does seem that this was the case at Cafetal Biajacas, and at least in one recorded incidence, an enslaved man, Francisco, who had been designated a Congo on a previous list, told the appraiser of the estate in 1841 that he was not Congo but Maená (ANC Galletti leg. 934, no. 6).

If these ethnic designations are self-identifications, then I would add that these may be the identities that enslaved people acquired in the Americas through their associations with others with whom they shared a mutually intelligible language and similar cultural practices, rather than their ethnicities at the time they became victims of the slave trade in Africa. Hall admits that ethnic designations appear on records not when the enslaved people first enter the Americas but many years later when they are listed on estate and other kinds of records. Because of the time lapse between when Africans entered the Americas and when these designations were recorded, we should not assume recorded ethnicities reflect how these Africans identified themselves when they were in Africa. It is, however, very likely that there is a close relationship between the two. Scholars formerly treated African cultural groups as timeless and unchanging entities; failing to consider ethnicity is often fluid and situational, as numerous Africanists have shown.[2]

Clearly, the meanings and usages of these ethnic designations changed through time and place, and Hall (2005:122–25) demonstrates many of these changes for the 400 years of the transatlantic slave trade. Using "Minas" as a primary example, she traces the use of the term and challenges the widespread assumption that Minas referred to enslaved people taken from the Elmina. The Portuguese established the fortress they named Elmina primarily for trading gold and ivory, not Africans, and even after the Dutch capture of Elmina in 1637, only a very small number of Africans were shipped from Elmina (Hall 2005:122). The noun *mina*, a "mine" in both Spanish and Portuguese, often described enslaved people of various ethnicities who worked in mines or possessed skills in gold production and processing during the sixteenth and early seventeenth centuries when slave labor played a major role in mining operations.

After 1650, "Mina" increasingly referred to peoples shipped from the Slave Coast, present-day Republic of Benin, who spoke Gbe languages, which includes the ethnic groups Ewe, Fon, and Aja. In Brazil, the term broadly referred to peoples shipped from the Gold and Slave Coasts that sometimes included the Yoruba (Torres de Souza and Agostini 2012:106–7). In Cuba and Louisiana, from 1750 to 1850, however, *Mina* referred to specific self-identified communities who spoke a common language, but it is unknown what that language was (Hall 2005:123–24). Hall (2005:125) concludes that the term *Mina* varied in time and place and in the language of the document, but the term most often referred to an ethnic or coastal designation from the Bight of Benin and sometimes the Gold Coast.

The naciones listed on the inventories for Cafetal Biajacas mirror those found in various Cuban colonial documents and traveler accounts of the nineteenth century. By that time, there were eight major naciones in Cuba: Mandinga, Gangá, Mina, Arará, Lucumí, Carabalí, Congo, and Macuá (Barcia 2014:297). Considerable debate continues regarding the relationship between African groups and the ethnic designations found in the Americas. However, the contributions of Hall (2005) and Barcia (2008:18–24) suggest that the Cuban naciones listed for the dotación at Cafetal Biajacas broadly correspond to the following African ethno-linguistic groups and geographical regions: 18 Carabalí (Igbo, Ibibio, Efik, and other groups from southeastern Nigeria); 17 Congo (Kikongo speakers of West Central Africa from present-day countries of the Republic of Congo, Democratic Republic of Congo, and Angola); 13 Gangá (Mande-speaking peoples primarily from present-day Sierra Leone and Liberia); 12 Lucumí (Yoruba-speaking peoples of southwestern Nigeria); 6 Maená (an unknown designation, possibly a misspelling of Maní, a subgroup of Gangá from near the Mano River located between Guinea and Liberia [Basso Ortiz 2005:44–45], or a misspelling of Macuá, a designation for Bantu-speaking people who embarked from East African ports from present-day Mozambique (see Barcia 2008:21, 23); 4 Minas (peoples taken from the Slave Coast of present-day Republic of Benin and Togo, who presumably spoke a Gbe language); and 11 Criollas (born in Cuba).[3]

The distribution of naciones at Cafetal Biajacas indicates that no one group was in the majority. It is difficult to know whether or not Ignacio O'Farrill intentionally acquired a diverse group of naciones or simply purchased people based on market availability. Hall (2005:68) rejects the idea that slaveholders deliberately fractionalize new Africans to prevent communication among them in order to minimize revolts. Instead, she provides examples from Louisiana of the opposite situation, slaveholders bringing in new Africans of the same nations already on the plantation for the purpose of using established slave residents to assist in the indoctrination of the newcomers. Manuel Barcia (2008:14) suspects similar practices occurred on Cuban plantations.

Yet the fact that the dotación at Cafetal Biajacas consisted of enslaved people from five or six of the eight major naciones of nineteenth-century Cuba suggests that deliberate efforts may have been taken to balance the cultural diversity to prevent one group from overpowering the others. Drawing on her extensive research in Cuban archives, Gloria García (2003b:24) argues that the ethnic composition of Cuban dotaciones did not make integration easy, but "actúan distanciando más que como fuerzas aglutinadoras" [worked more as a distancing rather than a unifying force] that made the creation of slave communities difficult. She expresses some skepticism regarding the use of "community" to describe Cuban dotaciones because the restrictive character of chattel slavery, being someone's possession, and the physical boundaries of the plantation itself drastically reduced opportunities for forming social networks. But, despite these obstacles, enslaved laborers formed social relationships that vaguely resemble African traditions, and they submitted to a slave-created hierarchy of subordination regardless of nación, age, or gender. She acknowledges the need for subsequent research, however, to clarify if the external manifestation of ethnic diversity masked a more unified situation among enslaved peoples in Cuba (García 2003b:23–24).

Inventories of the dotación at Cafetal Biajacas provide important information on the demographic composition and cultural backgrounds of the enslaved people who lived within the enclosure. To understand how they lived, we must look at the recovered artifacts they left behind along with other kinds of written records.

Provisioning and Independent Production

Historian Kathleen Hilliard (2010:693–97) has shown that one of the ways in which students of slavery have sought to find slave voices and insights into slave agency has been to analyze slave independent production. This included producing food and finished products (e.g., baskets, furniture, or pottery) for themselves and for sale, raising livestock, marketing their own products, and consuming or saving the proceeds from these activities. These and other activities form the "slaves' economy" (Berlin and Morgan 1991).

Analysis of the slaves' economy has become a standard if not an expected theme to address in slavery studies, but opinions differ on how these activities are interpreted. Several contributors to Berlin and Morgan's (1991, 1993) edited volumes and others (Penningroth 2003) view slave independent production as a means by which enslaved people undermined the planter economy while establishing a degree of autonomy and empowerment for themselves. Other scholars, however, argue that slave independent production was directly tied to, and constrained by, staple crop production; therefore, it should be understood as "auxiliary production" (Kaye 2007:9, 103–5). No doubt, slaveholder provisioning and slave independent production varied through time and from place to place.

The study of slave independent production began in the Caribbean with the classic study of anthropologists Sidney Mintz and Douglas Hall (1960) on modern-day internal markets of Jamaica, the origins of which they traced to the early eighteenth century during the time of slavery. Initially, slave laborers in Jamaica produced food for themselves, but in time they began taking surplus food to local markets and selling their crops for money or exchanging them for other goods. Market days, established on Sundays, avoided disruption of the work routine on plantations, and in time these Sunday markets became an important social and economic institution (Mintz 1974:183). Through the study of statutes, Mintz and Hall (1960:15–17) demonstrated the growing importance of the crops and handicrafts enslaved people produced that allowed them to establish a place for themselves in the free economic activity of Jamaica. Mintz and Hall's work set the stage for subsequent studies in Jamaica and inspired similar studies on other Caribbean islands.

Analysis of slave independent production in the southern United States began in the 1980s after examination of Reconstruction-era records of the Southern Claims Commission (SCC) revealed the claims from former slave laborers of non-real property—poultry, cows, horses, crops, wagons, and other possessions—they owned during slavery (Penningroth 2003:47). Following the Civil War, the federal government established the SCC to hear the claims of Unionist southerners who lost property during the Union army occupation and raids. The commission sought to reimburse white Unionist southerners and, to its surprise, also received claims from formerly enslaved African Americans. Consequently, the SCC agents recorded what the claimants acquired while they were enslaved and how they earned money to acquire these items. More significantly, these records established that a slaves' economy operated in the antebellum South, a finding that has led to the reexamination of other overlooked sources with similar information on slave independent production and exchange (Hilliard 2010:696–98, 2014).

While the historiography of slave independent production influenced some archaeologies of the slaves' economy, archaeological research on slavery has always examined slave production and consumption focusing on the kind, quality, and quantity of objects enslaved people used and how they acquired these items. Some early studies proposed slaveholders provisioned enslaved people with ceramics and other household objects, some of which were possibly castoffs from the great house (Fairbanks 1972:78–79), but written sources supporting this interpretation remain scarce. On the other hand, using archaeological evidence to determine whether or not an object recovered from slave quarters was a castoff from the great house either has not been supported (Otto 1984:61) or has produced questionable results (Kelso 1997:90–91).

As many of the first slave sites investigated in the southern United States were located on the coastal areas of South Carolina and Georgia where task labor predominated, archaeologists reasoned that enslaved peoples obtained these artifacts and food resources from work they performed in their free time (Adams and Boling 1989; Crook 2001). But when sites from other regions of the South that employed gang labor also yielded significant quantities of household and personal goods, archaeologists began to recognize that they had been unearthing the spoils of the slaves' informal economy but had not interpreted their findings in that way.

The growing historical scholarship of the slaves' economy reinforced what many archaeologists had already suspected—that enslaved people acquired many, if not most, of their household possessions on their own. Since the 2000s, several archaeologists have conducted their own studies of slave markets and informal exchange by focusing on the production and trade of a particular commodity such as handcrafted pottery (Hauser 2008, 2011) or the acquisition and consumption of mass-produced objects (Galle 2010; Gibson 2007; Heath 2004; Wilkie and Farnsworth 2005:262–302). Studies of both types demonstrate the critical role archaeology plays in the analysis of slave consumption, production, and exchange.

No single published study comparable to those conducted on other Caribbean islands or in the southern United States has focused exclusively on the slaves' economy in Cuba, but studies of Cuban slavery describe tantalizing pieces of it. From the sixteenth century onward, Spanish law required Cuban slaveholders to provide their laborers with provision grounds known as conucos to grow their own food and to raise pigs and chickens (García 2003b:38). Account books of the second half of the nineteenth century show the sale of slave livestock and produce to plantation owners (R. Scott [1985] 2000:15–17). Unfortunately, similar records for coffee and sugar plantations of the first half of the nineteenth century have not survived or they have not been deposited and made available in Cuban public archives. Despite this gap in the written record, a variety of scattered sources indicate that enslaved Cubans on coffee plantations produced foods and handicrafts that they sold for cash or exchanged for other items. The following discussion examines slave independent production in western Cuba in general and, when possible, on coffee plantations specific to Matanzas jurisdiction.

Slaveholder Provisioning

Slave independent production and self-provisioning generally developed from insufficient slaveholder provisioning. Most of the nineteenth-century Cuban discourse on slaveholder provisions focuses on food rations, although clothing was also a problematical issue (Serrano 1837:48; Lowell 2003:84, 89; and chapter 7). Various sources indicate that workers on coffee plantations generally received better food provisions than on sugar plantations in Cuba. The smaller land requirements for coffee than for sugar usually afforded surplus acreage often dedicated to the cultivation of provision crops as shown in the plan of James DeWolf's Marianne plantation in figure 3.1.

Coffee planters typically reserved one caballería [33 acres] for growing *viandes* [root crops] such as *yuca* [cassava] (*Manihot esculenta*), malanga, also known as *yautia* [cocoyam] (*Xanthosoma* sp.), and *boniato* [sweet potatoes] (*Ipomoea batatas*) (González Fernández 1991:173). These and other viandes became major food sources for all Cubans and by the mid-nineteenth century formed an integral part of an emergent national cuisine (Dawdy 2002:59). Plantain and corn were also used for slave provisions, as many coffee planters interspersed these crops with coffee trees. Rice was produced on plantations with sufficient water, or upland rice, cultivated in dry soil, was substituted. At Cafetal Biajacas, yuca, malanga, sweet potatoes, and corn were all produced on 67 acres in addition to plantain grown alongside the coffee (ANC Galletti leg. 934, no. 6). This inventory also indicated that 300 pounds of rice en cáscara [in husks] was either harvested from the cafetal or potrero or purchased locally. All these foods supplied the dotación at Cafetal Biajacas with high-caloric, starchy vegetables, the bulk of the Cuban slave diet.

But food shortages still occurred due to crop failures, droughts, or storms. Joseph Goodwin, the mayordomo for George DeWolf, recorded periods of insufficient food supplies on the two coffee plantations he managed. On July 11, 1822, he wrote: "not anything for man, or beast, to eat, for those that belong on the estate. The cattle, horses & mules sent to barter, no grass there. The Negroes eat the last provisions this day, and for a month past not half enough" (Goodwin Diary). On May 4, 1825, Goodwin found his own food resources in short supply: "I am reduced to pork and plantains, and if it does not rain soon I shall go on the corn." The hurricanes in 1844 and 1846 were particularly devastating to food supplies and left many enslaved people scavenging for food because slaveholders were unable to provide for them (Pérez 2000:87–88).

During times of good crop yields, provisions of starchy vegetables were generally sufficient, but meat or fish rations were frequently sparse. Mary Gardner Lowell (2003:85) observed the distribution of weekly rations at Mr. Smith's coffee plantation in Camarioca: each adult received four mackerel, and each child got one. She referred to the fish ration as a "luxury" allowed to them because during the week their food consisted principally of plantains and some corn. Cuban planters provisioned dotaciones with imported *bacalao* [salted codfish] or *tasajo*, dried meat similar to jerky. James DeWolf shipped cod and menhaden (*Brevootia tyrannus*), an oily marine fish, from New England to feed workers at his coffee plantations from 1817 onward. In his correspondence, DeWolf indicated his preference for fish for slave provisions and reserved barrel pork and beef for consumption by the managers of his Cuban properties.[4] Most Cuban planters opted for imported meat and fish because of the high cost of locally produced meat, a concern James DeWolf shared with Stephan Hales on August 8, 1817, regarding the purchase of fresh beef from Madruga for his Mount Hope plantation. Due to the high cost of fresh meat, both black and white Cubans consumed imported salty meat and fish, but the quality of the imports fed to slave workers was generally poorer than those consumed by free Cubans (Sarmiento Ramírez 2009:149). Although enslaved people often raised their own livestock, they rarely consumed these animals but kept them for the purpose of making money from their eventual sale.[5] Chickens, for example, were kept for their eggs, a food product that was also sold.

By the 1840s, increased complaints about the quantity and quality of food provisions prompted discussion among members of the Sociedad Económica and the captain-general to develop standard requirements for slave food (ANC GSC leg. 945, no. 33309). In a letter that Gerónimo Valdés circulated to several members of the planter elite on slave housing (see chapter 5), he raised questions concerning food provisions as to the kind and amount of food and whether food should be distributed raw for enslaved people to prepare meals for themselves or cooked in central kitchens and served at designated hours. Responses from the planters varied with the specifics, but they employed similar practices. Most agreed that some portion of meals, usually the midday meal, should be prepared for slave laborers, because if slave laborers prepared their own food it would take too much time away from work.

Domingo Aldama strongly advocated for cooking slave meals in central kitchens because he believed some owners of taverns would accept uncooked rations from enslaved people as payment for *aguardiente*—a strong, distilled alcoholic beverage usually made from fermented sugarcane. Therefore, Aldama recommended providing only married slave laborers with uncooked provisions, and all others were given cooked food (ANC GSC leg. 940, no. 33158). The collective thinking of the slaveholders whom Valdés consulted formed the basis for article 6 in the 1842 slave code that provided a minimal daily requirement for slave food provisions: two or three meals consisting of six to eight plantains or the equivalent in sweet potatoes, yams, yuccas, and other edible root crops; eight ounces of meat or salted codfish; and four ounces of rice, flour, or a mixed vegetable stew (García 2003b:86). The law only stated recommendations for the amount of food, but left the matter of food preparation for planters to decide.

The recovery of iron kettle fragments and food-serving implements from within the enclosure at Cafetal Biajacas along with documentary sources suggest many Cuban plantations combined preparing slave meals in a central kitchen with meals that workers prepared for themselves. Abiel Abbot (1829:41) observed this practice on a plantation he visited in Matanzas jurisdiction: "They come to the cook-room with their gourd and take as much as they choose of the delicious plantain; they have rations of fish, indeed, of jerk beef. . . . A pretty good sized codfish is cut in three parts, and one of them given to a laborer for the day. . . . In addition to the common fare, they have their own favorite dishes, cooked in their private kettles, in which they put melanga [malanga], ochra [okra], and anything they please, raised in their own gardens. They cook their own suppers; and on Saturday evening, they make entertainments, and invite guests with as much form and ceremony as their hospitable masters." Abbot's observation of food provisioning resonates with archaeological findings found not only at Cafetal Biajacas but elsewhere in the Americas as well.

Archaeologists almost always turn up evidence of food preparation in their excavation of slave quarters, but the documentary records for many plantations often indicate that the preparation of slave food took place in central kitchens. Assuming these records are accurate, the food remains, preparation equipment, and serving utensils recovered from archaeological investigation most likely derived from evening and Sunday meals that workers prepared for their own consumption. Abbot's reference to the use of gourds for food consumption and social activities associated with food are both further examined. Cuban planters, like slaveholders throughout the Americas, usually provided laborers with some food rations. But enslaved people found they had to supplement these foods through their own efforts.

Slave Independent Production at Cafetal Biajacas

Undoubtedly, enslaved laborers at Cafetal Biajacas undertook some form of independent production for themselves, but it is unclear precisely what those activities were from either archaeological or documentary resources. One inventory for the cafetal refers to lands reserved for the dotación's use and a *corral* [an animal pen or farmyard] (ANC Galletti leg. 245, no. 1), possibly within the enclosure. This statement implies that the laborers farmed conucos as well as raised some livestock. The metal portions of farm tools recovered from the excavated slave bohíos include an axe, a mattock or hatchet, 13 identifiable machetes, as well as parts from unidentifiable metal objects that could have been used in tending gardens in addition to working the coffee fields.

Archaeological evidence, though slim, suggests that the dotacíon at Cafetal Biajacas may have produced handicrafts for their own use or for sale. The primary craft item archaeologists tend to associate with enslaved Africans and their descendants in the Americas is pottery. But the laborers at Cafetal Biajacas apparently did not produce pottery; slave-made pottery has not been reported in the investigations of other Cuban plantations. Written sources, however, allude to the possibility of Afro-Cubans producing pottery both on plantations and in towns. In his response to Gerónimo Valdés's question regarding food rations, Jacinto Gonzáles Larrinaga wrote that the laborers on his sugar plantation received their midday meal on earthenware plates made on the same plantation (García 2003b:83).

Additionally, Afro-Cubans may have participated in the local, hand-built pottery industry in Guanabacoa, a suburb of Havana established as an Indian town in the sixteenth century (Domínguez González 2004). Seventeenth-century documents describe the Indians of Guanabacoa as producing earthenware pots and jugs, and pottery production continued in Guanabacoa well into the nineteenth century when the population was no longer identified as Indian. José Marie Andueza (1841:159), a Spaniard, visited Guanabacoa in the 1830s and noted a family of potters whom he referred to as descendants from the Indian race, but who seemed unaware of their indigenous heritage, engaged in making *cazuelas* [a shallow cooking vessel with a wide opening], *búcaros* [vases], and *jarros* [jug or pitcher often with handles on each side] made in an old style. Later in 1851, Fredrika Bremer (1853:286) commented: "Among the memories which the Indians have left in Guanabacoa is a kind of earthen vessel made from a sort of porous clay, peculiar to the place, which is still made there." Bremer's statement suggests that the production of earthenware continued in Guanabacoa at least until the 1850s, but the makers were no longer of Amerindian descent.

Archaeologists excavating in Havana find the majority of wares associated with the Guanabacoa industry in contexts dating from the seventeenth and eighteenth centuries before the massive importation of Africans

Figure 6.1. Example of a bottle-glass fragment reworked into a razor-sharp tool (1.95 cm × 2.35 cm) recovered from excavations in the enclosure. Photograph by Lisette Roura Álvarez.

to Cuba in the nineteenth century. In addition, these recovered vessels possess attributes characteristic of traditional Arawakan pottery (Roura Álvarez, Arrazcaeta Delgado, and Hernández Oliva 2006:24–26). The only pottery recovered from archaeological contexts strongly linked to Afro-Cubans are those that Gabino La Rosa Corzo (1999:110–14) recovered from slave runaway sites in caves of Pinar del Río and Mayabeque provinces. These vessels were probably not traded but made for their own use.

Rather than making pottery, the dotación at Cafetal Biajacas possibly crafted items for themselves and for sale from perishable materials seldom recovered from archaeological investigations. Travelers' accounts describe enslaved Cubans making baskets and hats from palm leaves (Abbot 1829:141; Bremer 1853:2:335); household utensils—bowls, ladles, cups—and musical instruments from gourds or calabashes (Bremer 1853:2:277, 282; Townsend Diary, 126–27); jewelry and other forms of ornamentation from acacia and other seeds (Townsend Diary, 127); Bremer 1853:2:314, 353); and drums and canoes from hollowed out trees (Townsend Diary, 126) Hurlbert 1854:154; Howe [1860] 1969:165).

Handmade tools recovered from the enclosure were perhaps utilized in some way to produce such items. One type of tool consists of cutting implements made by chipping or flaking broken pieces of bottle glass to produce a sharp cutting edge in a fashion similar to making stone tools (figure 6.1). The other type of tool consists of broken pipe bowls that exhibit evidence of wear consistent with that found on implements used for polishing or buffing. It is unknown how the slave occupants at Cafetal Biajacas used these objects, but suggestions for their former uses are based on interpretations offered from other sites and inferred from the examination of the wear found on them.

The refashioned glass implements provided ideal tools for projects requiring a razor-sharp edge for delicate cutting, whittling, shaving, and perhaps carving and incising household implements or musical instruments made of gourds. Similar tools made from recycled glass have been found in Brazil, Jamaica, and Louisiana. Former residents of post-emancipation sites in Louisiana told archaeologists that they utilized these glass tools for the same purposes as one would use safety razor blades today, including shaving facial hair or shaving designs into the hair. The reworked glass offered a viable substitute for safety razor blades, which were expensive for poorly paid tenant farmers (Palmer 2011:149; Wilkie 1996:45–46).

The widespread geographic distribution of these reworked glass artifacts suggests enslaved peoples frequently made them. Archaeologists, however, have reported similar glass artifacts at sites occupied by indigenous peoples (Casella 2007:132–33) and European Americans; therefore, they should not be thought of as tools that people of African descent exclusively made nor should archaeologists use these artifacts to identify the presence of people of African descent.[6] These glass artifacts are usually found at sites where the former occupants had limited financial resources and may indicate impoverished living situations. These artifacts can also be thought of as "opportunistic implements" made on the spur of the moment to meet an immediate need (F. Smith 2008:26). Regardless of the circumstances for making them, they functioned as tools because they were handheld devices that aided in accomplishing a task. They were undoubtedly used for numerous purposes, and at Cafetal Biajacas they apparently were utilized for purposes that other cutting tools did not provide, as excavations in and around the slave bohíos yielded numerous machetes and a few knives.

The reused earthenware pipe bowl fragments recovered from within the enclosure offer another possibility of craft production. These fragments exhibit wear usually on interior and sometimes on exterior surfaces of the pipes similar to that observed on objects used for smoothing, polishing, or buffing materials such as wood, bone, hide, pottery, and possibly gourds.

Figure 6.2. Gaming pieces (diameters 1.35 cm to 2.2 cm) made from ceramic fragments recovered from slave enclosure at Cafetal Biajacas. Photograph by Lisette Roura Álvarez.

The wear apparently resulted from the use of pipe bowl fragments after the pipes broke. It is possible they were used in shaping and smoothing refined earthenware into the rounded forms recovered from the site (figure 6.2). These ceramic discs are found at sites of various periods worldwide, and most archaeologists interpret them as gaming pieces, although they were conceivably used in other ways.

Both the archaeological and documentary records show that the dotación at Cafetal Biajacas undertook various forms of independent production for themselves, but to what extent they sold or exchanged the products of their labor is unknown. The following discussion examines the forms of exchange Cuban slave laborers pursued.

Venues of Exchange: Tiendas, Tabernas, and Vendedores

Perhaps due to the absence of institutionalized Sunday markets in Cuba, enslaved Cubans had fewer options for the sale and exchange of the commodities they produced than their counterparts in the English-speaking Caribbean (R. Scott [1985] 2000:149). Cuban slave laborers sold their produce to their owners or nearby plantations or engaged in transactions with owners of local *tabernas* [taverns] and *tiendas* [general stores]. They also bought and sold items from *vendedores* [itinerant merchants] who travel from plantation to plantation selling a variety of goods. Julia Ward Howe ([1860] 1969:76) observed a peddler selling "white bread, calicoes, muslins, and cotton handkerchiefs" at the sugar plantation of Jacinto Gonzáles Larrinaga, a contributor to Gerónimo Valdés's 1842 slave code. Vendedores, along with tabernas and tiendas, supplied more than venues for the trade. They also provided an important social function, similar to the slave markets of the English Caribbean, as the conveyors of gossip, news, and other information beyond the confines of plantations. Consequently, slaveholders desirous of keeping enslaved people tied to the plantation and isolated from the outside world viewed these venues of exchange with contempt.

Suspicious of slave sales to tiendas and tabernas, many slaveholders accused enslaved people of exchanging plantation staple crops for aguardiente and tobacco. Captain-General Miguel Tacón attempted to curb this activity in 1836 when he issued a bando stating that anyone caught trading goods after the evening prayer without a license from their owners would be fined four pesos (ANC GSC leg. 996, no. 33048). Persistent complaints of slave nocturnal transactions at taverns suggest that Tacón's proclamation went unheeded. As discussed in chapter 5, slaveholders often used the nocturnal trade of goods as a rationale for locking up workers at night, a practice first legalized in the Matanzas jurisdiction in 1825 and later mandated for all slaveholders in the Slave Code of 1842. Locking up the dotación at Cafetal Biajacas at night to prevent them from trading at tabernas may partially account for the small quantity of household objects they possessed.

Planter essays and complaints to colonial authorities emphasized the so-called clandestine trade among enslaved Cubans rather than their sales of produce and livestock that benefited the interests of planters. James DeWolf, for example, required workers on his plantations to give him half of all proceeds they received from the sale of their crops and livestock. In a letter written to Alexander Griswold, the manager of his coffee plantation Mount Hope on June 15, 1831, DeWolf expressed his policy on slave independent production: "There appears to me to be no government of the negroes, that what work they do was mostly for their own account. I had formerly given orders that the negroes should have but one half the hogs they fatten, that a pig should be given them from the porero [potrero] when their hog was sold & the money divided, which rule I request you to enforce. And one half of whatever the negroes grow of stock of any kind or corn or anything to sell must be one half for the Estate" (JDWSFP, vol. 3). DeWolf's attitude may not have been typical of Cuban planters, but he provides an excellent example of a slaveholder who attempted to manipulate slave independent production to his advantage.

While planters like DeWolf demanded a share of slave laborers' profits, Cornelio Souchay, owner of the Angerona coffee plantation, restricted slave access to trade by setting up his own plantation store. According to Abiel Abbot (1829:141), Souchay encouraged his dotación to earn money and to spend it; therefore, he established a shop next to the coffee mill "with everything they may wish to buy that is proper for them; clothe cheap and showy; garments gay and warm; crockery; beads; guano, or the American palm that may form neat hats for themselves; little cooking pots, etc. He puts everything at low prices; and no peddler is permitted to show his wares on the estate." Abbot's description of a plantation store seems unique to Angerona because no references to other stores on coffee plantations were found in the numerous accounts and other documents examined for this study.

Similar stores, however, were established on large sugar plantations known as *tiendas mixtas* in the 1880s on the eve of slave emancipation in Cuba. Rebecca Scott ([1985] 2000:184–85) contends planters used these stores not only to exercise economic control over plantation workers but also to control information concerning opportunities for workers that existed beyond the plantation property. Souchay's plantation store possibly aimed toward a comparable objective—to constrict slave options for trade but also to reduce slave mobility and contact with the outside world in much the same way planters deployed other geographies of containment such as barracones de patio or the wall enclosure. Souchay possibly barred peddlers, who were often free people of color (García 2003b:38), from Angerona because like many slaveholders, he distrusted associations between enslaved blacks and free blacks.[7]

Unscrupulous plantation managers also found ways to profit from the slaves' economy, usually by stealing from enslaved laborers. Aristide des Chapelles wrote to Helene Bauduy on July 15, 1823, that he fired the mayoral of his coffee plantation in Lagunilla, Matanzas, because he "stole from the negroes 7 or 8 ounces" of gold (Bauduy Family Papers). This was $119 to $160, depending on the value of gold.[8] Although the circumstances of the theft are not stated, overseers sometimes kept account of the money that enslaved people earned (Howe [1860] 1969:167).

One of the most unconscionable offenses of robbing a slave laborer occurred on a *vega* [tobacco farm] in the present-day province of Pinar del Río. In 1849, Juan Lucumí, enslaved on the vega of Josefa Garro, entered into an agreement with Ramón de Avila, the mayoral, to help sell Juan's tobacco crop at current prices for part of the proceeds. Juan never received any money from the sale, so he angrily confronted Avila. Avila refused to give Juan money for the sale of his crop and subjected him to two hundred lashes and shackling for seven months. In addition, Avila destroyed Juan's conuco and removed his piglets and chickens (ANC GSC leg. 947, no. 33399).

In 1852, Juan sought legal action against Avila to obtain his lost property through a *síndico*, a local appointee charged to represent enslaved Cubans in legal proceedings.[9] Almost a year later, the governor-general's office ruled in Juan's favor, but it is unclear if Juan was compensated for his lost property. Regardless of any material compensation Juan received, Avila could never make up for the brutal physical treatment and mental anguish he inflicted upon Juan.

The previous examples of Cuban planters and managers exploiting the slaves' economy for their own purposes represent extreme cases. But they illustrate various ways slaveholders and their emissaries interfered with and impeded slave efforts to acquire cash and a few commodities for themselves. To examine the economy without also examining the challenges that enslaved independent producers faced distorts the reality of their lives and their ongoing struggles with their enslavers. Analyzing slave independent production from the perspective of the master-slave dialectic enables an evaluation of slave agency within the constraints of chattel slavery. Juan Lucumí, for example, took action against his oppressor but risked being defeated in his efforts. As Manuel Barcia (2008:104) observes, many who brought their cases to the colonial authorities often ended up frustrated or punished for their actions because colonial officials often sided with white Cubans in these legal proceedings.

The benefits of independent production for enslaved people depended upon their circumstances. Some earned enough money, usually through hiring themselves out rather than from the sale of produce and other commodities, to eventually purchase their freedom through *coartación*, an institution that permitted gradual self-purchase by making payments in installments (R. Scott [1985] 2000:13]. Cuban *coartados*, however, usually lived in or near cities and towns where there were more opportunities for self-hire than in the countryside (R. Scott [1985] 2000:76; García 2003b:41; Barcia 2008:95).

Ignacio O'Farrill held several hundred people in bondage, but only one of them was manumitted through self-purchase. Micaela of the Mandinga nation purchased her freedom when she was over 40 years old for 400 pesos (ANC Salinas 1829c:1977). Because she is not identified with any of O'Farrill's plantations, like all the other workers referenced in his property records, she most likely lived and worked in his town house in Havana. And, like other enslaved Cubans living in urban areas, she could have earned money by hiring herself out.

In contrast to Micaela, the enslaved people at Cafetal Biajacas, who lived within a massive enclosure locked at night, had fewer money-making possibilities. Based upon archaeological findings, their independent production only allowed them to supplement meager, monotonous food rations and acquire a few personal and household possessions. Their consumption of these items and the cultural practices associated with the usage of these things provide insights into life within the enclosure.

7

Consumption and Life within the Enclosure

Archaeologist Paul Mullins (2012:2) defines consumption as "a complex and far-reaching concept that encompasses the making, selling, buying, using, and discarding of material things." He goes on to say that "historical archaeologists have typically focused on how patterns of material consumption reveal, reflect, and confirm consumers' social identity and position and how individuals use things to shape their definitions of self and others." Previous discussion addresses the production and trade of slave consumption in Cuba. Here I examine how the enslaved people at Cafetal Biajacas used the objects recovered from the archaeological investigations within the enclosure and what these findings indicate about their living conditions and cultural practices.

How these objects were used to shape a collective identity is too difficult a question to tackle at this preliminary stage of archaeological research of Cuban slavery. Architectural historians and others have begun to examine material expressions of the Cuban creole elite in architecture and some aspects of the decorative arts, but this has not been the case for the study of enslaved Cubans' material expressions. A notable exception, however, is in the realm of Afro-Cuban religions. For example, archaeologist Lourdes Domínguez (1999:17, 22–23) and art historian David Brown (2003) draw historical links between the religious artifacts of enslaved Cubans and those used in present-day Afro-Cuban religious practices. A preliminary effort is made here, however, to suggest some ways in which enslaved Cubans used things to express their definitions of themselves.

Recycling and Refashioning Objects

One striking characteristic of the artifacts recovered from within the enclosure is the amount of recycling of broken and discarded items, some of which were refashioned into other kinds of tools. Cutting tools made from broken bottle glass, smoothing or buffing tools made from pipe bowl fragments, and round gaming pieces made from broken ceramics compose a very small percentage of the artifacts recovered from the enclosure. The most abundant artifact in the total collection, the horma de azúcar [sugar mold], an unglazed, coarse earthenware vessel used in sugar production, also appears to have been recycled, although the ways these vessels were reused remain unclear.

Of the 11,737 artifacts recovered from within the enclosure, 7,261 are fragments of sugar molds, used to produce raw, unrefined sugar from the boiled, semicrystallized cane product poured into the wide mouth and drained out of the small hole in the bottom (Mintz 1986:49). It is difficult to imagine another use for the horma because its conical shape was designed for this specific task. The sizes of hormas vary, but the one in figure 7.1 is 41.5 cm long (16.34 in) and the wide opening measures 39 cm (15.34 in). Fragments of hormas frequently turn up in slave settlements on sugar plantations and occasionally at the sites of slave runaways (La Rosa Corzo 2010:19). The runaways possibly obtained them by raiding a nearby sugar plantation or by trading with laborers on sugar plantations.

The presence of such a large number of sugar molds on a coffee plantation is puzzling. Many coffee plantations in western Cuba planted small amounts of sugarcane for feeding animals during the dry season and perhaps for use by plantation occupants. But this cane was not processed into sugar. Sugarcane was possibly planted at Cafetal Biajacas for this purpose as well, but none of the inventories or other detailed estate records mentioned anything about sugar growing or processing at Cafetal Biajacas.

A more likely source for the hormas as well as for any sugar and sugar products for the cafetal was the O'Farrills' nearby sugar plantation, San Juan de Nepomuceno, which contained all the workshops for the plantations, including a *tejar* [a tile factory] with kilns for producing hormas, *tejas* [roof tiles], and *ladrillos* [bricks]. The 1841 inventory listed 1,000 fired

Figure 7.1. An *horma de azúcar* [sugar mold], 41.5 cm long and opening 39 cm. Collection of the Archaeology Museum of Havana, Office of the Historian for the City of Havana. Photograph by Lisette Roura Álvarez.

hormas and 500 unfired hormas within the tejar at the time the inventory was taken (ANC Galletti leg. 934, no. 6). San Juan de Nepomuceno obviously produced large quantities of hormas for sugar production and was likely the source for the hormas at the cafetal. But did the workers at Cafetal Biajacas receive raw sugar in the hormas? Unless the hormas were damaged, it seems unlikely that raw sugar was brought from San Juan to Cafetal Biajacas in hormas, because these vessels were used again and again for sugar processing until they broke. The remains of hormas at Cafetal Biajacas were more likely either wasters—vessels damaged or broken in the firing process—or vessels discarded after their use in sugar making. In either case, the hormas came to Cafetal Biajacas as discards, unusable for sugar making, but presumably useful for other purposes.

Evidence for how hormas were reused at Cafetal Biajacas is admittedly slim. Nine fragments have mortar stuck to them, suggesting they were used in some kind of construction. A large piece was inserted into a masonry wall of locus C, the infirmary/almacen, apparently to line an airhole near the roof of the building; however, airholes on another wall of the same building were lined with roof tiles. Perhaps when roof tiles were in short supply, a broken horma was substituted. The hormas at Cafetal Biajacas were probably recycled in many ways that are not evident from the recovered fragments. For example, Anselmo Suárez y Romero (1859:203) described enslaved people placing straw in broken hormas for hens to lay their eggs. Suárez y Romero's observation suggests recycling of broken hormas was commonplace on Cuban plantations, and they were probably reused for a variety of farm-related and domestic purposes, including as troughs for animals. The hormas recovered from the enclosure were possibly recycled for similar purposes.

Slave sites frequently yield artifacts refashioned from discards. In addition to recycled glass scrapers, archaeologists have also uncovered an awl (a sewing or leather-working tool) made from a bone toothbrush handle and a chisel made from a horseshoe from plantations in the southern United States (Singleton 1991:62, figures 138 and 139). Recycling points to the resourcefulness of enslaved laborers and perhaps their limited access to certain kinds of materials and tools. People of all walks of life recycled throughout the eighteenth and nineteenth centuries. But refashioning discarded objects to make other objects is frequently observed on the sites of enslaved peoples and other agricultural workers, people with limited financial means, and those confined to prisons, asylums, and other institutions.[1]

Foodways

Food-related artifacts comprise the second-largest category of excavated materials recovered from the slave settlement. These materials include animal bones, fragments of iron kettles and coarse earthenware for cooking, earthenware and stoneware for food storage, and tableware. Excavations within the enclosure yielded only 107 fragments of animal bones—a sample size that zooarchaeologists generally consider too small to offer substantive interpretations of the occupants' food habits (see table 7.1). Yet

Table 7.1. Faunal remains recovered from the Cafetal Biajacas enclosure

Classification	Fragment no.	Minimum no. of individuals
Echinodermata (Marine bottom-dwelling invertebrates, incl. starfish and sea urchins)	1	1
Osteichthyes (Bony fish)	1	1
Selachimorpha (Sharks)	1	1
Aves (Birds)	7	
Gallus gallus (chicken)	5	1
Capromys pilorides (jutía conga)	4	1
Artiodactyla (Even-toed ungulates)	15	2
Capra sp. (goats)	1	1
Sus scrofa (pig)	27	2
Bos taurus (cattle)	22	1
Unidentified bone	23	
Total	**107**	

the small quantity of faunal resources is in keeping with the small quantity of recovered artifacts from the site overall, a finding that supports my argument that the dotación at Cafetal Biajacas possessed or had restricted access to provisions.

Despite the limitations of the faunal data, they do provide some insights into the foods consumed. More than half of the identifiable bones came from cattle, pigs, chickens, and goats—livestock the dotación possibly raised for themselves within the enclosure. The only nondomestic animal identified to species level was a jutía conga (*Capromys pilorides*), the largest endemic mammal of Cuba, which resembles a guinea pig. Past and present-day Cubans have hunted jutía for food.[2] Archaeological investigations of slave runaway sites indicate jutía was an important food resource for runaways in western Cuba living in the rock shelters and overhangs in the general vicinity of Cafetal Biajacas (La Rosa Corzo 2005:177). The jutía individual recovered at Cafetal Biajacas was a juvenile found together with pig and unidentified Artiodactyla [the order of hooved animals having an even number of toes, including pig, cattle, sheep, and goat] bones in one of the few postholes containing cultural materials. These animal remains appear to have been deposited as a onetime, discrete event, possibly the refuse from the preparation or consumption of a specific meal.

The other nondomestic faunal items present interesting curiosities that appear unrelated to food procurement. These include a shark tooth, a fish vertebra, and a pedicellaria, a claw-shaped structure commonly found on Echinoderms (the phylum containing marine bottom-dwelling invertebrates such as starfish and sea urchins). The shark tooth and the fish vertebrae could have been keepsakes possibly used as amulets, although neither item exhibited evidence of modification usually indicative of wearing a charm. In the Spanish world, fish parts were sometimes fashioned into amulets. In her study of Spanish colonial artifacts, archaeologist Kathleen Deagan (2002:92) describes an amulet made from a fossil shark tooth in the collection of Museo del Pueblo Español in Madrid.

The use of fish vertebrae for amulets or adornment is also associated with enslaved Africans in the Caribbean. The most notable example was recovered from a burial of an enslaved male wearing a necklace with fish vertebrae, cowrie shells, animal canines, and glass beads (Handler 1997:114–20). With the recovery of only one fish vertebra at Cafetal Biajacas, however, it is impossible to say how it was used. The pedicellaria, on the other hand, may not be associated with the cafetal. It was found at the deepest level of the excavations, more than 80 cm below ground surface, and may well predate the occupation of the cafetal. Although the small quantity of animal bones is difficult to evaluate with regard to their significance to slave foodways at Cafetal Biajacas, it reinforces the historical evidence that enslaved Cubans ate very little fresh meat. Unfortunately, tasajo and bacalao, the salted meats they did eat, leave few, if any, archaeological traces.

Food was cooked primarily in iron kettles and occasionally in earthenware pots as indicated by a few charred unglazed earthenwares. Other than the iron kettles, all other food preparation and serving vessels consisted of ceramic artifacts (table 7.2). The dotación at Cafetal Biajacas utilized a variety of unmatched ceramic vessels, a finding consistently observed at

Table 7.2 Ceramic artifacts from the Cafetal Biajacas enclosure

Ceramic Type	Form	No. of Fragments	MNV
COARSE EARTHENWARES			
Unglazed		7,261	
No surface treatment	horma de azúcar		
No surface treatment	hollow	119	
No surface treatment	unidentifiable	346	
Burnished	pot	2	
Charred	pot	17	
Painted, red (Mexican)	jar or tinaja	13	1
Glazed			
El Moro-like	hollow	277	
Triana polychrome	chamberpot	29	1
Triana blue-on-white	hollow	5	
Marine ware			
green/white	bowl/chamberpot	6	
blue	lebrillo	1	1
Tin-enamel, green	ointment jar	2	1
Unidentified types			
Interior white glaze	storage jar	33	
Blue/White		3	
Plain White		5	
REFINED EARTHENWARE			
Creamware			
Undecorated	flatware	3	1
Edged wares			
Scalloped rim	plates, platters		
Blue		196	3
Green		6	1
Embossed rim			
Blue-on-white		7	1
Unscalloped rim			
Blue		18	1
Non-impressed			
Blue		5	1
Green		8	1
Factory-made slipwares			
Banded/solid color	hollowware	209	
Cabled	bowl	17	1
Marblized	hollow	8	1
Mocha	hollow	46	2
Hand-painted			
Blue-on-white	hollow, flat	49	2
Polychrome	hollow	159	2

Transfer-print			
Blue-on-white	flat	136	1
Pink on white	hollow	3	1
Black-on-white	flat	3	1
Sponged			
Cut Sponged		2	2
Undecorated, white	flat	437	
	hollow	201	
	unidentifiable	409	
STONEWARE			
Ginger-beer bottle		27	1
Grey/Brown salt-glazed	jug	256	2
Miscellaneous ceramic artifacts			
Pipes, earthenware			
reed-stem	bowl	1 whole	1
	bowl	25	4
	stem	1	1
REFASHIONED REFINED EARTHENWARE	gaming pieces?	11	11

sites of enslaved and other peoples of limited means. Unmatched serving dishes suggest that ceramic pieces were acquired individually through diverse sources, including planter castoffs, other forms of gifting, purchases, exchanges, or pilfering. It may also suggest communal consumption where food is prepared in the kettles of different households but is later brought to another location for several households, with different types of tableware, to eat together. Cultural anthropologist Jack Goody (1982:87) observed communal consumption in this manner among the LoDagaa in northern Ghana, and he inferred that this style of communal consumption was characteristic of many village-organized societies. According to Toye Ekunsanmi (2010:8–10), a student of West African food traditions, sharing food and communal dining are widely practiced in West Africa.

Given the presently known dates of production for ceramic items, only a few eighteenth-century ceramics appear out-of-date for the occupation of the site, including creamware and possibly some Hispanic wares such as Marine ware, Mexican red-painted, and El Morro. Most of the ceramics are contemporaneous with the occupation of Cafetal Biajacas, 1815–46. This is an indication that the enslaved people primarily used ceramics that were in vogue at the time. This finding supports the proposition that the dotación at Cafetal Biajacas acquired these wares through purchase or exchange rather than as castoffs or gifting, which most often consists of out-of-date items as observed at other sites. A few ceramics postdate the cafetal era such as the nonimpressed, edged (1860–90), and cut-sponge (1845–70) wares. These and later materials were presumably deposited at the site after it was no longer a cafetal.

Due to the highly fragmented condition of most of the ceramics, it was often impossible to determine the vessel form or shape and a minimum number of vessels (MNV), an estimate for the amount of whole vessels that these fragments represent. Vessel form and MNV are two standard forms of artifact analysis that require reconstructing the ceramic vessel by piecing together the fragments recovered from excavations. When ceramic sherds were of sufficient size, it was possible to determine if a fragment came from a hollowware vessel (cup, bowl, pot) or flatware (plat, platter, saucer).

In other cases, partial piecing together of some vessels along with careful study of design motifs on decorated ceramics did permit approximations of vessel numbers for some ceramic types. For example, the 49 blue-on-white hand-painted refined earthenware fragments, all with the same design motif, were part of at least two vessels: a small bowl or cup and a saucer. Similarly, most of the blue-on-white transfer print sherds have the same repeating continuous design found on a marly (the flat border area of a plate between the rim and the flat base) of an oval flatware vessel, most likely a platter. This suggests that many of the flatware sherds with the same design were part of the same platter. Estimating the number of undecorated vessels, including the hormas, proved too difficult to offer reliable suggestions, but the fragment counts minimally indicate which undecorated wares were more numerous than others.

All the Hispanic wares, those produced in Spain or Spanish America, were coarse earthenware intended for food preparation and storage, water collection, or in the case of Triana polychrome, personal hygiene. Only a few Hispanic vessels appear to be tableware to serve food, whereas the refined English wares were primarily tableware. The notable presence of English tableware in Cuba is not surprising. Kathleen Deagan (1987:22, 2002:28–29) has shown that occupants of Spanish colonial sites in the circum-Caribbean region preferred English ceramics because they were less expensive and more durable than the Spanish ones. Spanish colonists often obtained the English wares through a lively illicit trade prior to Spain's passage of a free trade act.

In Cuba, Roger Arrazcaeta (1999) traced the growing importation of English ceramics to Cuba using archaeological contexts in Habana vieja [Old Havana] dating to the second half of the eighteenth through the nineteenth centuries. He found that small amounts of English ceramics trickled into Havana after the eleven-month British occupation of Havana during the French and Indian War in 1762. During the American Revolution (1776–83), English ceramics increasingly arrived in Cuba via a contraband trade in which English ceramics were transshipped from all the major North American ports along the Atlantic seaboard. After Spain established free trade in 1818, the Cuban market for the English wares proliferated so that in 1842, William Adams, an English manufacturer of ceramics, began producing transfer-printed wares with landmarks and other themes associated with Havana.

Still, English ceramics did not completely replace Hispanic wares at Cafetal Biajacas or at other nineteenth-century Cuban sites. Lead-glazed earthenware, often glazed only within the interior of the vessel and resembling the type known as El Morro (Deagan 1987:50–51), is the most abundant glazed Hispanic earthenware at Cafetal Biajacas. El Morro, originally assigned production dates of 1550 to 1770, occurs as late as 1820 in Argentina (Schávelzon 1998:98) and even later in Cuba at the sites of cimarrones (La Rosa Corzo and Pérez Padrón 1994:119). J. W. Joseph and Stephan Bryne (1992:53) propose that the El Morro they studied in Puerto Rico was produced locally because its low-fired, rough quality did not warrant shipping and trade. Analytical studies of the ceramics to determine if the El Morro recovered in Cuba was produced there or elsewhere, however, have not been undertaken. Either the dates for El Morro are in need of revision, or this later lead-glazed earthenware is not El Morro. Here it is classified as El Morro–like and fits the generic category of lead-glazed earthenware described in the digital collection of the Florida Museum of Natural History (hereafter FLMNH collection) and produced from 1400 through 1900.[3] When it was possible to identify the vessel forms for this earthenware, most appear to be holloware.

The other Hispanic wares occurred in very small quantities and most

Figure 7.2. Variant of Marine ware with thin blue glaze, possibly a fragment (7.35 cm × 3.75 cm) from a *lebrillo*, recovered from slave enclosure at Cafetal Biajacas. Photograph by Lisette Roura Álvarez.

likely represent only one or two vessels. A *mayólica*—tin-glazed earthenware—with a green-on-white glaze over an orange-colored paste resembles a variant of Marine ware, an earthenware of questionable date and place of manufacture in the FLMNH collection.[4] In the examples identified at Cafetal Biajacas, the glaze is severely deteriorated on all the fragments that appear to be from the same hollowware vessel. Another variant of Marine ware is represented by a single sherd of a cream-colored body covered with a thin blue glaze (figure 7.2). The sherd was possibly part of a *lebrillo* [pan or tub] or similar form. Triana polychrome, known as blue-green-basin in other Spanish American settings (Deagan 1987:93–94; Schávelzon 1998:67), is the only other mayólica identified from the artifact assemblage. In addition to the blue-green decoration outlined in black, it has touches of yellow paint. The recovered rim and body sherds suggest the vessel was a chamber pot.

Thirteen fragments of a thick-walled, coarse earthenware with a red surface resemble a type known as Mexican red-painted (FLMNH digital collection). Together the fragments appear to have belonged to a jug like a *cántaro* or a *tinaja*, a Cuban water-collection vessel. This ware was particularly popular in Havana from the 1650s to the 1770s, after which time it was supplanted by English, Dutch, and French ceramics that arrived in Havana via the contraband trade. Archaeologists and members of the

Figure 7.3. Red-painted earthenware fragments either imported from the Yucatán or made by Yucatecos in Cuba, recovered from slave enclosure at Cafetal Biajacas. Photograph by Lisette Roura Álvarez.

Cafetal Biajacas project team Mahé Lugo Romera and Sonia Menéndez Castro (2003:20–46) suggest that some of these red-painted wares (figure 7.3) were made in Cuba by indigenous people from the Yucatán in Mexico. Known in Cuba as Yucatecos, they lived in the Barrio de Campeche in Havana and arrived in Cuba in several waves from the late sixteenth through the late eighteenth centuries.

Analytical sourcing studies directed toward determining whether the red-painted pottery recovered from barrio Compeche was made in Cuba or the Yucatán proved inconclusive. Despite this drawback, Lugo Romera and Menéndez Castro (2003:42, fn2) posit that Yucatecos were responsible for introducing not only pottery but other Meso-American cultural characteristics to Cuba, such as use of the *mano* and *metate* [polished-stone mortar and pestle] for grinding corn and other foods, which are found in the excavations of colonial-period houses in Habana vieja.

Among the English ceramics recovered, edged wares and the machine-made slip or dipped wares predominate. Edged wares are primarily cream to white-bodied flat vessels with scalloped, impressed, embossed, or plain rims most often painted blue or green. They were the least expensive ceramics with color decoration from 1780 to 1860 (Miller 1994:443). Factory-made slipwares, on the other hand, are almost always hollowwares with a wide range of colorful decorative designs, including color bands, marbleized, Mocha (a treelike pattern), cables resembling a worm, and cat-eyes. These slipwares were the cheapest available hollowwares with color decoration from the late eighteenth through the nineteenth centuries (Miller 1991:6).

The low cost of these ceramics may partially account for their presence at Cafetal Biajacas and other slave sites, but some archaeologists believe the decorations like those found on the factory-made slipwares aesthetically appealed to enslaved peoples and therefore may explain why these specific types were acquired. Laurie Wilkie and Paul Farnsworth (2005:274–75) compare the bands of color and designs on the slipware vessels with the stripping of colors and patterns found in an African textile, an African American quilt, and a garment of a Saramaka maroon in Suriname to suggest enslaved Bahamians purposefully selected these ceramics for their aesthetic value. Such visual analogies are always evocative, but they undermine the specific historical circumstances that might account for these similarities. In any event, this interpretation does not account for the large amount of undecorated white or minimally decorated tableware with blue edging that comprises more than half of the tableware found in the enclosure. Given the diverse cultural origins of the dotación at Cafetal Biajacas, a variety of aesthetic practices no doubt influenced the colors or designs that enslaved people selected for household and personal items.

To gain insights into how food was served and eaten, archaeologists customarily examine the vessel forms of tableware. At Cafetal Biajacas, both flatware and hollowware are more or less equally present in the total artifact collection recovered from the enclosure, a finding that differs from most discussions of slave foodways that emphasize the use of hollowware in the consumption of soups, stews, and pottages. Without a doubt, bowls were important in slave foodways and were the predominant vessel forms of slave-made pottery found in the southern United States and Caribbean. And, indeed, soupy, one-pot meals form a major component of traditional Cuban cuisine. The famed *ajiaco*, a meat and vegetable soup containing several *viandas*, is most certainly a creole dish. Ajiaco, with a name presumably derived from the Arawakan language (Villapol 1997:25), was analogous to Spanish stews, but with African, Asian, and French elements. The convergence of these varied cuisines and the peoples from whom they originated prompted Fernando Ortiz to refer to Cuba as an ajiaco (Sarmiento Ramírez 2009:147).

Other dishes consumed, however, were undeniably of African origins, and some of them possibly were served on flatware. Paramount among them was the dish *fufú*, referenced in several nineteenth-century Cuban sources, made by boiling starchy vegetables such as yams, cassava, or plantain and then pounding them into a doughlike mixture. It is popular throughout western and central Africa, where it is typically eaten with a soup or stew. In the Spanish Antilles, however, plantain became the favored vegetable for making it, where it is known today as *mangú* in the Dominican Republic and *mofungo* in Puerto Rico. In Cuba, it retained the name fufú, and a nineteenth-century cookbook (Langarika [1862] 1996:88–89) indicates it was prepared in the African style, pounded with a wooden mortar and pestle and not simply mashed as it is often prepared in the Caribbean today. White Cubans appropriated fufú, adding their own twists such as *chicharrones* [pork skins, usually fried] (Gil Recio and Cardenas Alpízar 1993:111), creating a dish comparable to mofungo (Cabanillas and Ginorio [1956] 2002:62). Fredrika Bremer (1853:409–10) referred to fufú as "the favorite dish of negro slaves," which she found "remarkably good and wholesome" and ate many times for her own breakfast.

Funche, made from dried ground corn, water, salt, and animal fat (Pichardo 1953:311), was a standard dish prepared, usually as a porridge, in plantation central kitchens. Enslaved Cubans possibly modified the basic recipe for it by adding other ingredients or by frying or baking it when they prepared it for themselves. While the word *funche* originated in central Africa (Sarmiento Ramírez 2009:144), the dish itself is found in numerous cuisines worldwide from the boiled corn mushes of indigenous Americans to Italian polenta. Planters fed ground corn to enslaved Africans throughout the Americas, and funche, also known as fungi, funchi, and funjie, is still widely consumed in the Caribbean.

In Cuba, funche, also known as *serensé*, was not necessarily made from cornmeal. According to food historian Nitza Villapol (1997:36), it was also made from coarsely ground or grated *maíz tierno* [tender kernel maize], which has a pasty consistency. Bremer (1853:2:333) described a dish served for breakfast to laborers on a sugar plantation "made of boiled maize, which they bruise and mix with wild tomatoes, the fruit of plantain, or vegetables." Unlike fufú, which many free Cubans consumed, funche became known as "slave food" and was denigrated as "bad food" (Sarmiento Ramírez 2009:144n8). This may possibly account for the curious absence of recipes for funche among traditional Cuban recipes even though dishes similar to it are found in these sources and are still consumed today.[5]

Rice was a major staple of enslaved Africans, particularly for those originating from Senegal, Gambia, Sierra Leone, and Liberia. Rice dishes also arrived in Cuba via planters and their slave laborers from Saint-Domingue at the end of the eighteenth century, such as *congri*, a bean and rice pilaf (Sarmiento Ramírez 2009:144). The name congri derives from the words *Congo* and *riz* [French for rice] (Villapol 1997:52), and it remains a popular dish among Cubans today. Other rice pilafs using okra, tomatoes, or salted codfish possibly originated during slavery. In West Africa, rice is boiled, fried, or ground into porridge. Among some West African groups, rice was of ceremonial significance and cooked primarily on holidays, special occasions, and for communal feasting (Ekunsanmi 2010:35). Some Cuban planters provisioned laborers with rice, but enslaved Cubans also produced rice on their own.

Fufú, funche, or rice dishes were the mainstay of the Cuban slave diet. These foods could have been served on flatware or hollowware depending on the other foods that accompanied them. For example, if they were served with a soup or stew, hollowware would be necessary for eating them. But if they were eaten plain or with a little sauce and other vegetables, flatware could have been used. In the tableware assemblage recovered from the enclosure, most hollowware vessels appear to be small bowls and most of the flatware are plates and platters. Archaeologist Leland Ferguson (1992:106) suggested enslaved people on South Carolina plantations used small earthenware bowls as containers for serving sauces as well as for eating and drinking.

Enslaved Cubans possibly used small bowls in similar fashion, although calabashes, as several traveler accounts suggest, were used primarily for eating and drinking (Abbot 1829:41; Bremer 1853:2:277, 282; Lowell 2003:85). Assuming food was eaten from calabashes, all the tableware was possibly used only for serving foods—plates and platters for solid items like fufú or rice, large bowls for porridges, soups, and stews, and small bowls for sauces. These vessels were possibly laid out on a table or on the ground and passed around a group eating communally. Although few in number, references suggest that when enslaved Cubans prepared food for themselves, it was prepared and eaten communally, particularly on Saturday evenings or Sundays when they entertained. According to Gloria García (2003b:39), enslaved Cubans used the money they earned from the sale of pigs to buy necessities and food for "las diversiones y los convites frecuentes" [frequent entertaining and get-togethers]. Abbot's description of slave meals quoted previously suggests slave laborers shared the food they prepared with invited guests. Cooking food in excess of one's household needs in order to share with neighbors or friends is a traditional practice found among many groups in West Africa (Ekunsanmi 2010:8–10).

They also prepared and drank a variety of fermented beverages. They tapped the sap of the Guinea palm (*Elaeis guineensis*) to make palm wine, a practice that has a long tradition in Africa. Abiel Abbot (1829:44–45) visited a plantation in Camarioca where Guinea palms were planted for the purpose of extracting palm oil for cooking and palm wine for drinking. Other beverages slave laborers made were similar to the grain- and fruit-based drinks of West Africa (Ekunsanmi 2010:116–18), but the herbs, spices, and grains used in Cuba differed from those used in Africa. One such drink was *agualoja* made of water, honey or sugar, vanilla, mint, pepper, and other ingredients. In another drink, *sambumbia*, a mixture of water, molasses, and pepper, was combined with charred corn cobs for several days, after which time it was ready for drinking. A third frothy drink known as *pru* combined various roots, barley, sassafras, black pepper, anise, vanilla, sugar, and pineapple peel. This drink was made and consumed primarily in eastern Cuba (Sarmiento Ramírez 2009:145).

A total of 869 fragments of dark-green bottle glass were recovered from the enclosure. These bottles were most likely recycled to hold beverages or other liquids enslaved Cubans made for their own consumption. In addition to glass bottles, recovered fragments for at least two stoneware jugs and at least one ginger-beer bottle indicate these ceramic containers could also have been reused.

The assemblage of food remains, food preparation, serving, and storage equipment from the enclosure provides insights into the kinds of foods and the manner in which the enslaved people at Cafetal Biajacas consumed them. Documentary sources indicate that many of these foods and beverages were similar to those consumed in Africa, while others derived from combining different culinary traditions. Many of these creole dishes are now items considered traditional Cuban cuisine.

Adorning the Body and Home: Personal Objects

Only a few objects associated with clothing, adornment, and furnishings were recovered from the enclosure that date to the period of the cafetal. They include three glass beads, a white metal button, a gold, stamped-decorated fragment possibly part of a decorative trim from an unknown object, and a Chippendale-style drawer pull made of a copper alloy. A blue glass bead, identical to the one found in the enclosure, and a mass-produced, five-hole bone button were recovered from the small room of locus C (the infirmary warehouse). The context of these two artifacts strongly suggests that they were associated with enslaved occupants at the cafetal.

The small number of these objects could easily be dismissed as insignificant, and formerly archaeologists only reported on the physical or functional attributes of such finds. Small finds, however, are receiving increased attention, because such personal objects are among the best sources of material culture for investigating agency, identity, ideology, and economic and social status (Deagan 2002:5; Loren 2010:9).

Artifacts of adornment and clothing are particularly important in understanding the embodiment of self and identity. Many archaeologists following the ideas of third-wave feminist Judith Butler (1990) view the body as the site for analysis of how people experience the world, establish self and identity, engage in social exchanges, and negotiate social constructions of race, gender, power, and age. Archaeologist Diana Loren (2010:9) has shown how this theoretical perspective to the study of clothing and adornment is particularly insightful in investigating the ways colonizers attempted to control the bodies of colonized peoples through the imposition of restrictive sumptuary laws as well as how the colonized chose "to express their bodies and identities." In a similar vein, studies of slave clothing and adornment artifacts provide information on the clothing slaveholders imposed upon enslaved peoples as well as how enslaved peoples embellished plantation-issued clothing and created their own attire.

Most descriptions of Cuban slave clothing refer only to the mass-produced work clothes, known as *esquifación*, sewn in local mills or imported from factories abroad (Moreno Fraginals 1978:2:63, 66). Twice yearly Cuban law required that each man receive pants, a shirt, a felt jacket, and a blanket and that each woman receive a dress, kerchief, hat, jacket, and blanket (2:63). Wearing the same clothes daily and the failure of some planters to supply their dotaciones with the required two sets of clothing frequently resulted in enslaved Cubans wearing rags or going around nearly nude.

The singular focus on the clothing provided to enslaved laborers, however, neglects the important role of garments and bodily adornments they chose to wear. Studies of slave clothing in the southern United States indicate enslaved peoples took pride in purchasing garments in stores (Foster 1997). Entries in store ledgers further confirm that they frequently purchased fabrics, sewing notions, and ready-made garments (Heath 2004:29–30; Martin 2008:184). Although no artifacts associated with sewing were recovered from Cafetal Biajacas, enslaved Cubans apparently purchased fabrics and garments from peddlers (Howe [1860] 1969:76) and stores (Abbot 1829:141), thus creating their own fashion sense. Unfortunately, scant description exists for the attire they fashioned for themselves on Cuban plantations. Nineteenth-century artists such as Victor Patricio Landaluze depicted the attire of Afro-Cubans in many of his paintings, but most of these images document the clothing worn in urban areas, not in the countryside.

The two buttons recovered associated with enslaved occupants at Cafetal Biajacas are both typically found on nineteenth-century slave clothing in the Americas and do not necessarily provide insights into embellishments to slave clothing. The recovered buttons were possibly affixed to plantation-issued garments. Both buttons, like most of the recovered ceramics from Cafetal Biajacas, were in vogue when the cafetal was operating. The white metal button stamped "treble Gilt Standard" is identical to a metal button recovered from a slave quarter at Rayfield Plantation on Cumberland Island, Georgia. Buttons such as these were becoming fashionable for men's wear in England starting around 1830 (Ascher and Fairbanks 1971:13). The five-hole bone button, also mass-produced during the first half of the nineteenth century, is similar to others recovered from slave sites. Both buttons were primarily utilitarian—to fasten clothing—rather than for a strictly ornamental purpose.

The small quantity of buttons recovered from Cafetal Biajacas stands in stark contrast to several slave sites in the United States that yielded sizable quantities of buttons. For example, at Thomas Jefferson's plantation Poplar Forest, 122 buttons were recovered from three slave houses and their adjoining yards (Heath 1999:53), an area comparable to the excavated portion of the slave dwellings within the enclosure. Because so few buttons were found at Cafetal Biajacas, it may indicate the enslaved people wore clothing with fasteners other than buttons or that buttons were made from perishable materials. Descendants of enslaved communities in Dutch Antilles told archaeologist Jay Haviser that they used rounded ceramic pieces, like those in figure 6.2, which most archaeologists interpret as gaming pieces, as forms for making homemade buttons. Cloth was wrapped around a rounded disc and then sewn onto the garment (Haviser 2013, pers. comm.). Using rounded ceramic pieces as forms for making buttons was a possibility, but interviews with other Afro-Caribbean communities (Pulsipher and Goodwin 1999:30fn57), plus the recovery of these artifacts at numerous sites among diverse peoples and time periods found worldwide, strongly support their use as gaming pieces.

The recovered beads, unlike the buttons, provide insights as to how the slave community at Cafetal Biajacas chose to adorn their bodies. Anselmo Suárez y Romero (1859:207) noted that women dressed up their plantation-issued tunics and kerchiefs by wearing necklaces of brightly colored glass beads, particularly on Sundays when they sang and danced.

Fredrika Bremer observed men and women of all ages wearing beads. She described observing on the plantations she visited several incidences of enslaved Cubans adorning their bodies with beads and head wraps as well as with "tattoos" (scarification): "All the negroes here are tattooed in the face; some around the eyes, others around the cheekbones, and so on according to the custom of their nation to which they belong. The greater number—even of the men wear necklaces of red or blue beads—the red, the coral-like seed of a kind of tree on the island; and the greater number, men as well as women wear striped cotton handkerchiefs around their head" (1853:2:314). On another occasion, she remarked, "I have seen a couple of young women at work here who are really splendidly beautiful, with their dark glancing eyes, white teeth, and their coral necklaces round their throats, and pink handkerchiefs bound round their heads" (1853:2:324). In a third reference to beads, Bremer observed children wearing beads, "the very little Bambinos . . . dance upon their mother's knees, generally with a blue or red string of beads around the loins, and another round the neck; they are the very prettiest little things one ever saw; and their mothers, with their strings of beads around their necks, their showy kerchiefs fastened, turban-wise, around the head, look very well too" (1853:2:335). Bremer's observations indicate the wearing of beads was ubiquitous among enslaved Cubans, and the primary colors of the beads were blue and red.

Of the four beads recovered from Cafetal Biajacas, coincidently, two are blue and two are red. All are glass. Of the three faceted beads, two are similar to the blue faceted beads frequently found on other slave sites. The recovery of blue beads has generated considerable discussion among archaeologists. Some have suggested the color blue was of spiritual or other symbolic significance (Stine, Cabak, and Groover 1996:63–64), and at least one documentary source suggests blue beads held a special meaning for some enslaved persons in the southern United States (Singleton 2010:177).

The fourth bead resembles and partially corresponds to the formal description of a short tubular bead of Venetian origin produced from the seventeenth to the early nineteenth centuries sometimes referred to as *galet rouge*. The color of this bead type is described as a dull opaque brick red over a transparent green illustrated in type 76 (DeCorse, Richard, and Thiaw 2003:97). The example from Cafetal Biajacas measures 4.2 mm × 3.8 mm, and the red color matches that of type 76, but it is over an opaque white with brown pigment on the surface of the white. The beads DeCorse and his coauthors analyzed were found in Senegal and used in the European trade with Africans; therefore, the bead from Cafetal Biajacas was possibly an item an African person was wearing when he or she became a victim of the slave trade.

Another possibility is that enslaved Africans acquired the beads from their captors. From his study of the British slave trade, anthropologist Jerome Handler (2009:6) notes that beads were sometimes distributed to enslaved Africans, particularly women, during the Middle Passage as a

Figure 7.4. Strings of seeds for sale in a Cuban market, Old Havana, 2013. *Left*, black seeds from the *jaboncillo* [soapberry tree, *Sapindus saponaria*]; *right*, red seeds from the *coralina* [coral acacia tree, *Adenanthera pavonina*]. Photograph by author.

diversion for them to make ornaments. Whether enslaved Africans were wearing beads at the time of capture or were given beads on slave ships, it is possible that Africans arrived in Cuba wearing some beads and acquired others after they resettled on plantations through purchases and other exchanges.

The red-beaded necklaces Bremer (1853:2:353) described, however, were made from red seeds, not glass, from a tree she identified as an acacia. She was most likely describing the coral acacia or coralina (*Adenanthera pavonina*). Native to India and southeast China, the tree was introduced to the Caribbean and other humid tropical areas. It produces pods containing red seeds about 7.5–9 mm in size that are still widely used to make jewelry today (figure 7.4, right), not only in Cuba but worldwide.[6] Peter Townsend observed a slave woman whose upper body was ornamented with seeds he identified as acacia while she was performing a dance (Townsend Diary, 127). Enslaved Cubans utilized acacia and other seeds, like those from the jaboncillo [soapberry or chinaberry] tree (*Sapindus saponaria*) (figure 7.4., left), not only for adorning their bodies but also for making percussion instruments such as the *chekeré*—a dried gourd wrapped with a mesh of beads or shells (figure 7.5). Maracas, another musical instrument, made from hollowed-out gourds, were filled with dried seeds or beans. Seeds were obviously very important in the craft items that enslaved Cubans made. In exuberant displays of beads, seeds possibly substituted for glass beads or were used along with them as well as beads made from other kinds of materials.

The small number of beads from Cafetal Biajacas is not necessarily unusual when compared with many other slave quarter sites in the Americas. But compared with other Afro-Cuban sites, the number is quite small. Lourdes Domínguez (1998, pers. comm.) recovered 15 beads from one slave burial and 23 from another from excavations of a slave cemetery at Taoro plantation. In addition to the glass beads, she found a pierced coin, animal canines with drilled holes, and a large bone bead associated with one of the burials (1999:17, 33). Similarly, at the slave runaway site known as el Grillete—a cave in Matanzas where a slave shackle [*grillete*] was found—42 glass beads of several colors and shapes were recovered (Hernández de Lara, Rodríguez Tápanes, Arredondo Antúnez 2012:102–5). Both Domínguez (1999:17) and Hernández de Lara and his colleagues (2012:105) interpreted the beads as having had a religious association, perhaps as precursors to the beaded *collares* [necklaces] that modern-day adherents of Santería wear to be protected by a particular *orisha*, one of several saints or deities of the Cuban-Lucumí religion. The small number of beads at Cafetal Biajacas may be another example of the enslaved

Figure 7.5. Cuban *chekeré,* percussion instruments made from dried gourds with a mesh of seeds and beads. Exhibit display at the Museum of Guanabacoa, Havana. Photograph by author.

workers' limited access to trade due to the constraints of living within the enclosure.

Wearing head wraps and other headgear was another way of adorning bodies. In Africa, everyday head coverings combined the practical need of protecting the wearer from the elements, meeting African notions of proper decorum, and displaying aesthetic preferences. Christine Kreamer (1995:83) explains that covering one's head among many African groups is considered socially appropriate when outside the home. Mary Jo Arnoldi (1995:11) adds that in many African and African diaspora societies, "the head, itself, is a potent image that plays a central role in how the person is conceptualized." Thus headgear often expresses shared cultural beliefs and values toward ethnicity, gender, life stages, status, authority, occupation, and social decorum (Arnoldi 1995:13–14).

Although enslaved peoples were denied the opportunity to decorate their heads in the ways of their native cultures, the widespread African practice of wrapping the head with cloth persisted in many slave communities. Slaveholders, however, in Spanish Louisiana and in the southern United States redefined the African hair wrap as a "badge of servitude" by requiring women to bind their hair in kerchiefs (Foster 1997:273). This may explain why Cuban slave codes mandated a *pañuelo* [handkerchief or kerchief] among the few clothing items issued to enslaved workers (García 2003b:86). Yet Bremer's glowing description of slave head wraps conveys that women styled them eloquently from colorful fabrics comparable to the elaborate head ties women wear in many African societies. By wearing head wraps in the manner they chose, Cuban slave women reappropriated the meaning and aesthetic value of an African cultural practice.

Bremer (1853:2:335) also observed a slave laborer "constructing a fine head-dress of showy patches and cock's feathers," which further suggests ways enslaved men and women in Cuba displayed their creativity in personal adornment, specifically in headgear. Dancers in carnival processions held on saint feast days and holy days often donned feathered headdresses (Brown 2003:35, fig. 1.7). Fernando Ortiz ([1906] 1995b:87, figures 26 and 27) described and illustrated two feathered headdresses that Afro-Cuban religious specialists wore for special rituals.

Another artifact that may be related to adornment is a stamped-decorated fragment made of gold (figure 7.6). It was possibly affixed to a mirror,

Figure 7.6. Gold-filled or -plated, stamped-decorated fragment (1.6cm × 0.9cm) possibly used as trim on or to frame an object, recovered from slave enclosure at Cafetal Biajacas. Photograph by Lisette Roura Álvarez.

a decorative comb, hairbrush, or other small object. Given the paucity of recovered objects and the fact that all the other artifacts are clearly mundane objects, this piece stands out as a prestige or high-status object. At the same time, it was not unusual for enslaved Cubans to own gold or silver objects. Juan Manzano ([1840] 1996:117) wrote in his autobiography that after the death of his enslaved mother, he found within an old box in her house "some fine gold jewelry in the hollow. Among them, the most valuable ones were three old bracelets, each nearly three fingers wide and very thick, and two rosaries, one made of solid gold and the other gold and coral, although broken and very dirty." He later described a reliquary that also belonged to his mother: "It was large, trimmed with gold-braid engravings of the same metal, and had the divine face of Jesus in the middle" ([1840] 1996:119). The description of the gold trim around the picture offers an example of how the recovered golden fragment may have once framed an object or picture in a similar manner.

According to the inventories, Padre Ignacio O'Farrill, the owner of Cafetal Biajacas, possessed gold-trimmed religious and secular objects. He possibly gave enslaved people reliquary and medals, or the dotación acquired such items for themselves. It is also possible that after O'Farrill's death, some of the objects in the great house were given to occupants of the slave settlement.

The drawer pull was the only artifact recovered that definitely was associated with furniture, most likely with some type of chest or a trunk with drawers. Like the gold-trimmed object, the drawer pull may have been on a piece of furniture that was recycled from the great house or manager's house.

Diversions: Drinking, Smoking, Gaming, Music, and Dance

Enslaved laborers in Cuba had little time for diversions. They worked very long days, and during harvests they often worked every day including Sundays and holidays. While Sundays were usually reserved for their own affairs, a considerable amount of that time was spent preparing food, mending and washing clothes, building and maintaining their houses, tending to their own gardens and livestock, and gathering a variety of plant resources (seeds, gourds, palm leaves, wood) to use to make items for their own use and perhaps for sale. But they also found time to entertain guests, and they organized social activities where they played musical instruments, invented games, and danced. Recovered artifacts suggestive of these social or recreational activities include several previously mentioned artifacts—glass bottles, ceramic jugs, gaming pieces, and tobacco pipes. These artifacts are briefly reexamined here to discuss their usage as diversions.

Alcohol consumption among enslaved peoples was widespread throughout the Caribbean, and most slave-occupied sites have yielded evidence of alcoholic beverages (F. Smith 2008:118–24). Enslaved Cubans drank a variety of homemade and store-bought alcoholic beverages. Cuban slaveholders frequently complained to colonial authorities about slaves' abuse of alcohol both on and off the plantation, but they unknowingly contributed to the problem by dispensing the highly potent aguardiente as an elixir to energize, medicate, or reward slave laborers. Ismael Sarmiento Ramírez (2009:133, 135) provides examples of slave traders and Cuban planters giving aguardiente to enslaved people to revive, stimulate, and prepare them for their daily activities. They considered this alcoholic beverage a part of the *alimentos*, foods provisioned to the enslaved. Jacito González Larrinaga, for example, wrote to Gerónimo Valdés that he provided his dotación with *guarapo*—a fermented sugarcane beverage—during the sugar-processing season and a little aguardiente mixed with lemon extract and brown sugar in the morning before work and when field laborers became wet from rain (García 2003b:82).

Similar practices were adopted on coffee plantations. Joseph Goodwin wrote in his daybook on June 19, 1821, that slave laborers were served aguardiente when they worked in the rain. On the other hand, Eulalia Keating noted in her travel diary on February 17, 1839, that aguardiente was distributed to enslaved dancers before performing a dance in honor of her recently born granddaughter on the coffee plantation of her son-in-law's family, the Bauduys. Unlike the previous examples, Keating's example appears as an inducement to get the dancers in the mood, possibly to assist in making the dancers more animated for the amusement of a white audience. While this interpretation is perhaps stretching the available information, this was at a time when whites poked fun at black cultural production in parodies prevalent in Cuban popular culture (Moore 1997:20–21).

The remains of presumed alcohol consumption recovered from the enclosure were most likely beverages that enslaved people acquired on their own. Plantation managers and overseers usually kept the plantation-issued aguardiente under their care. Enslaved Cubans obtained alcoholic beverages from various sources, and they also prepared them. In addition to the archaeological remains suggestive of alcohol consumption, perishable materials such as gourds or coconut shells sometimes replaced bottles for holding alcohol (F. Smith 2008:119).

Like alcohol, tobacco usage was common, and pipes are almost always recovered from slave quarters. The pipe fragments recovered from the enclosure are like those found at excavated sites of cimarrones near San José de las Lajas in Mayabeque (La Rosa Corzo 2002) and at the cave El Grillete in Matanzas (Hernández de Lara, Rodríguez Tápanes, Arredondo Antúnez 2012:106–7). The pipes consist of molded, reed-stemmed pipe bowls with floral and other ornamental relief designs (figure 7.7). This style of pipe developed in France at the end of the eighteenth century and was later manufactured in Cataluña, Spain, and elsewhere during the nineteenth century. These pipes are found throughout Cuba on various kinds of sites, and one recovered in Old Havana was stamped with the name and place of manufacture, "Palamos en Cataluña FCA. De Estevan Gorcoll" (Prado Flores, Rossi Álvarez, and Arrazcaeta Delgado 2004:37).

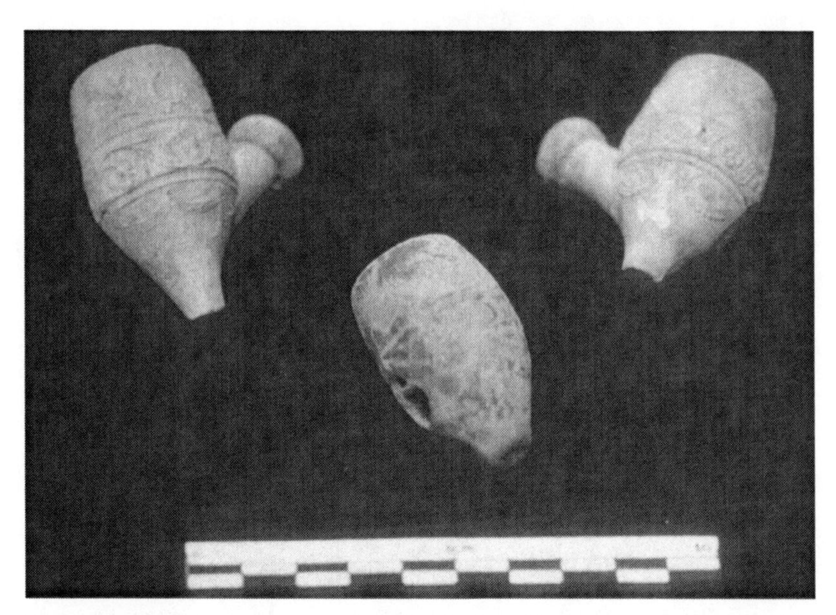

Figure 7.7. Reed-stemmed pipes with relief designs. *Upper row*, two complete pipes recovered from excavations in Old Havana; *lower row*, partial pipe recovered from slave enclosure at Cafetal Biajacas. Photograph by author.

The pipe fragments from the enclosure represent four or five pipes. But, unlike those reported from the sites of cimarrones, most of these pipe fragments were reused for polishing or buffing, indicating that the pipes may have belonged to other plantation residents, discarded elsewhere on the plantation, and later scavenged for reuse. Such pipes, however, were inexpensive, and enslaved Cubans could easily have purchased them from country stores (La Rosa Corzo and Pérez Padrón 1994:128). Excavations within the enclosure did not yield handmade earthenware pipes like those recovered from some slave runaway sites (La Rosa Corzo 1991a:72–73; 2010:19), which provides additional support that the dotación at Cafetal Biajacas did not produce pottery of any kind. The enslaved workers at Cafetal Biajacas may have also smoked cigars and cigarettes, both of which leave few archaeological traces.

Playing board games and other games offered another diversion. Games of chance were popular both in Spain and in Spanish colonies (Deagan 2002:291). Laborers on Cuban plantations gambled, and perhaps white overseers occasionally joined them, as Joseph Goodwin suggested in his diary on March 23, 1822: "Gambling at night by the hands very late adjourned until next morning." The Spanish passion for playing games and gambling may explain the occurrence of gaming pieces made from broken pottery found at various Spanish colonial sites, including Cafetal Biajacas.

The games played that utilized the recovered gaming pieces could include backgammon and checkers. A description of a game that specifically used pieces made from broken ceramics comes from the Caribbean island of Montserrat where descendants of the enslaved population played a gambling game known as "Chiney money." The name refers to the blue Chinese-inspired decoration often found on one side of a disk (Pulsipher and Goodwin 1991:30fn57). A game called *chinata* was played in Cuba, but its name was derived from small smooth stones known as *china pelonas* originally used as playing pieces. Eventually, however, gaming pieces made from various kinds of materials substituted for the smooth stones. Pichardo (1953:248) defined chinata as a game children played with many variations that utilized rounded gaming pieces. It is unknown how the ceramic gaming pieces were used in Cuba, but they have been recovered at other Cuban sites. Excavations at the Castillo San Severino in the city of Matanzas unearthed approximately 50 of the reworked ceramic gaming pieces from the areas where soldiers and prisoners resided (Hernandez de Lara 2006, pers. comm.). In Cuba, diverse groups of people made and used these gaming pieces.

Enslaved Cubans drank alcoholic beverages, smoked, or played games in the evenings after long hours of plantation labor, but major social gatherings took place on Sundays and feast days. These events usually consisted of drum playing, singing, and dancing that sometimes involved religious rituals. Drum beatings known as *toques de tambores* occurred throughout Cuba and often attracted large numbers of both enslaved and free blacks. When local authorities complained about the disorderly behavior that transpired at some dances, Captain-General Joaquín de Ezpeleta issued a proclamation in 1839 requiring white supervision of these events (ANC GSC, leg. 938, no. 33102).

The plantation dances that Bremer and Suárez y Romero described, however, seem quite tame, and both observers regarded them highly. Bremer (1853:2:328) liked that "everyone in company may take part in it,

Figure 7.8. "Negro Dance on a Cuban Plantation," *Harper's Weekly*, January 29, 1859, vol. 3, p. 73. Image HW0006 as shown on http://www.slaveryimages.org, compiled by Jerome Handler and Michael Tuite and sponsored by the Virginia Foundation of the Humanities and the University of Virginia Library.

either in the singing, dancing, or applauding." Suárez y Romero (1859:200) referred to the dances as "la inocente diversion de la negrada" [innocent fun of the blacks], and he particularly liked the songs (figure 7.8). He noted that each sugar plantation and coffee plantation had its particular songs that were sung not only at feast days but at baptisms, weddings, during coffee harvests, the sugar-milling season, and even for the distribution of work clothing.

African music and dance on Cuban plantations were not simply diversions but formed integral aspects of the expressive culture of enslaved Cubans. Unfortunately, such cultural production rarely leaves archaeological traces, and only one artifact related to making music—a mouth harp—was recovered at Cafetal Biajacas. A mouth harp is a musical instrument of great antiquity and found on many archaeological sites (Deagan 2002:302–3). Slave sites in the United States like Andrew Jackson's plantation home, the Hermitage (Battle-Baptiste 2007:242), and others have yielded these artifacts.[7] At Cafetal Biajacas, it was possibly used with instruments of African origins to make music. Like other enslaved Cubans, the dotación at Biajacas expressed themselves in music and dance.

Identity, Artifact Paucity, and Religiosity

Without a doubt, enslaved Cubans drew upon their African heritage to create new ways of life and to shape their Afro-Cuban identities. Previous discussion considered how African customs influenced slave consumption habits, particularly in the areas of adornment, headgear, domestic architecture, foodways, music, and dance. Two other issues, mentioned but not fully explored earlier, shape the conclusion of this chapter: first, the small number of artifacts recovered from the enclosure and, second, the absence of material expressions of African-inspired religiosity. Although these are completely different issues, they are discussed together here because similar factors may have played a role in producing them.

Interpreting Artifact Paucity

The paucity of artifacts at any archaeological site is always difficult to evaluate, because the small number could be the result of unknown factors such as unidentified trash disposal practices or an undetected disturbance to the site after the occupants abandoned it. The archaeological premise for the interpretation that the slave laborers at Cafetal Biajacas possessed few objects is based upon the low density of artifacts recovered from within the enclosure—an average of only 39 artifacts from each of 303 excavated 1 m × 1 m units within the enclosure, the large amount of recycled materials within the artifact assemblage, recovery of relatively few ceramic vessels, and a negligible number of personal artifacts. These findings could be explained as peculiar to the archaeological deposits at Cafetal Biajacas. If this is the case, any archaeological interpretation regarding the quantity of household and personal possessions among enslaved Cubans must await future investigations of slave quarters at other Cuban plantations.

Documentary evidence, however, supports the interpretation that enslaved Cubans owned fewer things than many other enslaved peoples in the Americas. The discussion presented thus far has emphasized the restricted opportunities that they had to trade and to acquire goods, which some Cuban slaveholders further exacerbated by quartering slaves in housing that they locked at night to stop anyone from leaving plantations to participate in the exchange of goods; preventing itinerant merchants from trading on their plantations; and claiming a sizable share of the profits that enslaved

Figure 7.9. Calabash tree (*Crecentia cujete*) in Rafael María Moscosco National Botanical Garden, Santo Domingo, Dominican Republic. Photograph by Victor Manuel Camilo Bencosme.

people obtained from their independent production. These obstructive slaveholder practices reduced the possibilities for laborers to engage in trade.

Along with limited opportunities for trade, the small quantity of recovered household and personal objects may be related to the greater use of, and perhaps even a preference for, perishable materials for household items. Again, written sources describe enslaved people in Cuba eating from cups, bowls, and ladles made of gourds harvested from the calabash tree (*Crecentia cujete*), a tropical tree native to the Americas (figure 7.9). Pierre Laborie's (1798:26) widely distributed treatise on coffee production strongly advised coffee planters to plant calabash trees to supply slave workers with material for making eating vessels.

In addition to household utensils, enslaved people in Cuba made musical instruments from gourds, including chekeré, *güiro*, and maracas. They also strung seeds together like beads to adorn their bodies. Archaeologists working in the tropics often acknowledge the importance of gourds and other perishable materials used to make artifacts, but they rarely consider the relationship between objects made of perishable materials and those made of more durable materials, like ceramic and glass recovered through archaeological investigations. These perishable items were often more readily available than mass-produced items, and some Africans would have been familiar with crafting items from gourds prior to their arrival in Cuba. And some Africans possibly preferred gourds for some household items. Assuming perishable housewares were more commonly used than the artifacts made of ceramic and glass, the small quantity of ceramic tableware may be an indicator that these artifacts merely supplemented gourds and were not used on a regular basis or were special-use items for serving meals prepared at weekend gatherings.

The slave community at Cafetal Biajacas was predominantly male, and some lived as single adults. Archaeologists are just beginning to consider slave household composition in their interpretation of the archaeological record. Garrett Fesler (2004:360–401), an archaeologist working in the Chesapeake area of Virginia, found slave quarters that housed single adults yielded considerably fewer artifacts than quarters used to house family units. The small quantity of artifacts at Cafetal Biajacas may be an indication of a situation comparable to what Fesler observed in Virginia. Thus far, archaeological studies of gender on plantations primarily emphasize women's roles (Galle and Young 2004).

Efforts to analyze possible archaeological signatures (artifacts suggestive of a particular activity or social group) of an enslaved community primarily of men have received little attention. It is tempting from the artifact analysis of Cafetal Biajacas to suggest certain artifacts are associated with men and others with women. For example, the absence of sewing equipment, artifacts stereotypically associated with women, and the large quantity of machetes, stereotypically associated with men, support the predominance of men. But such an assessment only reinforces these gender stereotypes rather than helps us to understand how gender operated at Cafetal Biajacas or other plantations. Gender definitely mattered within slave communities, and on some Cuban plantations consistent with the customs of certain African societies, enslaved men and women carried out domestic chores, consumed meals, and socialized separately (García 2003b:28). Perhaps future studies will permit us to interpret these gendered activities from archaeological sources.

The paucity of artifacts at Cafetal Biajacas most likely resulted from a combination of factors. Artifact paucity is also culturally relative—a small quantity of things in one context is not necessarily applicable to another. Lynn Meskell (2005:11) discusses how a paucity of goods is often equated with an "impoverished culture," a view she attributes to the persistent influence of social evolutionist E. B. Tylor in which material sophistication becomes an index of social complexity, while material lack determines underdevelopment. Archaeologists initially interpreted the inhabitants of some sites of the African diaspora as impoverished. Whitney Battle-Baptiste (2011:129–30) questions the basis for such claims and challenges archaeologists to critically examine the criteria they use to identify poverty in the archaeological record. Poverty is almost always defined by the dominant culture—those who have money, power, and plenty of things—and not by the people they identify as poor. A paucity of artifacts does not necessarily imply poverty, nor is it an index of an "impoverished" culture. The enslaved community at Cafetal Biajacas had few objects for many reasons. They may have been unable to obtain a lot of artifacts, or they may have chosen to use their earnings from their independent production in other ways. In either case, the cultural world they created was far from impoverished.

African Religiosity on Cuban Plantations

African religious beliefs and practices occupied a prominent position in the lives of enslaved people on Cuban plantations. They consulted with religious specialists, made and used "fetishes" (Van Norman 2013:101–3), participated in special rituals (Barcia 2008:123), held toques de tambores (Ortíz [1916] 1988:215), and performed dances to invoke religious deities that often resulted in spirit possession (Ortiz [1906] 1995b:93–95). Very little archaeological evidence of African-inspired religious practices, however, has been reported in Cuba with a few notable exceptions. These include the previously described necklace recovered from a slave burial at Taoro plantation that included glass beads, animal canines, and a pierced coin. Lourdes Domínguez (1999) believes the buried individual was possibly a religious specialist similar to the individual excavated in Barbados (Handler 1997). Second, isolated finds of amulets such as pierced coins recovered from sites in Old Havana may be indications of African religious beliefs. Third, pictographs found on the walls of caves once occupied by slave runaways are believed to depict Afro-Cuban religious rituals and symbols (Enrique Alonso 1998, pers. comm.; Garcell Domínguez 2009).

An intriguing possibility of a ritual burial was unearthed during excavations of a house lot at Obrapía no. 55 in Old Havana, but its association with Afro-Cuban religions is highly questionable. Excavations yielded three adult craniums, one of which appears to have been autopsied, and three nearly complete skeletons of infants in a late nineteenth-century deposit. The careful positioning of human remains, large stones, iron fragments, and animal bones within the corners of the area strongly suggested this was a ritual burial. The archaeologists initially proposed the ritual to be that of the Congo-Cuban religion of Palo Monte, but efforts to support this attribution remain unsubstantiated (Roura Alvarez 2002:5–7). As of this writing, it is unknown whether the ritual burial is related to any Afro-Cuban religion. The date of the deposit coincides with the time when Afro-Cuban religious practitioners, particularly those of Palo Monte, were falsely accused of performing rituals involving child sacrifice. Investigations revealed in many of these cases that whites committed these murders, but they implicated blacks by making victims' bodies appear like they were killed for religious rituals (Moore 1997:31; Brown 2003:57–59). The burials at Obrapía 55 could have been a similar effort to malign adherents of Afro-Cuban religions.

With the exception of the slave burials at Taoro, no religious artifacts have been recovered from Cuban plantations. This contrasts with identification of intentional caches of artifacts in the United States and in Brazil (Agostini 2013) found in and around the living and working areas of enslaved people associated with the ritual practices of various African cultural groups. These deposits are sometimes compared with the *nganga* or prenda [religious altar or shrine] of Congo-Cuban religion (Brown and Cooper 1990; Fennell 2007). But no discrete deposits containing objects associated with prendas were recovered from Cafetal Biajacas, and such finds appear to be rare on Caribbean plantations as a whole. Matthew Reeves (2014) tentatively attributed African spirituality to a deposit of bottles purposefully buried upright near a slave quarter on a Jamaican plantation, but this is one of the few exceptions.

The Afro-Cuban practices that North American archaeologists used as analogies for interpreting prendas emanated from urban institutions initially from the *cabildos de naciones*, mutual aid and religious societies organized around a particular African ethnic designation. Later, charismatic religious leaders established *casa templos* [house temples] and began the process of institutionalizing many of the practices now considered fundamental characteristics of these religions today (Brown 2003:62–112). Students of both the (Yoruba) Lucumí-derived Santería and the Congo–Palo Monte date the genesis of these present-day, African-inspired, but clearly creole religions to the last quarter of the nineteenth and early twentieth centuries (Brown 2003:75–76; Ochoa 2010:9).

Religious expression among enslaved people in the Cuban countryside appears to have been less structured and more individualized than in urban areas. George Brandon (1993:74–75) suggests that on Cuban plantations enslaved people poured libations, used divination to settle disputes, collected herbs to brew plantation medicines, and made shrines of the trees, hills, fields, or a collection of appropriate objects. He points out, however, that communal worship and an organized African priesthood found in the urban cabildos were absent in the countryside. The toques de tambores that accompanied Sunday dances and celebrations of Catholic saints and holy days provided one form of communal worship for enslaved people laboring on plantations. The best-known carnival took place on El Día de Reyes [the Day of the Kings] or the Epiphany on the sixth of January. These carnivals occurred in cities and towns all over Cuba, and the dotación at Cafetal Biajacas most likely participated in those organized in nearby Madruga. But it is unlikely that enslaved people were able to establish cabildos or casa templos on Cuban plantations, though some were possibly connected to these institutions through their social networks located in nearby towns.

Of the religious activities Brandon describes for plantations, collections of "appropriate artifacts" are potentially recoverable through archaeology. Identifying evidence of African religious expressions on plantations has been a very challenging proposition throughout the Americas because the particular context in which the artifacts are found is a key to making a claim of religiosity (Fennell 2007:65–66). The absence of material evidence of African religiosity at Cafetal Biajacas and other excavated Cuban plantations may certainly be related to the use of perishable items for many of these rituals. Fernando Ortiz ([1906] 1995b:46–108, figures 1–41) described many of the objects used by Afro-Cuban religious practitioners at the beginning of the twentieth century. Most of these items were made from perishable materials. Those that are likely to be recovered through archaeology—nails, iron objects, and ceramic vessels—need to be unearthed in concentrated deposits with other materials indicative of rituals and not scattered throughout the site.

At the site of Cafetal Biajacas, the large quantity of recovered machetes in and around the slave houses may have held some religious significance. Machetes have symbolic meanings in both Cuban-Congo and Lucumí religions (Brown 2003b:188, plate 13). Additionally, Ortiz illustrates a dance that utilized machetes as props, the *danza guerrera* [war dance], performed on Kings' Day and other festivals in Cuba and on some islands of the English Caribbean (1992:58–59). The machetes at Cafetal Biajacas, however, were dispersed throughout the excavated spaces and not in a specific context suggestive of a prenda, shrine, or other ritual object.

The idiosyncratic nature of Cafetal Biajacas, owned by a Catholic priest, possibly played a significant role in the absence of material evidence of African-derived religion. O'Farrill very likely proselytized to his slave workers and confiscated any amulets or other African-inspired religious objects belonging to them that came to his attention. Slaveholders and colonial officials regarded African religiosity as *brujería* [witchcraft], a punishable offense. Enslaved Cubans with devout Christian owners may have been especially secretive about their religious beliefs. Fredrika Bremer (1853:2:315) wrote about an enslaved man everyone thought was an "upright Christian" until his death revealed "he wore upon his breast an African amulet, a piece of folded paper printed very small, with letters and words in an African tongue, and to which the negroes appear to ascribe a supernatural power." The slaveholder had known the enslaved man for many years and was shocked to learn he was an adherent to African religious beliefs.

The absence of archaeological evidence of African religiosity at Cafetal Biajacas is likely the result of several factors. But, as with the paucity of artifacts, slaveholder intrusion in slave lives at Cafetal Biajacas and the use of perishable materials to make many religious objects offer strong possibilities to explain why these kinds of artifacts were not recovered. The absence of material evidence of African religiosity, however, is not an absence of African religiosity. The enslaved people at Cafetal Biajacas very likely participated in toques de tambores and other rituals that allowed them to express their religious beliefs through music, dance, and other forms of performance.

8

Conflict and Compromise

On Christmas Day 1837, Ramos León, the mayoral of Cafetal Santa Ana de Biajacas, discovered that about 20 slave runaways had blended themselves among the dotación of the cafetal within the wall enclosure for a few days. Startled by the presence of runaways and fearful of what would happen to him if they stayed, León went to local authorities to report this incident. By the time the local patrol arrived, the runaways had departed. Mariano Paradas, the head law enforcement officer for the partido Ceiba Mocha, reported to Antonio García Oña, governor of Matanzas jurisdiction, "Todo queda tranquilo sin que del arrancamiento que se hizo de los cimarrones hubiese resultado capturado ninguno, pues según se me informó por los cabos de ronda que concurrieron con la comitiva al registro de los montes no se encontraron sino vestigios antiguos de haber estado otros negros" [Everything is now quiet without the destruction slave runaways make, none of them were captured, but I have been informed that patrol officers participated in a search with a convoy to the mountains and did not encounter them; they only found old remnants of the living conditions left by another group of blacks] (AHPM GPC leg. 12, no. 50).

This all-too-brief document raises numerous questions regarding the role that the enslaved community at Cafetal Biajacas played in providing refuge to the runaways. What kind of relationship did the slave community there have with cimarrones who lived intermittently in nearby caves and overhangs? Had similar incidents with cimarrones occurred at the coffee plantation but gone unreported? Why was the slave community at Cafetal Biajacas not accused or implicated in any way for providing refuge to the runaways? These questions are posed to examine how slave resistance was executed and dealt with at Cafetal Biajacas. From the episode described above, it appears that the wall enclosure proved ineffective at keeping out cimarrones or other unwanted visitors. It also did not deter four men who ran away and were never captured.

If the wall was ineffective in these two examples, it was possibly ineffective in others. How then did O'Farrill and his managers deal with these and other forms of slave resistance? They may have tolerated some activities that went against legal statutes or unwritten rules of slave conduct. But the archaeological recovery of a shackle, chain links, and the small room possibly used for confinement, together with a documentary reference to a 14-hole cepo [restraining device] listed on the inventory for Cafetal Biajacas (ANC Galletti leg. 934, no. 6), provide compelling evidence that O'Farrill and his emissaries meted out brutal treatment when they deemed it necessary.

This chapter examines the circumstances regarding slave actions that prompted O'Farrill, as well as the other nearby planters, to authorize brutal treatment and those actions in which they compromised with the enslaved in order to maintain the smooth operation of their plantations. Thus the objective is to evaluate the master-slave dialectic by considering examples of slave action and slaveholder reaction indicative of compromise and conflict.

Archaeologies of Resistance

Enslaved peoples ran away, planned and incited revolts, assaulted and murdered their owners, and even took their own lives. They also engaged in more subtle forms of protest on a daily basis, such as work slowdowns, feigned illness, pilfering, or other actions that did not free them from slavery but possibly helped them to cope. Douglas Egerton (2010:455–56) observes that some students of slavery traditionally delineate between everyday resistance and organized forms of resistance aimed at ending the institution of slavery. He argues that the distinction between the two is a misleading one because small acts of insubordination helped lay the foundation for organized, politicized resistance. In Cuba, Manuel Barcia (2008:9) distinguishes between violent forms of resistance (conspiracies, homicides, revolts, suicides, and marronage) and those he characterizes as nonviolent (use of the legal system and cultural practices including music, dance, religion, gossip, folktales, and jokes). Using James C. Scott's (1990:4–5) concept of hidden transcripts—disguised actions that critiqued the power of the dominant class—Barcia persuasively argues that nonviolent forms of resistance are critical to understanding those who did not resort to violence to oppose their enslavement (2008:5–6). This chapter follows Barcia's lead and examines examples of violent and nonviolent slave resistance at Cafetal Biajacas, one inferred from archaeological evidence and the other from documentary sources. Both provide insights into slave resistance generally in western Matanzas.

Archaeologists have recovered evidence of resistance for diverse subjugated groups. In Foucault's notion of power, all levels of society have access to power, making it possible for all people to engage in social action. This kind of practical *power to* differs from *power over* that dominant classes like slaveholders and factory owners wielded over those forced into subordinate social positions (Shackel 2011:52). Studies of industrial workplaces, for example, have yielded archaeological data on how workers sabotaged machinery, broke tools, discarded manufactured products, and concealed their consumption of alcoholic beverages on the job (Shackel 2011:56–61).

Power relations and resistance are also important themes in the archaeological study of slavery and plantations. Archaeological investigations of the places where enslaved people fled to liberate themselves from slavery are testaments to overt slave resistance (Agorsah 1993; Orser and Funari 2001; Weik 2012). In Cuba, Gabino La Rosa Corzo has conducted numerous archaeological investigations of both short-term occupation sites of cimarrones and their long-term, semipermanent settlements known as palenques throughout Cuba. His publications examine archaeological evidence of defensive strategies, weapons, spatial organization of settlements, pottery making, hunting, and raiding of livestock and supplies from nearby plantations (1989, 2003, 2005, 2008, 2010). His archaeological study of slave runaway sites is the most comprehensive of any investigator in the Americas.[1]

Archaeologists interpret slave resistance on plantations as well, but it is often difficult to demonstrate how artifacts or artifact contexts are suggestive of resistance. Like factory workers, enslaved peoples sabotaged machinery, broke tools, and destroyed crops. In a number of subfloor pits dug beneath the floor boards of slave houses on plantations in the states of Virginia, Tennessee, and Kentucky, farm tools found in good condition may indicate the deliberate hiding or discarding of tools to keep from doing plantation work. The action of digging these subfloor pits may also have been considered an act of resistance. The handful of written sources referring to these pits suggest the slaveholders were not pleased with enslaved people digging these pits and were concerned that the items contained within them were pilfered goods (Fesler 2004:280; Kelso 1984:201). Expensive or high-status objects, like the decorative gold fragment from the enclosure, are sometimes interpreted as evidence of pilfering and therefore an act of insubordination. At Cafetal Biajacas, the gaming pieces suggestive of gambling or glass and stoneware bottles suggestive of imbibing alcoholic beverages certainly denote activities strictly prohibited on some Cuban plantations. Other slaveholders, however, permitted these activities and regarded them as small indulgences to placate or to reward workers.

Archaeologists also draw on Leland Ferguson's (1992:119–20) concept of ideological power of enslaved peoples to interpret various cultural practices as forms of resistance. Ferguson proposed that enslaved South Carolinians resisted slavery through their ideological power that allowed them to reject the world of their masters in favor of their own. This includes aspects of their material world, such as the making and use of pottery, building mud-walled houses, or using earthenware vessels with crosses marked on them in religious rituals. Ideological power most certainly played a key role in the religious practices, as they performed rituals in order to take control of their world and to weaken the power of their oppressors.

As discussed previously, discrete deposits of objects suggestive of African-derived religious practices were not identified from excavations of Cafetal Biajacas, and archaeologists working on the Caribbean plantations have rarely reported such evidence. Analyzing slave resistance through archaeology poses numerous challenges, but in the study of slavery and other subjugated peoples, resistance should always be considered one feasible (but not the only) avenue for interpreting suspect objects. These objects will vary greatly according to the type of site being investigated and the objects used to infer resistance. Such objects are likely to be multivalent and therefore do not immediately convey the theme of resistance.

Subverting the Authority of the Wall

One can only imagine the various ways the enslaved laborers at Cafetal Biajacas undermined the authority of the wall. Escape from the enclosure either permanently or temporarily presented the most serious affront to it, because its purpose was to contain the residents. No doubt the residents engaged in prohibited activities and undermined the wall through tactical everyday activities (de Certeau 1988:xix–xx). Archaeological evidence hints at some of these activities, such as imbibing or gambling, but O'Farrill and his overseers were possibly aware that these activities took place and permitted them. Two other possibly unauthorized activities suggest how enslaved people defied the wall while living within its enclosure: the concealment of machetes—potential weapons—within their houses and the harboring of slave runaways.

Machetes: Artifacts of Labor and Resistance

Despite the difficulty of demonstrating that a specific artifact, a group of artifacts, or an artifact context is suggestive of slave resistance, the machete is proposed here as a plausible artifact of slave resistance. Machetes are large knives, like cleavers, used for clearing thick vegetation and agricultural chores. In the Caribbean and Latin America, they are most often associated with cutting sugarcane, but they were general agricultural tools. On coffee plantations, machetes were used daily in the routine maintenance of coffee plants.

At first glance the recovery of about 13 machetes within the enclosure does not seem unusual. Archaeological investigations at other Cuban plantations found large numbers of machetes and other cutting tools (Domínguez González 1991:267; Moreno Fraginals 1978:2:30). But unlike those found at Cafetal Biajacas, machetes from these other sites were recovered from the ruins of mills and warehouses, not from slave quarters. At Cafetal Biajacas, a few machetes were found outside the enclosure. One of these—hand-forged, with a maker's insignia (figure 8.1)—was collected at the surface of an agricultural field designated area F (see figure 4.2). But the vast majority of the recovered machetes came from inside and around the slave houses. Enslaved Cubans most likely used them for tending to their own

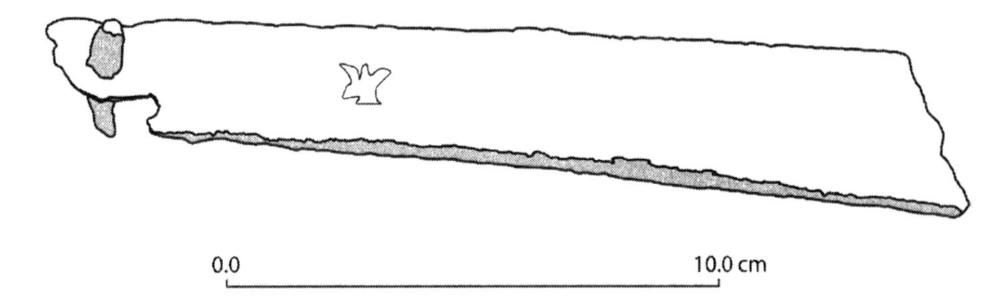

Figure 8.1. Hand-forged machete with maker's insignia and a slant-cut blade, recovered from surface collection outside of slave enclosure. Drawn by Syracuse University Cartographic Laboratory.

gardens or harvesting fruit, gourds, palm leaves, and bark from a variety of trees.

Yet the machete was also a weapon: an Afro-Cuban adage states that "a machete can also cut the master" (Barcia 2008:120). This is exactly what happened to José Cantos Valdespino, the owner of Cafetal Empresa in Havana jurisdiction, who was murdered with a machete during a slave uprising on his plantation (ANC GSC, leg. 939, no. 33131). But this is just one example of violent acts in which enslaved Cubans utilized machetes (Barcia 2008:31–41; Garcia 2003b:112–28). Slave violence was particularly rampant in Matanzas, with as many as 399 cases recorded from 1825 to 1850 for that jurisdiction alone (Paquette 1988:72). In the 1825 slave rebellion, the rebels relied on "machetes, knives, clubs, and other working tools" to carry out the insurrection (Barcia 2012:132).

Access to machetes and other agricultural tools when slave laborers were not working alarmed colonial authorities and slaveholders. Consequently, the 1842 slave code contained three statutes requiring owners to restrict access to agricultural tools. These laws stipulated that all instruments of labor be collected at the end of each day and stored in a locked depository, the key to which was never to be entrusted to an enslaved person. In addition, enslaved laborers were not permitted to leave plantation grounds with any instrument of labor unless accompanied by a master or overseer (García 2003b:80).

Many of the statutes of the 1842 code, like those described above, merely institutionalized preexisting plantation practices. The first inventory for

Cafetal Biajacas (1838) indicates that all plantation tools were stored together in a building outside the enclosure (ANC Galletti leg. 245, no. 1). When the item-by-item valuation was later taken, this building contained 42 machetes (ANC Galletti leg. 934, no. 6). So why were so many machetes found associated with the slave bohíos? Did the dotación of Cafetal Biajacas conceal these tools and conceivable weapons from O'Farrill and his managers? Did machetes serve purposes other than those of tools or weapons? The discussion that follows describes the recovered machetes, and considers how they might have been acquired and what their multivalent usages and meanings might be.

Machetes and other agricultural tools rarely receive attention in archaeological literature primarily because they are usually highly fragmented and therefore unidentifiable. When archaeologists do recognize these artifacts, they simply classify them as agricultural tools without considering other possible uses. From the slave enclosure at Cafetal Biajacas, a whole machete, 8 handles, 15 large blade fragments (6 of which do not appear to go with any of the handles and together represent 4 separate machetes), and 37 smaller blade fragments were recovered. Together these remains suggest that there were at least 13 machetes in the enclosure, if not more.

In Jamaica, Barry Higman (1998:214) recovered three bill hooks (a short and broad tool with a sharp hook) and four cutlass (machete) blades from slave houses at Montpelier plantation. Jamaican planters distinguished between bills and machetes. Bills were used to clear lands and to harvest sugarcane, whereas the cutlass, a long, narrow tool, was a general farm tool for planting, weeding, harvesting, and butchering, among other tasks (Higman 1998:211). In Cuba, both the bill and the cutlass were considered machetes, but two distinct forms. The machetes with the rounded cutting edge in figure 8.2 were variations of a bill, sometimes referred today as *machetes mocha*.

Ramos Zúñiga (1984) illustrates several forms of machetes and swords historically used in Cuba, and figure 8.2 depicts those he associates with agricultural labor. Although he describes the various styles in the text, he does not identify them on the illustration. The names for the point types indicated in figure 8.2 are based on the patterns manufactured by Collins Company in Collinsville, Connecticut. Collins did not begin to manufacture machetes until 1845 (one year before the final demise of Cafetal Bi-

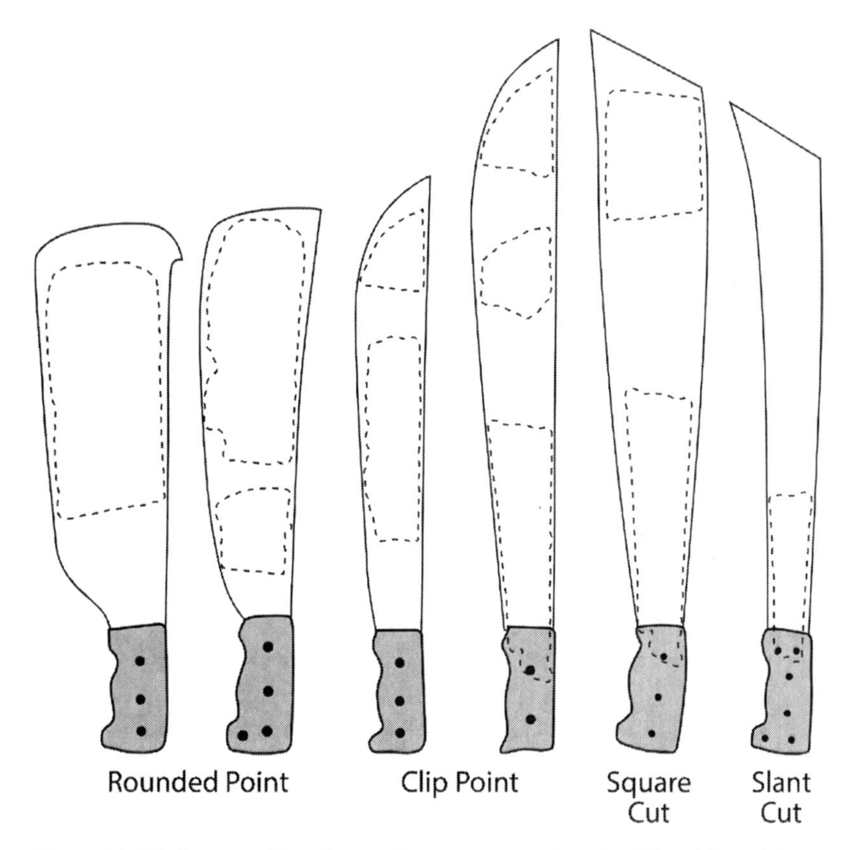

Figure 8.2. Machetes used in nineteenth-century agriculture in Cuba. Adapted from illustration in Ramos Zúñiga (1984). Drawn by Syracuse University Cartographic Laboratory.

ajacas), but Collins machetes made for the Latin American market were usually based on preexisting popular forms (Henry 1995:33). All the machetes recovered from Cafetal Biajacas appear to have been hand-forged and most likely were made in local foundries, prior to the importation of Collins and other mass-produced machetes.

An attempt is made in figure 8.2 to match some of the machete fragments from Cafetal Biajacas with Ramos Zúñiga's agricultural machetes to determine which forms were represented in the assemblage. The illustration also aided in establishing a minimum number of machetes represented from the 61 identifiable machete fragments. Fragments of what appear to match these basic forms were recovered, but there was and still is considerable variation in the shapes of machetes. For example, Ramos Zúñiga (1984:54) describes the machete calabozo used widely on Cuban plantations around 1820 as lacking a point, with a slightly convex cutting edge and straight on the side away from the edge. Examples are illustrated in the slant point machete in figure 8.2. Some illustrations, however, depict calabozos with a completely squared cutting edge (Hernández de Lara, Rodríguez Tápanes, and Arredondo Antúnez 2012:98). Many slaveholders preferred that enslaved laborers use the calabozo because it lacked a pointed cutting edge, but these machetes were heavy and greatly slowed down the harvesting of sugar. Their use prevailed on coffee plantations, however. Local law enforcement officers in Matanzas recorded incidences when slave runaways were in possession of machetes and particularly noted their possession of machetes calabozos on several occasions.[2]

Without an account book containing details about the distribution of machetes at Cafetal Biajacas, one can only speculate as to whether or not the dotación had permission to keep the machetes in their houses. Higman's (1998:211–14) study of the Montpelier plantation in Jamaica offers some insights into the distribution of machetes that may be applicable to other Caribbean plantations. He found that the plantation managers recorded the distribution of bills, specialized tools for sugar production, but not for cutlasses. Not every slave worker received a bill, and if the worker lost one, he or she would have to negotiate with the manager to get another one. Only bills, hoes, and dung drays, items considered plantation property, were distributed this way. All other items allocated to laborers were considered slave property. Therefore, the recovered cutlasses were possibly the personal property of the slave residents at Montpelier and therefore not recorded. Similarly, the dotación at Cafetal Biajacas very likely acquired the machetes within the enclosure through their own efforts, and they considered these tools their personal property. Gloria García (2003b:37) purports that rural taverns became notorious places where knives, machetes, ammunition, and even rifles were sold to anyone, including enslaved laborers, with cash in hand and no questions asked.

The source of the machetes, however, is secondary to the fact that enslaved people at Cafetal Biajacas kept machetes in their houses that could be used as weapons. Given the number of uprisings and violent acts committed by enslaved Cubans, it seems surprising that O'Farrill or his managers would have permitted the residents to keep machetes within their enclosure. More to the point, it seems at odds with forcing them to live within the massive enclosure intended to restrict their movement and suppress rebelliousness. Their living situation and access to potential weapons presented conditions likely to foment an uprising or other violent acts of resistance. It seems more plausible that the dotación concealed the machetes and kept them in their houses without the approval of O'Farrill and his managers. Although no records indicate that workers at Cafetal Biajacas used machetes in assaults or murders, many other enslaved Cubans did use them in violent acts.

In the study of Afro-Cuban heritage, machetes are multivalent artifacts—containers of multiple meanings and usages. They are at once tools and weapons as well as symbols of oppression and of resistance that have special significance in Afro-Cuban religions. Although it was not possible to make a claim that the machetes recovered from the enclosure were used in religious practices, they could have been kept for religious or other symbolic purposes. In the Congo-Cuban religion of Palo Monte, machetes are sometimes found with other metal objects in prendas [altars or shrines], particularly those made for Zarabanda, a deity or spirit with warrior characteristics (Brown 2003:188; Ochoa 2010:109). The principal tool for Ogún, Zarabanda's counterpart in the Lucumí-Cuban religion of Santería, is the machete (Brown 2003:370). Additionally, *santeros*, practitioners of Santería, transformed the oppressive connotations of machete usage on plantations along with the overseer's whip-and-sword—equipment used to inflict brutal physical treatment on the enslaved—into instruments of "strength, liberation, and healing" (Brown 2003:188). Thus the machete evokes many concepts, memories, and virtues and is one of the most multivalent objects of Afro-Cuban heritage.

Los Cimarrones en Cafetal Biajacas and Marronage in Matanzas

In the episode of the cimarrones at Cafetal Biajacas used to introduce this chapter, it may seem unusual for slave runaways to seek refuge at a plantation rather than running away from one. But cimarrones frequently interacted with the enslaved on Cuban plantations. Fredrika Bremer

(1853:2:349–50) remarked, "Sometimes they [slave runaways] will come down in the night-time to the plantations for sustenance, which they obtain from the negroes of the plantations who never betray the fugitives." Other primary sources support Bremer's observation. Enslaved people not only provided cimarrones with food and shelter but often engaged in trade with them (Barcia 2008:67; García 2003b:40). And this covert trade partially accounts for the recovery of items at slave runaway sites that are similar to those found on plantations. But cimarrones also obtained food and supplies as well as recruits by raiding plantations. A slave runaway who called himself Mayumbe became notorious for the successful raids he led on plantations in Matanzas during a two-year period beginning in 1842. His guerilla strategy of moving often and dividing his followers into dispersed settlements known as "bite and run" proved very effective until someone revealed his tactics to his pursuers, who located some of his party's settlements and destroyed them (Landers 2010:222).

The cimarrones targeted Cafetal Biajacas either to raid it or to secure assistance from people they knew. In a similar occurrence of cimarrones seeking refuge on a coffee plantation, Francisco "Pancho" Mina, a maroon leader, told local authorities that they chose Cafetal Landot to seek refuge because the enslaved people there had been friendly to them on a previous occasion and one of the 10 cimarrones in his party, Pablo Criolla, had run away from that plantation. For eight days, the runaways hid within the slave quarters at Cafetal Landot (García 2003b:172). In the report to the governor of Matanzas, Mariano Paradas claimed that cimarrones did not loot Cafetal Biajacas; therefore, they appear to have sought refuge there rather than to raid it.

During the period 1837–38, a group of about 20 slave runaways inhabiting a large cave in the mogotes of El Grillo, just northeast of Madruga, frequently came down at night and pilfered from neighboring plantations. Because they sometimes performed toques de tambores that greatly alarmed plantation residents, both the cave and the cimarrones associated with it became known as El Tambor. La Rosa Corzo and Pérez Padrón (1994:104) posit that the runaways at Cafetal Biajacas were possibly those of El Tambor. William van Norman (2013:102), however, surmises the slave runways fled from another plantation, possibly a sugar plantation where the labor regime was more onerous than on a coffee plantation. For that reason, the runaways attempted to incorporate themselves among the dotación of Cafetal Biajacas with the expectation of staying there indefinitely.

Regardless of where the runaways originated, their presence at Cafetal Biajacas ignited a concerted effort to destroy the cimarrones of El Tambor. A month later, a group of *rancheadores* [bounty hunters] found 8 or 10 cimarrones living on the forested lands of Cafetal Santa Brigada (see figure 2.1). One of the runaways was assaulted, but the others escaped into the forest. Later, the presumed leader of the group, Leandro of the Gangá nación, was captured. He had fled a sugar plantation two years earlier and led a group of about 20 runaways, but for shelter they employed the bite-and-run tactic of separating into smaller groups. Using Cafetal Santa Brigada for their base of operation, the rancheadores launched intensive searches for 15 days and captured five men and two women. On February 11, 1838, colonial officials announced their belief that the slave runaways in the area of Madruga had been exterminated because active pursuits of runaways left them with few places to hide and those that survived most likely left the area (La Rosa Corzo and Pérez Padrón 1994:104–6). Four years later in 1842, however, a planter reported another group of runaways on his plantation around Madruga. He attempted to pursue them but was unsuccessful, and later, rancheadores captured a few of them (AHPM GPC 1842 leg. 12, no. 71). As late as 1870, slave runaways were still being reported in the area of the Cafetal Biajacas (AHMP GPC 1870 leg. 17, no. 16).

With its sizable slave population, Matanzas jurisdiction developed as a hotbed for slave runaways in the nineteenth century (Franco 1973:90). Although documentation of the numbers of slave runaways is sparse, a few surviving records indicate that the number of runaways reported to colonial officials was substantial. For example, in 1817, slaveholders reported 159 enslaved persons had run away from plantations in five partidos of Matanzas (Yumurí, Ceiba Mocha, Camarioca, Guamacaro, Santa Ana) within a month (AHPM GPE leg. 12, no. 5a). And in 1829, 17 slaveholders in the partido of Yumurí reported 38 members of their dotaciones ran away in the month of November (AHPM GPC 1eg. 12, no. 25).

Slave flight resulted in several forms of *cimarronaje* [marronage], which

Cuban officials variously defined. Based on his studies of Cuban maroons, Gabino La Rosa Corzo (1991a:64–66) refined these definitions to include three general categories prevalent in western Cuba:

1. *Cimarronaje simple*: one or a small group of runaways who fled within a short distance (7–8 miles) of the plantation where they labored.
2. *Cimarronaje en cuadrillas* [in gangs]: a larger group than the cimarrones simples, these runaways wandered the countryside constantly and lived in simple thatched huts, in caves, or under overhangs, and hunted, fished, and robbed for subsistence.
3. *Apalencamiento* [palenque settlement]: fortified or semipermanent settlements in mountainous or other difficult-to-access areas.

Of the three, only *apalencados* eluded capture for long enough periods to farm and craft the hand-built pottery and pipes recovered from their sites. All three types of marronage were abundant in Matanzas, but apalencados in Matanzas apparently did not build substantial settlements like those La Rosa Corzo (1989; 1991b; 2003) studied in eastern Cuba. Instead, they usually occupied large caves, and one reported to the governor of Matanzas in July 1829 reputedly had 300 men, women, and children living within it. It was also noted that this maroon community was armed with machetes and knives (AHPM GPC leg. 12, no. 23a).

Sightings of runaway gangs and communities reported to colonial authorities in Matanzas indicate that Cafetal Biajacas was in close proximity to slave runaways in three directions: to the north, east, and south (see figure 8.3). Given the location of the cafetal, it is not surprising that cimarrones came to the plantation seeking assistance from the slave community, and other runaways possibly came at times that went unrecorded. On the other hand, Ignacio O'Farrill must have considered using the wall enclosure not only as a way to contain the dotación but also to deter slave runaways or other intruders from entering the slave settlement. Although the wall failed in the one documented incidence, it may have been more effective in other situations.

Intruders of all kinds, not just runaways, preyed on Cuban plantations. While visiting a sugar plantation in Matanzas, Richard Dana ([1859] 1966:75) commented that noises heard on plantations at night, like the

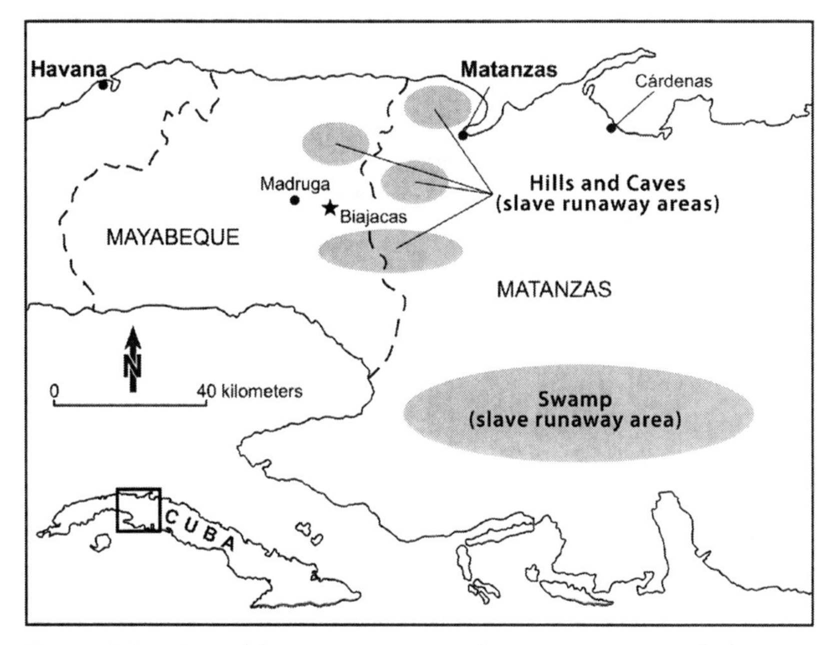

Figure 8.3. Locations of slave runaway gangs and communities near Cafetal Biajacas reported to Cuban colonial authorities from sources in AHPM Fondo Cimarrones and in La Rosa Corzo's publications, particularly 1991a, 2005, 2008, 2010. Drawn by Syracuse University Cartographic Laboratory.

tramp of horses, caused considerable uneasiness for planters. "A Negro may have attempted to steal out, or some strange Negro may be trying to steal in, or some prowling white, or free black, has been reconnoitering. These are the terms on which this system is carried on." Several decades earlier, Joseph Goodwin noted on February 12, 1823, nine armed robbers stole $1,500 from a nearby plantation and rode off into the night (Goodwin Daybook). James DeWolf alluded to the potential threats posed by slave runaways, other intruders, or perhaps slave uprisings in a letter dated August 20, 1817, to Stephan Hales, a manager of his coffee plantations: "I desire you to always be well armed at night" (JDWSFP, vol. 2). Fourteen years later, DeWolf's fears were realized when an unidentified assailant attacked Alexander Griswold, the manager at his coffee plantation Mount Hope (Lowell 2003:69–70). Given the constant threat of intruders, O'Farrill most likely took precautions to deter interlopers from entering the plantation.

Slave runaways occupied the caves and overhangs near Cafetal Biajacas intermittently as some of these environments, like El Grillo, were not suitable for continuous or long-term settlement. With the assistance of enslaved laborers living on plantations, as in the case of Cafetal Biajacas, slave runaways prolonged their existence in these marginal areas until they were captured, surrendered, or took their own lives.

Evaluating the Master-Slave Dialectic

The two examples of slave resistance at Cafetal Biajacas presented in this chapter—the concealment of potential weapons and the harboring of slave runaways—suggest ways in which the enslaved community used the wall enclosure to their advantage. In doing so, their actions contravened the slaveholder's purposes for the wall: to restrict slave movement, suppress rebelliousness, and keep intruders out. The written information available, however, does not reveal how O'Farrill and his managers handled such contravention or on what occasions they resorted to violence to control slave laborers by cepo, shackles, or possibly the small room for solitary confinement.

A few months after the death of Ignacio O'Farrill in October 1838, 40 of the enslaved workers at Cafetal Biajacas were relocated to the sugar plantation San Juan de Nepomuceno (table 6.1), O'Farrill's most lucrative plantation. The inventory indicated that 118 enslaved persons already worked there (ANC Galletti, leg. 240, no. 1, pieza 1). The addition of 40 slave laborers from Cafetal Biajacas made a total dotación of 158, 37 fewer workers than were listed in 1822 (ANC GSC, leg. 871, no. 29460).

Based on the estate papers, after O'Farrill's death and the relocation of laborers from Cafetal Biajacas, life became intolerable for the enslaved people at San Juan. They received little food and clothing, prompting some of them to pilfer from nearby plantations. Two men caught taking plantains from the Cafetal de Brown were abused and constrained in a cepo at that cafetal until they were released to the custody of the mayoral for San Juan (ANC Galletti, leg. 240, no. 1, pieza 7). In 1840, 39 of the slave workers rebelled, and 20 ran away; a few injured runaways were captured and held by local law enforcement, but the rest were presumed to be living in palenques

(ANC Galletti leg. 240, no. 1, pieza 5). A year later, between 45 and 50 members of the dotación ran up into the mountains near Madruga. The captain of Madruga organized a patrol to search for them. Most were captured, and a few returned to San Juan de Nepomuceno voluntarily (ANC GSC, leg. 617, no. 19712).

This large-scale escape prompted both the captain of Madruga, Francisco Rodríguez, and the administrator of O'Farrill's estate, Francisco Galarraga, to question what motivated this drastic action and would this event have occurred if O'Farrill had been alive? Rodríguez pondered whether or not the incident was an isolated case of little significance and the customary behavior of the dotación when they lived under O'Farrill's management. The enslaved workers told Rodríguez that the reason for their action was that all they wanted was a change in the mayoral's treatment toward them. Rodríguez believed them and ordered 50 lashes for the organizers of the escape, which included two contramayorales, 25 lashes for the remaining participants, and imprisonment for all of them. He chose not to go through the court because doing so would further delay the settlement of the estate for O'Farrill's heirs (ANC GSC leg. 617, no. 19712).

Galarraga, on the other hand, did not believe the reason given for the escape. He claimed while O'Farrill lived, his dotaciones were pampered and that after his death the dotación at San Juan received little discipline from the manager. When the new manager tried to correct these problems without the use of "un latigazo ni se puso a nadie en cadena" [a lash nor was anyone put in chain], the slave workers rebelled and fled (ANC Galletti leg. 240, no. 1, pieza 8).

Galarraga, and to some extent Rodríguez, thought O'Farrill had been too accommodating to his dotaciones. If the word *accommodating* characterized O'Farrill's management style, it may partially explain the absence of recorded slave uprisings while he was alive. But enslaved laborers did run away from Cafetal Biajacas and his other plantations during O'Farrill's life. Additionally, O'Farrill's so-called benevolent treatment resulted in only one recorded manumission, that of Micaela of the Mandinga nation, who purchased her freedom. The archaeological evidence suggests ways in which O'Farrill compromised with his slave laborers, for example, in the building of their bohíos on their own terms, and perhaps in granting them small indulgences such as consuming alcoholic beverages, smoking, or gambling. He may have even been willing to have the cimarrones who sought refuge at Cafetal Biajacas remain on the plantation indefinitely (Van Norman 2013:110). When the incidence with the runaways occurred, however, Ignacio O'Farrill was a feeble old man and perhaps not fully aware of his actions. Ten months after the appearance of the cimarrones at the cafetal in December 1837, O'Farrill died at the age of 82 (ANC Galletti leg. 245, no. 1, pieza 1).

O'Farrill's age was possibly a factor in his so-called indulgent management style. He was 50 when he established San Juan de Nepomuceno with Ignacio Méndez in 1807 and 58 in 1815 when he most likely began developing Cafetal Biajacas. Julia Ward Howe ([1860] 1969:77) observed what she considered the undisciplined behavior of the slave laborers on the plantation of Jacinto González Larrinaga and commented, "Don Jacinto is an old man,—a very old man; and where discipline cannot be maintained, peace must be secured on any terms." Eighteen years earlier, González Larrinaga portrayed his management of enslaved laborers on his plantation as a well-oiled operation when he wrote to Gerónimo Valdés as a contributor to the slave code of 1842. Perhaps, as time passed, he relaxed some of his rules.

Nonetheless, Cuban planters conceded to their enslaved charges in many incidences totally unrelated to the age of the slaveholder for the purpose of keeping peace to ensure the smooth operation of their plantations. Ebenezer Sage, for example, seemed delighted when five of six slave runaways voluntarily returned to his plantation in January 1821, after hiding in the mountains for five months. The runaways returned when Sage was scrambling to find enough laborers to complete the coffee harvest (Sage letterbooks). Although Sage does not say how he handled the runaways, he possibly gave them what he considered a mild reprimand because he needed their labor. This was similar to when Rafael Montalvo pardoned all those who fled his sugar plantation following an uprising. He made that concession to get everybody back to work.

Many Cuban planters recognized they lived in a world that required good judgment in negotiations with the enslaved to prevent violent acts of resistance. The threat of uprisings loomed large for many white residents of Cuba, as Joseph Goodwin learned after working in Cuba for six months. Following a suspicious fire that destroyed between 1,500 and 2,000 coffee trees at George DeWolf's Arca de Noe plantation on June 28, 1821, Goodwin wrote, "Sooner or later many of the plantations will be destroyed by fire in this island of fear" (Goodwin Diary). Goodwin's statement epitomizes the trepidation of many slaveholders and managers in Cuba and offers a rationale for why some of them chose to overlook some acts of resistance or refused to build housing for locking up laborers at night.

Yet to refer to O'Farrill as an indulgent slaveholder seriously undermines how he exercised his power over the dotación at Cafetal Biajacas. While we will never know his reasons for building the wall enclosure, the mere presence of the wall points to an overall strategy of controlling people, their activities, and their spaces. Walls also designate boundaries, define flows of circulation, and set paths for people to follow (Brighenti 2010:322). The wall restricted slave movement both within and beyond the plantation. Previous discussion showed how the wall separated, created distance, and concealed the laborers from the rest of the plantation. Controlling slave mobility limited the dotación's access to economic opportunities and social interactions with enslaved people at other plantations. The recycling and refashioning of artifacts recovered from within the enclosure resemble artifacts excavated at various institutions of confinement, particularly those found at prisons (Casella 2007:87).

Moreno Fraginals (1977:189) advanced the idea that Cuban slavery became like a jail in which enslaved people lived in lockdown after they completed their daily work. Gloria García (2003b:40), however, refutes Moreno's characterization and posits that the jail-like image existed only as an ideal type that some planters espoused. She explains further that enslaved Cubans challenged slaveholders' efforts to isolate and imprison them by creating their own channels of communication, social networks, and trade.

The archaeological study of the enclosed slave settlement at Cafetal Biajacas enhances our understanding of slave life in lockdown by providing empirical data on the ways slave life was constricted as well as how the enslaved pushed the boundaries of their containment. They subverted the slaveholder's geography of containment by creating *rival geographies*. Although the wall reduced opportunities for the enslaved to engage in trade and social interactions, the workers at Cafetal Biajacas participated in some form of exchange evident in the objects recovered from their houses that were most likely acquired either from itinerant merchants or by leaving the plantation at night, in spite of the wall, to trade at taverns. Additionally, they found ways to interact with other people beyond the confines of the plantation at weekend dances, feast and holy days, and again in taverns and other shops when they found ways to leave the plantation.

The enslaved laborers at Cafetal Biajacas defied the authority of the wall and slaveholder meanings of it by aiding and harboring slave runaways who came to the cafetal. In addition, many of the artifacts found within the enclosure suggest that the dotación could have concealed some of their activities such as drinking, gambling, or keeping machetes in their houses. The absence of discernible artifacts of religiosity, however, was possibly due to Padre O'Farrill's efforts to control the religious lives of the enslaved. O'Farrill may have been tolerant regarding some slave activities, but it is doubtful that he would have approved of workers openly practicing their African religions. The dotación most likely concealed their religiosity in music, song, and dance.

In the final analysis, the wall served as a powerful symbol of slaveholder authority that restricted slave movement and subjugated laborers by reinforcing their subservient status through screening their slave quarters from the idyllic gaze of the avenues, orchards, and gardens. At the same time, it facilitated slave activities that undermined the wall's authority. The enslaved at Cafetal Biajacas engaged in some form of trade, interacted with other enslaved peoples, and ran away. The enslaver and the enslaved used the wall for their own purposes and imbued it with opposing meanings. Whether one studies walls of the past (Samson 1992) or those of the present (Caldeira 2000; Brighenti 2010), people build walls to define their territory, to confine a group of people to a specific location, or to keep a group of people out of a location. Thus a wall is an object that brings into focus the interplay between social relations and the use of space.

By framing this study around the wall to understand the role it (as well as other aspects of material culture) played in the master-slave relationship at Cafetal Biajacas, this study privileged an examination of power relations, a materialist rather than a materiality perspective (DeMarrais, Gosden, and Renfrew 2005:2) Yet this study engages with materiality by considering how the wall shaped the lives of those living within the enclosure and to a lesser extent those living outside of it. The wall at Cafetal Biajacas was built to control the enslaved occupants for myriad reasons. Yet, like other walls (Caldeira 2000:296), it exposes the fear, suspicion, and desire for segregation from others by the slaveholder who was responsible for its construction.

9

Conclusion

The Enduring Legacy of Cafetal Biajacas

When Patricio Pérez came to settle at the site of Cafetal Biajacas in the 1890s, the batey of the cafetal had been abandoned, and all the former plantation buildings were in ruins. After the hurricanes of 1844 and 1846, the property had been deserted and later subdivided into small subsistence farms. San Juan de Nepomuceno, O'Farrill's nearby sugar plantation and the recipient of many of the enslaved laborers from Cafetal Biajacas, endured. In 1862, Francisco de Cordova was identified as its new owner, with 100 enslaved and 20 Chinese indentured workers (ANC GG, leg. 562, no. 27528).

Patricio told his grandson, Genaro Vidal, that the roofs of the great house and the other standing structures were gone, only a few coffee dryers were still visible, and nothing was standing within the enclosure when he arrived at Cafetal Biajacas. In between the extant coffee dryers and ruins of a building of unknown function (locus H, figure 4.2), Patricio built his house. At some later time, either a house was built on the foundation of G (see figure 4.2), or the ruins of the former structure were rebuilt into a house for a woman named Gollita and her family. As time passed, the coffee dryers, Gollita's house, the unknown buildings, and Patricio's house were all razed.

Genaro sometimes planted his *frijoles* [beans] within the vast enclosure, and at least on one occasion while tending his crop, he found a *cachimba* [pipe], presumably used by the former enslaved residents. When Genaro was a boy, Patricio told him the big enclosure was probably the barracón where the enslaved workers lived, but that was all he knew about it. But Genaro remained curious about the site and was delighted when a team of archaeologists came to investigate (figure 9.1).

Figure 9.1. Genaro Vidal (deceased) with Sonia Menéndez Castro and Adrián Labrada Milán, members of the archaeological team, and Dinki (the dog, deceased), 2005. Genaro frequently visited the team while working at Cafetal Biajacas. Photograph by Lisette Roura Álvarez.

This study has sought to accomplish two goals: to tell the story of the enslaved people who were forced to live behind a wall and to examine various ways that material things contribute to the telling of their story. Analyses of material culture yield diverse insights into life on a Cuban cafetal, but these studies also provide numerous examples of how to think about material culture more generally.

Slavery and Spatiality

Historian Walter Johnson (2013:210) writes that "enslavement was a material and spatial condition as much as an economic and legal one." Archaeological research uniquely contributes to discussions of the material and spatial dimensions of slavery. But the emphasis of this study is the spatiality of slavery, a growing research interest pursued from diverse disciplinary perspectives (Camp 2004; Delle 2014; Ellis and Ginsburg 2010; Mack and Hofficus 2008).

The enclosed slave settlement at Cafetal Biajacas appears to have been an anomaly among Cuban plantations, yet it was deployed to achieve a goal common to all slave societies—restricting slave mobility. Few slaveholders in the Americas utilized slave housing to control laborers as conspicuously as those who built barracones de patio or wall enclosures. But even less conspicuous ways of quartering laborers produced landscapes of control, or "carceral landscapes," as Johnson (2013:209–43) refers to them. The construction of buildings, walls, and designated paths on Cuban plantations formed a carceral landscape that restricted slave activities and movement to specific areas. By contrast, the cotton kingdom of the southern United States was transformed into a carceral landscape by the opening up of space. Clearing forests for fields, roads, and trails in many cotton districts rendered enslaved people visible, vulnerable, and with few places to hide (Johnson 2013:221–22). Although enclosing and opening up space are completely opposite undertakings, Michel Foucault (1979:200) discusses how visibility can be a trap, particularly when deployed in a panopticon or similar methods of surveillance. Making people visible by opening up space can be used to achieve goals similar to enclosing people within a space.

Despite panopticons or other forms of surveillance, enslaved people negotiated these landscapes by creating their own spatial discipline—local knowledge of where to hide, whom to trust, which paths to take, and so forth—that made resistance possible (W. Johnson 2013:218). Sometimes these spaces were within their quarters and adjacent yard areas that archaeological investigations continue to inform us on the diverse domestic, social, and religious activities that took place in them. Other spaces, described in written sources, were on the outskirts of plantations: nearby forests, swamps, and other areas marginal to agriculture made excellent sites for short-term absences from the plantation (Camp 2004:36) or nocturnal gatherings. Slave runaways sometimes claimed these unused plantation lands as their own, like the small group caught living in the forested areas of Cafetal Santa Brigada near Cafetal Biajacas. Runaways often squatted on the undeveloped property of plantations. On a sugar plantation in northeastern Brazil, runaways established a semipermanent settlement, known as a *quilombo*. And the planter had considerable difficulty in getting rid of the runaways and the settlement (Catherine LaVoy 2012, pers. comm.). Very likely spaces on the periphery of plantations became sites where enslaved residents and runaways interacted and exchanged goods and information.

Unfortunately, locating these sites poses obstacles to archaeological research. Unless the same areas were subjected to repeated usage, and the occupants left behind materials preserved in archaeological deposits visible on the ground's surface, the likelihood of finding these spaces is remote. These areas may also be difficult to find for another reason—they have not been the focus of archaeological research on plantations. With a few exceptions, archaeologists concentrate on the plantation areas where houses or other buildings are evident. The spaces between plantation settlements receive far less attention, even though James Deetz (1990:1–4) advocated that the investigation of such spaces is necessary to understand the proper context of the sites that archaeologists investigate. In Deetz's vision, the investigation of both spaces with buildings and the spaces in between buildings and settlements constitute landscape archaeology. With this understanding of landscape archaeology, the project team for Cafetal Biajacas conducted surveys beyond the plantation batey, but we were unsuccessful in finding archaeological remains of other kinds of occupation.

The karstic terrain of large portions of Cuba, however, facilitates archaeological study of the spatiality of slavery beyond the plantation batey.

During the time of slavery, this landscape offered numerous hiding places in caves and rock shelters for both temporary and long-term escapes from plantations. Many of these sites like those that Gabino La Rosa Corzo investigated appear to have been occupied long enough for the runaways to craft pottery and pipes and carry out rudimentary farming. Other caves served as temporary refuges; some of these were perhaps special or sacred places (Garcell Domínguez 2009). And, for some runaways, caves became their final resting places. Archaeologist Alexa Voss found the remains of a man in a cave near the city of Cienfuegos while investigating a pre-Columbian site. She determined that he was a slave runaway based on dental modification, a form of beautification practiced among many African peoples, and nineteenth-century buttons and a metal buckle from the clothing he was wearing at the time of his death (Voss and Voss 2008).

Archaeologists have emphasized the spatial condition of slavery for over three decades, and it continues to be an important theme in the study of slavery and plantations. At this stage, more attention needs to be directed at the spaces beyond the planter-established settlements of plantations. Finding these sites will no doubt pose challenges, particularly in tropical areas where thick vegetation makes finding them very difficult. But they hold potential promise for understanding the rival geographies of enslaved people other than those located within their quarters and yard areas.

Historical Archaeology and Heritage in Cuba

Cuban historical archaeology has focused primarily on the colonial era (1511–1898) and plays a major role in the public history and heritage management in Cuba. While the objectives for archaeological projects vary widely, the vast majority of archaeological projects are undertaken to address heritage management issues. In other words, few projects are conducted solely for academic research, but to obtain archaeological data needed for architectural restoration, to establish and/or to interpret historic sites opened for public visitation, or to salvage information from sites slated for redevelopment.

Archaeological studies also have contributed to the nominations for some of the UNESCO World Heritage sites of Cuba, and one, "Archaeological Landscapes of the First Coffee Plantations in Southeastern Cuba," specifically denotes the significance of archaeological resources for deeming a site noteworthy of universal value to world heritage. As of June 2014, Cuba had nine World Heritage sites (and other nominations, I am told, are in progress). Cuba has more World Heritage sites than its Caribbean and many of its Latin American neighbors, as well as some European, African, and Asian nations (Scarpaci and Portela 2009:73). In addition to World Heritage sites, Cuba has close to 300 museums (4 archaeological) and 471 national, local, and protected zones and sites identified as of 2008 (Scarpaci and Portela 2009:102–5). Of the coffee plantations discussed in this work, Angerona is a national monument (La Rosa Corzo 2012), and La Dionesia is part of a protected zone (Hernández de Lara 2010).

Efforts are now under way to nominate the site of Cafetal Biajacas as a local monument to preserve for its historic significance to the local community. In addition to its contributions to the scholarship on Cuban slavery, the research at Cafetal Biajacas contributed to demystifying the site. In a similar vein as La Manuela, one goal of the project was to establish that the ruins were those of a coffee plantation and to identify its owner. While Genaro Vidal and others knew that the site was once a coffee plantation, some local residents were unaware of its former usage. A few people knew the site was called "El Padre," but they believed that the great house was once a church and that a residence for the priest was located nearby, possibly within the enclosure.

By far, the greatest myth that this research debunked concerns the owner of the Cafetal Biajacas. Some Cuban scholars speculated that the owners were French expatriates because of the H-shaped floor plan of the great house at Cafetal Biajacas (Álvarez Estévez 2001:59–60). Documentary sources did not support this assessment. Although there are some gaps in record of ownership of the property, Ignacio O'Farrill was always identified as the owner when Cafetal Biajacas was functioning as a coffee plantation. It is possible that he obtained the property from the French owners, but with vast O'Farrill landholdings in the Madruga dating back to the 1780s, it seems more likely that Ignacio acquired the property from his family.

The fact that the floor plan of the great house contributed to ascribing the ownership of the cafetal to French coffee planters points to another popular myth—French immigrants introduced neoclassical architecture to Cuba. To attribute the introduction of neoclassicism in Cuba to one source grossly oversimplifies the ways that this international artistic movement influenced the art and architecture of Latin America (see Niell and Widdifield 2013). French immigrants may well have introduced the H-shaped floor plan to the Cuban countryside. But Ignacio O'Farrill was possibly introduced to neoclassical architecture in Havana, where his brothers built grand houses in that style during the first decade of the nineteenth century.

More significant than debunking local myths, the research undertaken for this study yielded artifacts and details on the extant ruins that have been recorded for future study and comparison with other Cuban plantation sites. The investigation of Cafetal Biajacas has been the most extensive archaeological study of a plantation in the Madruga area. Like all first-time research efforts, the findings and interpretations offered here are tentative and subject to change with additional investigations.

The legacy of Cafetal Biajacas endures. Archaeology is not just about the past but also about the present and how we engage with those who want to know about the past from the tangible remains around them. Although Genaro has passed away, other descendants of Patricio Pérez still live near the ruins of the Cafetal Biajacas. Over the years, they have assumed the role of unofficial stewards of the site, pointing out the location of artifacts, building foundations, and other areas of potential archaeological interest. Their knowledge of the site proved invaluable. The effort to conserve the site of Cafetal Biajacas as a local monument will make the site available for future generations to learn about the plantation and the enslaved people who lived behind the wall.

Abbreviations

AGT	Administración General Terrestre
AHPM	Archivo Histórico Provincial de Matanzas
ANC	Archivo Nacional de Cuba
Cotés	Escribanía de Cotés
FLMNH	Florida Museum of Natural History Digital Type Collections
Galletti	Escribanía Archivo de Galletti
GG	Gobierno General
GPC	Gobierno Provincial de Cimarrones
GPE	Gobierno Provincial Esclavos
GSC	Gobierno Superior Civil
JDWSFP	James DeWolf and Seymour Family Papers
ML	Miscelánea de Libros
MRH	Escribanía Mayor de Real Hacienda

Notes

Chapter 1. Introduction: The Object World of Cuban Slavery

1. Please note my usage of the words "slave" and "enslaved Cubans." I use the word "slave" as an adjective to describe a house, a laborer, clothing, etc. I do not use the word "slave" as a noun to denote a person or a people. I use "enslaved Cuban" to refer to any enslaved person who lived in Cuba, whether he or she was born in Africa or Cuba.

2. The late Enrique Sosa Rodríguez told me in 1999 of archaeological studies of two plantations, La Harmonica and La Luz, both in what was then Havana province that predated the Cuban Revolution. But I have been unsuccessful in finding more information about these investigations.

3. The building that houses the Archivo Histórico Provincial de Matanzas [AHPM] was closed from 2003 to 2008 due to a collapsed roof that damaged many of the records. When I used the archives in 2009, many of the records I wanted to examine were undergoing restoration and were unavailable to researchers.

Chapter 2. Locating Cafetal Biajacas

1. This map consolidates information from Pichardo (1860, 1872), United States (1899/1914), and a map of unknown provenance in a private collection that identified some of the plantation names or their owners in the area of Madruga.

2. José Ricardo O'Farrill y Herrera is often associated with Hotel Palacio O'Farrill, but it was Rafael who had it built. It is possible that Rafael's son, also named José Ricardo (1816–82), may have owned the house at some point.

3. The peso is used here to refer to what became known in English as the Spanish dollar. The peso was the coin upon which the original U.S. dollar was based, and it was used as legal tender in the United States until the 1857 Coinage Act forbade the use of foreign coins. The symbol ($) used to denote the dollar in the United States may also have originated from the Spanish peso (Aiton and Wheeler 1931:198; Nussbaum 1957:56–57).

Chapter 3. Cuban Coffee Sector

1. In my examination of the business correspondence in both the Lynch and Aymar Company Papers and the Moses Taylor Papers at the New-York Historical Society, Haitian coffee is curiously absent. Coffee from Santo Domingo, however, is always present on the coffee price lists. During the period from 1822 to 1843 when Haitian coffee was competing on the world market, the Spanish part of Hispaniola was under Haitian rule (Nicholls 1983:95). Therefore, coffee identified as Santo Domingan at that time was, in fact, Haitian.

2. The DeWolfs operated the largest slave trading business in the United States. After the abolition of the slave trade in 1808, James, George, and William DeWolf established coffee and sugar plantations in Cuba, and some of their correspondence suggests that they continued slave trading between Africa and Cuba. See DeWolf (2008) and the film *Traces of the Trade*, http://www.pbs.org/pov/tracesofthetrade.

3. Around the time the Goodwin diary ends, George DeWolf had developed serious financial problems and was unable to meet his obligations to the Bank of Bristol or to manage his other debts (George DeWolf Letters, 1827–28, A-1).

4. Cuban architectural studies have emphasized the townhouses rather than the plantation homes of Cuban elites. Llanes states that country houses "did not match the grandeur of those in town" (1999:158). While this is an accurate assessment, many Cuban plantation houses, now in ruins, have not been sufficiently studied to determine how grand they were. This is certainly the case with the casa vivienda at Cafetal Biajacas.

5. In the first half of the twentieth century, colonos—many of whom were recent immigrants to Cuba from Spain—produced coffee and cacao [chocolate]. Sarah Fidelzait and Juan Pérez de la Riva ([1973?] 1987) conducted a study of a community in Pinar del Río engaged in the production of these crops.

6. Information on present-day growing conditions was obtained from visits to coffee farms in the Dominican Republic and from www.coffeeresearch.org (accessed January 10, 2012).

7. Plantain, bananas, eucalyptus, and local indigenous plants are used today to produce shade-grown coffee. Though considerably more expensive than sun-grown coffee, shade-grown coffee is considered more environmentally sustainable than sun-grown varieties, introduced in the 1970s, that require chemical fertilizers and pesticides to produce high yields. Advocates of shade-grown coffee claim it tastes better, is healthier, creates bird habitats, and promotes biodiversity. Most fair-trade coffee is shade-grown, which helps small coffee producers. See www.coffeeresearch.com (accessed 02/11/12) and http://nationalzoo.si.edu/scbi/migratorybirds/coffee/default.cfm (accessed 9/22/13).

8. The remains of coffee plantations and the canals, dams, and reservoirs in the

Sierra Maestra region are one of UNESCO's World Heritage Sites: "Archaeological Landscape of the First Coffee Plantations in Southeast Cuba," located in the provinces of Santiago and Guantanamo. See http://whc.unesco.org/en/list/1008.

9. R. R. Madden (1853:172–74) estimated the length of the workday for enslaved laborers as 15–16 hours at a coffee plantation and 19–20 hours at a sugar plantation. As a staunch abolitionist, however, Madden possibly exaggerated these numbers, but two sources—Goodwin Diary (1820–27) and Amory Diary (1843)—suggest slave workers labored on coffee plantations an average of 12 hours a day.

10. Goodwin (1821–27) required enslaved workers to work on the following feast or holy days, official holidays in nineteenth-century Cuba: December 8, 1823, January 6, 1824, March 29 and 31, 1825, and April 1, 1825.

Chapter 4. Built Landscapes of Cuban Coffee Plantations

1. Although Sage owned these Cuban properties with his brother-in-law, Webster, Sage presents himself in his correspondence as the primary owner, and he was possibly their principal financier. The Cuban records, however, attribute these properties only to Webster (Barcia 2012:87–88; pers. comm. 2014).

2. William Deal described J. J. Latting's house in the city of Matanzas as "built more after the American style 90 feet front with a balcony on the second story which is the part we live in the lower story being occupied for bedrooms for the kitchen, servants, offices etc." (W. S. Deall to Sister Carolina, February 5, 1822, Latting Family Papers, box 1, folder A). On March 7, 1839, Eulalia Keating recorded in her diary a description of the Macomb plantation house at Santa Victoria as built in "the American Style—Basement story, parlors and pantries on the first floor and the chambers on the 2nd floor"; on the next day, she described Mr. Howland's house at a plantation named Trinidad as "a nice American house" (Bauduy Family Papers).

3. Some local residents remembered bulldozers being present on the site of Biajacas in the 1980s, but they were unaware of their purpose. Bulldozing was not evident in site stratigraphy of Biajacas, but the mixture of archaeological materials, particularly in the excavations of locus D, may be an indication of such activity.

4. Interiors of historical Cuban houses are found in García Santana (1999) and Llanes (1999). Over the years, I have visited numerous Cuban museums that recreate the interiors of nineteenth-century houses once belonging to elite Cubans.

5. In units excavated in and around locus C, we were able to recognize three distinct strata. The uppermost stratum contained building debris, particularly from the *teja* roof. Below the building debris, a second stratum contained only cafetalera artifacts and presumably the original earthen floor within the small wing. The third and lowest stratum was devoid of artifacts.

6. Shovel test pits (STPs) refer to a field strategy used to identify buried archaeological resources. By digging small test pits (about 30–50 cm) at regular intervals, it is possible to discover areas of artifact concentration and to locate foundations and other intact remains. We attempted STPs in the slave settlement but abandoned them because they did not yield the desired results.

7. The legal and ethical considerations involved in archaeological investigations of burials were nonissues in Cuba at that time. Even so, though I was uncomfortable about excavating what might be a cemetery, I agreed with my Cuban colleagues to the testing because we thought that by locating and identifying the cemetery we could possibly protect it from future destruction. The Cuban team investigated Area E in December 2005, as I was unable to travel to Cuba at that time.

8. This slave revolt was fictionalized by Mercedes Santa Cruz y Montalvo, the Countess de Merlin, in her *La Havane*, a three-volume work published in 1844 and set on the plantation of her cousin, Rafael Montalvo (Méndez Rodenas 1998:170–71). Both the Countess de Merlin and Rafael Montalvo were related to the O'Farrills through marriage (Cornide Hernández 2008:245–46, 501; Méndez Rodenas 1998:20, 24).

Chapter 5. Housing Enslaved Cubans

1. Many of the Cuban slave codes have been translated into English. On the 1789 royal decree and for excerpts from the 1842 slave code, see García Rodríguez (2011:55–73, 80–84); on the codes following the 1825 slave revolt, see Barcia (2012:162–79); and for the 1842 and 1844 codes, see Paquette (1988:267–74).

2. The word *cuje* has several unrelated definitions in Cuba. Here, the word refers to a flexible plant material used to build the woven basketlike lattice of a wattle structure. Carley and Brizzi (1997:73) define *cuje* as a "native cane fiber." García Santana (1999:56, 63 fig. 29, 64 fig. 34) uses *cuje* to refer to a type of building construction found predominantly in Santiago de Cuba that is similar to wattle-and-daub but that instead of earth or mud uses a lime-based plaster with gravel inclusions.

Examples of the yagua bohío in nineteenth-century fiction include Ramon de Palma ([1838] 1929:43) and Mary Peabody Mann ([1887] 2000:39).

3. Examples of enslaved people building African-style housing in North America can be found in Du Bois ([1908] 1969:49); Georgia Writers Project (1940:179); Ferguson (1992:63–82); and McDaniel (1982:34–35).

4. The word *barracón* is found on the 1824 list of costs for the cafetal of Rafael O'Farrill y Arrendondo. See González Fernández (1991:179).

5. References to clandestine slave activities in bohíos are sometimes mentioned in legal proceedings and reports of local law enforcement officials. See, for example, Barcia Zequeira (2003:144–45); Escoto Collection, Ms. 712, "Conspiracies."

6. The project team observed and inspected the standing ruins of barracones-nave at the former Cafetales Carriera, Santa Brigada, and Zangroniz, all which are located near Cafetal Biajacas see (figure 2.1), and at Cafetales Santa Ana Azabache and Bocalandro (also known as Nuestra Señora del Carmen) near San José de las Lajas in Mayabeque province. We also visited the presumed ruins of a barracón-patio at the ingenio la Luz and another one at the ingenio Potugalete that had been converted into apartments, also near San José de las Lajas. Note that Zangroniz, originally a cafetal, was converted into a *cafetal-ingenio* (coffee and sugar plantation) but is indicated as an ingenio on the Pichardo maps.

7. Except when noted, Spanish measurements are based upon units of measure issued from Spain in 1801 that can be accessed at http://www.convert-me.com.

8. Note that this proposed configuration of slave bohíos is different from that published in Singleton (2003).

9. A few present-day bohíos near Cafetal Biajacas were measured to determine their dimensions.

Chapter 6. Enslaved Actors and Provisioning

1. Studies using the testimony of enslaved Cubans from judicial proceedings include Barcia (2008, 2012); Barcia Zequeira (2003); Childs (2006); García (2003b, 2011); and Van Norman (2013).

2. Hall appears somewhat ambivalent on the fluidity of ethnicity. On one hand, she embraces this approach to ethnicity when she cites Boubacar Barry (1998) to describe the ongoing process of the making of ethnicity in Africa (2005:52). At the same time, she insists that ethnic designations used in the Americas originated in Africa because they were self-identifications. For archaeological case studies that approach African ethnicity as fluid and situational, see DeCorse, ed. (2001).

3. Hall and Barcia are in general agreement on the relationship between specific ethnic designations in the Americas and corresponding African cultural groups, with the exception of Minas. Barcia (2008:19–20) associates Minas with Elmina and assumes they were related to the Gold Coast groups such as the Fante. Hall (2005:12) associates the nineteenth-century use of Minas in Cuba with an ethnicity exported from the Slave Coast.

4. References to James DeWolf's provisioning of his Cuban coffee plantations include the following: "Invoice of Sundries shipped by James DeWolfe on board Brig Neptune Simon and Liscomb master for Matanzas and consigned to rep. Drake and Coit to be forwarded to the Mount Hope Estate," DeWolf Papers, MSS 382, RHS; James DeWolf to Stephan S. Hales, August 17 and October 20, 1817; James DeWolf to Drake & Coit, May 11, 1831; James DeWolf to Alex Griswald, August 1, 1831, JDWSFP.

5. Several travel accounts indicate that enslaved people in Cuba raised livestock

primarily for sale. See Abbot (1829:97); Ballou (1854:194); Bremer (1853, 2:318); Dimock (1998:96); Lowell (2003:84); Wurdemann ([1844] 1970:144–45).

6. I was first introduced to these artifacts when I was a graduate student. A fellow graduate student recovered them from a late nineteenth-century site near Gainesville, Florida. None of the historically known occupants of the site was African American. White descendants of the former occupants said they used the glass scrapers to shave off sugarcane husks.

7. Local tradition depicts Souchay as a benevolent, antiracist slaveholder to the enslaved people at Angerona, perhaps because he hired Úrsula Lambert, a free black woman born in San Domingue, to manage the domestic affairs of his plantation and allegedly had a love affair with her. Despite his relationship with Lambert, Souchay still may have disapproved of interactions between enslaved people on his plantation and free blacks.

8. Abiel Abbot (1829:97) estimated the value of an ounce of gold in Cuba to be between $16.60 and $20.00 in 1828; Mary Gardiner Lowell (2003:85) indicates that an ounce was worth approximately $17.00 in 1831.

9. A Spanish resolution passed July 1, 1837, authorized the síndico to assist in the defense of enslaved persons and required their owners to pay the expenses (Barcia Zequeira 2003:49).

Chapter 7. Consumption and Life within the Enclosure

1. Casella (2007:132) describes how inmates in prisons refashioned spoons and forks into a lock pick and skeleton key (2007:99) and how Native American students, placed in a mandatory boarding school, made tools similar to the glass scrapers at Cafetal Biajacas from window glass, bottle fragments, and even ceramic plates).

2. I am grateful to archaeozoologist Osvaldo Jiménez of the Gabinete de Archaeología (my host institution in Cuba) for identifying the jutía conga remains as well as for his overall guidance in confirming my identifications of the faunal remains.

3. For examples of these lead-glazed earthenwares, see the Digital Type Collection, Historical Archaeology, FLMNH. http://www.flmnh.ufl.edu/histarch/gallery_types/type_index_display.asp?type_name=LEADGLAZEDCOARSE EARTHENWARE.

4. For examples of marineware variants, see the FLMNH collection at http://www.flmnh.ufl.edu/histarch/gallery_types/type_index_display.asp?type_name=MARINEWAREVARIANT.

5. A recipe for *maiz de finado criollo* in Langarika ([1862] 1997:79) is a variation of funche made from coarsely ground dried corn boiled in water. A Cuban dish known today as *tamal en cazuela* may also be a variation of funche.

6. Adenathera pavonia, *World Agroforestry Database 4.0* (Orwa et al. 2009), at http://www.worldagroforestry.org/treedb/AFTPDFS/Adenanthera_pavonina.pdf (accessed January 22, 2015).

7. Mouth harps also have been recovered from slave quarters at Monticello and Poplar Forest and are on display in exhibitions at both sites.

Chapter 8. Conflict and Compromise

1. The works by Gabino La Rosa Corzo cited herein represent a small selection of his publications on Cuban maroons and related topics.

2. For specific references to the possession of calabozo machetes by runaway slaves, see AHPM GPC, 1828 leg. 12, no. 23; 1829, leg. 12, no. 23a; 1870 leg. 17, no. 16.

References

Manuscript Collections

Amory, Thomas

1843 Thomas Amory Diary and Other Writings. Amory Family Papers. Massachusetts Historical Society, Boston.

Archivo Histórico Provincial de Matanzas (AHPM)

Fondo: Gobierno Provincial de Cimarrones (GPC)

AHPM GPC legajo 12, no. 23. 1828. Comunicación A. D. Ceillo Ayllon, gobernador de Matanzas sobre ranchería contra un palenque de Negroes situado entre la vega de Guerra, espinal y los hatos los alrededores de puerto Escondido y orillas de las playa, capturando 2 negroes y una negra.

AHPM GPC legajo 12, no. 23a. 1829. Comunicación al Gobernador de Matanzas sobre la captura de 2 negros cimarrones, los que declaran que se hallaban ocultos en una cueva cerca de 300 ellos de ambos sexos.

AHPM GPC legajo 12, no. 25. 1829. Comunicaciones al Gobernador de Matanzas adjuntando relación de cimarrones en el partido, correspondiente al mes de Noviembre incluyendo apalencados en el pan y cuevas de Espinal.

AHPM GPC legajo 12, no. 50. 1837. Don Mariano Paradas, Capitán de Ceiba Mocha al Gobernador de Matanzas. Ceiba Mocha, 25 de diciembre de 1837 Comunicaciones a Antonio García Oña, Gobernador de Matanzas, sobre ranchería contra una partida de cimarrones apostados en los barracones del cafetal Santa Ana de Biajacas, del Presbítero O'Farrill a los que se les incorporaron negros de esa finca.

AHPM GPC legajo 12, no. 71. 1842. Comunicaciones acerca de agresiones de cimarrones que huyeron en dirección a las lomas de Cayajabo, capitanía de Madruga; orientación acerca de que los gastos ocasionados por la captura de cimarrones se paguen por la Junta de Fomento correspondiente; aprehensión de tres negros y presentación de 7.

AHPM GPC legajo 17, no. 16. 1870. Comunicaciones del Gobernador de Matanzas sobre batida en los montes de Biajaca, partido de Madruga, en busca de cimarrones, capturados 2.

Fondo: Gobierno Provincial Esclavos (GPE)

AHPM GPE legajo 12, no. 5a. 1817. Estadísticas de Esclavos y libres de Color Extranjeros y cimarrones en el partido y mes de la fecha.

Archivo Nacional de Cuba (ANC)

Fondo: Administración General Terrestre (AGT)

ANC AGT legajo 170, no. 16. 1823. El 20 de octubre de 1823 el Presbítero Don Ignacio O'Farrill vendió a Basilio Perdomo in Toma de razón de las escrituras que a partir de 26 de agosto de 1813 al 29 de marzo de 1829 se otorgaron.

Fondo: Escribanía de Cotés (Cotés)

ANC Cotés legajo 227, no. 7. 1849–53. Expediente seguido para cobrar a los bienes del Sr. Pbo. D. Ignacio O'Farrill reditos del impuesto que sufre el Cafetal la Vija o Viajaca a favor de los cultos del Santísimo Sacramento y corre agregado el cuaderno de competencia para reclamar el concurso y testamento del Sr. Pbro. O'Farrill.

Fondo: Escribanía Archivo de Galletti (Galletti)

ANC Galletti legajo 240, no. 1. 1838–39. Concurso del Sr. Presbítero Don Ignacio O'Farrill, 8 piezas.

ANC Galletti legajo 242, no. 15. 1839. Incidente la testamentaría concursada del Sr. Pbro. D. Ignacio O'Farrill formado sobre que D. Gabriel J. Valdés rinda las cuentas de la administración de los bienes que dejó dicho señor.

ANC Galletti legajo 245, no. 1. 1838–39. Testamentaría de Señor Presbítero Ignacio O'Farrill, 2 piezas.

ANC Galletti legajo 934, no. 6. 1841. Incidente a la testamentaría del Sr. Presbítero Don Ignacio O'Farrill sobre la venta de bienes.

Fondo: Escribanía Mayor de Real Hacienda (MRH)

ANC MRH legajo 142, no. 2662. 1834. Testamentaria del Presbítero Don Ignacio O'Farrill y Herrera.

Fondo: Gobierno General (GG)

ANC GG legajo 562, no. 27528. 1862. Padrón de fincas rústicas de la jurisdicción y parroquia de Madruga.

Fondo: Gobierno Superior Civil (GSC)

ANC GSC legajo 1158. 1768. Fomento del café. 8 de marzo de 1768.

ANC GSC legajo 871, no. 29460. 1822. Expediente sobre las Ordenanzas municipales y plan describiros del pueblo de Madruga.

ANC GSC legajo 1469, no. 57999. 1825. Reglamento de Policía Rural del La Jurisdicción del Gobierno de Matanzas.

ANC GSC legajo 997, no. 33070. 1835. Expediente sobre Gobernador sobre sublevación en Macuriges.

ANC GSC legajo 996, no. 33048. 1836. Sobre multar á los negros que después de la oración salgan á vender por las fincas.

ANC GSC legajo 998, no. 33105. 1838. Sobre la denudes y escaso alimento Ingenio Lima, Matanzas.

ANC GSC legajo 938, no. 33102. 1839. Sobre del permisión experimentan las fincas con el baile tambores y reiterando la prohibición que las negradas se gobiernen mayorales.

ANC GSC legajo 939, no. 33131. 1840. Sobre el alzamiento de los negros de cafetal José Cantos Valdespino situado entro los partidos de la Ceiba del Agua y Vereda Nueva.

ANC GSC legajo 617, no. 19712. 1841. Expediente en que el Capitán de Madruga participa haberse fugado varios negros del Ingenio San Juan de Nepomuceno, perteneciente al Presbítero Don Ignacio O'Farrill.

ANC GSC legajo 940, no. 33158. 1842. Expediente sobre los informar pedidos acerca de un reglamento higiénico para la esclavitud de la Isla.

ANC GSC legajo 941, no. 33186. 1842. Expediente sobre para reformar el sistema moral, higiénico, y alimentario de los siervos que se emplean en la agricultura.

ANC GSC legajo 942, no. 33246. 1843. Expediente sobre la falta seguridad en las habitaciones de los negros en las fincas.

ANC GSC legajo 945, no. 33309. 1846. Establecer mejoras su los alimentos de los esclavos de nuestro campos.

ANC GSC legajo 947, no. 33399. 1852. Expediente instruido a consecuencia de la reclamación que hace el negro Juan [Lucumí] Garro contra D. Ramón de Abila [Avila], sobre productor de conucos de tabacos y otros efectos.

ANC GSC legajo 1129, no. 41699. 1856. Expediente sobre los hacendados vecinos de Cayajabo Don Antonio Ramos, Don Agustín Méndez, Don Sebastián Sánchez, Don Tomás Alvarez, Don Juan Fragoso, Don Manuel Rabelo y Don José Crespo solicitan que se le avecinden en el partido de Madruga y no en el de Cayajabos donde se hallan por estar a cinco leguas de la Capitanía y a nueve de la Cabecera.

Fondo: Miscelánea de Libros (ML)

ANC ML legajo 1149. 1772–79. Libro índice de fincas rústicas. Imposiciones sobre corrales, hatos y haciendas de las jurisdicciones de La Habana y Matanzas (1772–79).

Fondo: Protocolo de Salinas

1788. Adjudicación de Doña Luisa Herrera a sus hijos.

1829a. Cancelación de Don Ignacio O'Farrill a Don José Basilio Perdomo.

1829b. Imposición de Don Ignacio O'Farrill a Don Nicolás Manuel de Escovedo y Rivero.

1829c. Libertad a Doña Micaela de Don Ignacio O'Farrill.

1829d. Obligación de Don Ignacio O'Farrill a Juan Almazy.

Bauduy Family Papers, Bauduy Family Letters, and Eulalia Keating Journal during Trip to Cuba, 1838–39. Hagley Museum and Archives, Wilmington, Del.

DeWolf Papers. Rhode Island Historical Society, Providence, R.I. MS 382, Plantation Accounts, 1818–52, box 8, folder 1.

DeWolf, George. Letters, 1827–28 A-1. Bristol Historical Society, Bristol, R.I.

DeWolf, James, and Seymour Family Papers (JDWSFP), 1795–1904. Historical Collections MS 766, D534, 4 vols. Baker Library, Harvard School of Business, Boston.

Emerson, George. Diary, 1846. George B. Emerson volumes, 1825–48 diaries. Massachusetts Historical Society, Boston.

Escoto, Jose Augustus Collection, ca. 1574–1922. Cuban Literature and History Collection. MS no. 712: Report of incidents of revolt at plantations in Camarioca (Matanzas, Cuba). Houghton Library, Harvard College Library, Harvard University, Cambridge.

Goodwin, Joseph. Diary of Joseph Goodwin, son of Joseph Goodwin, Hudson, Columbia Co., New York, June 26, 1820, to March 6, 1827, while employed on plantations [Buena Esperanza and Arca de Noe], near Matanzas, Cuba. New-York Historical Society, New York.

Latting Family Papers, 1806–45, 2 boxes. Long Island Studies Institute, Rare Books and Manuscripts, Hofstra University, Long Island, New York.

Lynch and Aymar Company Papers. New-York Historical Society, New York.

Moses Taylor Papers. New-York Historical Society, New York.

Sage, Ebenezer William. Three Letterbooks, 1813–25, and Ebenezer William Sage Papers. Massachusetts Historical Society, Boston.

Townsend, Peter S. Diary of P. S. Townsend of New York, Matanzas—Island of Cuba—Charleston, S.C., 1830[?]. Peter S. Townsend Diaries Series 3, Vol. 2. New York Academy of Medicine, New York.

United States 1899, Adjutant General Office, War Department, RG 77 WDMC, 132 Cuba. Military Map of Section of Cuba, "Mariel to Cardenas, Based on Pichardo." Cartographic Collection, National Archives of the United States, College Park, Md.

United States 1914, Adjutant General Office, War Department, series E 723, Sheet 3884 IV. "Madruga." Geography and Map Collection, General Staff Map Collection, Library of Congress, Washington, D.C.

Published and Secondary Sources

Abbot, Abiel

1829 *Letters Written in the Interior of Cuba, between the Mountains of Arcana, to the East, and of Cusco to the West, in the months of February, March, April, and May.* Bowles and Dearborn, Boston.

Adams, William H., and Sarah J. Boling

1989 Status and Ceramics for Planters and Slaves on Three Georgia Coastal Plantations. *Historical Archaeology* 23(1):69–96.

Agorsah, Kofi E.

1993 Archaeology and Resistance History in the Caribbean. *African Archaeology Review* 11:175–95.

Agostini, Camilla

2013 A sombra da clandestinidade: Práticas religiosas e encontro cultural no tempo do tráfico ilegal de esclavos. *Vestígios: Revista Latino-Americana de Arqueologia Histórica* 7(1):75–104.

Aiton, Arthur S., and Benjamin W. Wheeler

1931 The First American Mint. *Hispanic American Historical Review* 11(2):198–215.

Álvarez Estévez, Rolando

2001 *Huellas francesas en el occidente de Cuba (siglos XVI–XIX).* Editorial José Martí, Havana.

Andueza, José M.

1841 *Isla de Cuba, pintoresca, histórica, política, mercantil e industrial: Recuerdos y apuntes de dos épocas.* Boix, Madrid.

Armstrong, Douglas V.

1990 *The Old Village and the Great House: An Archaeological and Historical Examination of Drax Hall.* University of Illinois Press, Urbana.

1999 Archaeology and Ethnohistory of a Caribbean Plantation. In *"I, Too, Am America": Archaeological Studies of African-American Life,* edited by Theresa A. Singleton, 173–92. University Press of Virginia, Charlottesville.

Armstrong, Douglas V., and Kenneth G. Kelly

2000 Settlement Patterns and the Origins of African Jamaican Society: Seville Plantation, St. Ann's Bay, Jamaica. *Ethnohistory* 47(2):369–97.

Arnoldi, Mary Jo

1995 Introduction. In *Crowning Achievements: African Arts of Dressing the Head,* edited by Mary Jo Arnoldi and Christine Mullen Kreamer, 9–25. Fowler Museum of Culture History, Los Angeles.

Arnoldi, Mary Jo, and Christine M. Kreamer (editors)

1995 *Crowning Achievements: African Arts of Dressing the Head.* Fowler Museum of Culture History, Los Angeles.

Arrazcaeta, Roger
1999 Cerámica inglesa en la Habana colonial. *Opus Habana* 3(3–4):45–49.
Ascher, Robert, and Charles H. Fairbanks
1971 Excavation of a Slave Cabin, Georgia, U.S.A. *Historical Archaeology* 5:3-17.
Ballou, Maturin
1854 *History of Cuba; or, Notes of a Traveller in the Tropics*. Phillips, Sampson, Boston.
Barcia, Manuel
2008 *Seeds of Insurrection: Domination and Resistance on Western Cuban Plantations, 1808–1848*. Louisiana State University Press, Baton Rouge.
2012 *The Great African Slave Revolt of 1825: Cuba and the Fight for Freedom in Matanzas*. Louisiana State University, Baton Rouge.
2014 West African Islam in Colonial Cuba. *Slavery and Abolition* 35(2):292–305.
Barcia Zequeira, María del Carmen
2003 *La otra familia: Parientes, redes, y descendencia de los esclavos en Cuba*. Casa de las Américas, Havana.
Barry, Boubacar
1998 *Senegambia and the Atlantic Slave Trade*. Translated by Ayi Kwei Armah. Cambridge University Press, Cambridge, UK.
Basso Ortiz, Alessandra
2005 *Los Gangá en Cuba: La communidad de Matanzas*. Fundación de Fernando Ortiz, Havana.
Battle-Baptiste, Whitney
2007 "In This Here Place": Interpreting Enslaved Homeplaces. In *Archaeology of Atlantic Africa and the African Diaspora*, edited by Akinwumi Ogundiran and Toyin Falola, 233–48. Indiana University Press, Bloomington.
2011 *Black Feminist Archaeology*. Left Coast Press, Walnut Creek, Calif.
Bennett, Hugh, and Robert Y. Allison
1928 *The Soils of Cuba*. Tropical Plant Research Foundation, Washington, D.C.
Bentmann, Reinhard, and Michael Müller
[1970] 1992 *The Villa as Hegemonic Architecture*. Translated by Tim Spence and David Craven. Humanities Press, Atlantic Highlands, N.J.
Bergad, Laird W.
1990 *Cuban Rural Society in the Nineteenth Century: The Social and Economic History of Monoculture in Matanzas*. Princeton University Press, Princeton, N.J.
Bergad, Laird W., Fe Iglesias García, and María del Carmen Barcia
1995 *The Cuban Slave Market, 1700–1880*. Cambridge University Press, New York.
Berlin, Ira, and Philip D. Morgan (editors)
1991 *The Slaves' Economy: Independent Production by Slaves in the Americas*. Frank Cass, London.

1993 *Cultivation and Culture: Labor and the Shaping of Slave Life in the Americas.* University Press of Virginia, Charlottesville.

Berman, Mary Jane, Jorge Febles, and Perry L. Gnivecki

2005 The Organization of Cuban Archaeology: Context and Brief History. In *Dialogues in Cuban Archaeology*, edited by L. Antonio Curet, Shannon Lee Dawdy, and Gabino La Rosa Corzo, 41–61. University of Alabama Press, Tuscaloosa.

Bernard Bosch, Luciano, Victor Blanco Conde, and Alexis Rives Pantoja

1985 *La Manuela: Arqueología de un cafetal habanero.* Editorial de Ciencias Sociales, Havana.

Bourdieu, Pierre

1985 The Social Space and Genesis of Groups. *Theory and Society* 14(6):723–44.

Boytel Jambú, Fernando

1961 Restauración de un cafetal de los colonos franceses en la Sierra Maestra. *Revista de arqueología y etnología* 5(1):27–56.

Brandon, George

1993 *Santería from Africa to the New World: The Dead Sell Memories.* Indiana University Press, Bloomington.

Braudel, Fernand

1979 *The Wheels of Commerce: Civilization and Capitalism, 15th–18th Century.* Vol. 2. Harper and Row, New York.

Bremer, Fredrika

1853 *Homes of the New World: Impressions of America.* Vol. 2. Translated by Mary Howitt. Harper and Brothers, New York.

Brighenti, Andre M.

2010 At the Wall: Graffiti, Writers, Territoriality, and the Public Domain. *Space and Culture* 13(3):315–32.

Brooks, James F., Christopher R. N. DeCorse, and John Walton (editors)

2008 *Small Worlds: Method, Meaning, and Narrative in Microhistory.* School for Advanced Research Press, Santa Fe, N.M.

Brown, David H.

2003 *Santería Enthroned: Art, Ritual, and Innovation in an Afro-Cuban Religion.* University of Chicago Press, Chicago.

Brown, Kenneth L., and Doreen Cooper

1990 Structural Continuity in an African-American Slave and Tenant Community. *Historical Archaeology* 24(4):7–19.

Buck-Morss, Susan

2009 *Hegel, Haiti, and Universal History.* University of Pittsburgh Press, Pittsburgh.

Burroughs, Charles

2013 The Plantation Landscape and Its Architecture: Classicism, Representation, and Slavery. In *Buen Gusto and Classicism in the Visual Cultures of Latin America, 1780–1910*, edited by Paul Niell and Stacie G. Widdifield, 114–35. University of New Mexico Press, Albuquerque.

Butler, Judith

1990 *Gender Trouble: Feminism and the Subversion of Identity*. Routledge, London.

Cabanillas, Berta, and Carmen Ginorio

[1956] 2002 *Puerto Rican Dishes*. 4th ed. Editorial de la Universidad de Puerto Rico, San Juan.

Caldeira, Teresa P. R.

2000 *City of Walls: Crime, Segregation, and Citizenship in Sao Paulo*. University of California Press, Berkeley.

Camp, Stephanie M. H.

2004 *Closer to Freedom: Enslaved Women and Everyday Resistance in the Plantation South*. University of North Carolina Press, Chapel Hill.

Cantero, Justo G.

[1857] 2005 *Los ingenios: Colección de vistas de los principales ingenios de azúcar de la isla de Cuba*. Edited by Luis Miguel García Mora and Antonio Santamaría García. Ediciones Doce Calles, Havana.

Cantón Navarro, José

2001 *History of Cuba: The Challenge of the Yoke and Star: Biography of a People*. SI-MAR, Havana.

Carley, Rachel, and Andrea Brizzi

1997 *Cuba: 400 Years of Architectural Heritage*. Whitney Library of Design, New York.

Carraz Hernández, Orlando, and Ramón González Caraballo

2004 Informe preliminar de los trabajos geofísicos realizados en áreas del cafetal "El Padre." Unpublished report. Departamento de Geociencias, Instituto Superior Politécnico José Antonio Echeverría (ISPJAE), Havana.

Casella, Eleanor Conlin

2007 *The Archaeology of Institutional Confinement*. University Press of Florida, Gainesville.

Casella, Eleanor, and James Symonds (editors)

2005 *Industrial Archaeology: Future Directions*. Springer, New York.

Certeau, Michel de

1988 *The Practice of Everyday Life*. Translated by Steven Rendall. University of California Press, Berkeley.

Chapman, William

[1991] 2010 Slave Villages in the Danish West Indies: Changes in the Late Eighteenth and Early Nineteenth Centuries. In *Cabin, Quarter, Plantation: Archi-*

tecture and Landscapes of North American Slavery, edited by Clifton Ellis and Rebecca Ginsburg, 99–120. Yale University Press, New Haven, Conn.

Chappell, Edward

2010 Accommodating Slavery in Bermuda. In *Cabin, Quarter, Plantation: Architecture and Landscapes of North American Slavery*, edited by Clifton Ellis and Rebecca Ginsburg, 67–98. Yale University Press, New Haven, Conn.

Chateausalins, Honorato Bernard de

1854 El Vademécum de los Hacendados Cubanos o Guía Práctica para curar la mayor parte de las enfermedades. Imprenta de Manuel Soler. http://www.archive.org/details/elvademecumdelos00bern.

Childs, Matt D.

2006 *The 1812 Aponte Rebellion in Cuba and the Struggle against Atlantic Slavery*. University of North Carolina Press, Chapel Hill.

Cornide Hernández, María Teresa

2008 *De la Havana, de siglos y de familias*. 2nd ed. Editorial de Ciencias Sociales, Havana.

Cremé Ramos, Zoe, and Rafael Duharte Jiménez

1994 ¿Barracones en los cafetales? In *Colección Santiago de Cuba*. Publicigraf, Havana.

Crook, Ray

2001 Gullah and the Task System. *Anthropology of Work Review* 22(2):24–28.

Dana, Richard Henry

[1859] 1966 *To Cuba and Back*. Edited and with introduction by C. Harvey Gardiner. Southern Illinois University Press, Carbondale.

Davis, Dave D.

1996 Revolutionary Archaeology in Cuba. *Journal of Archaeological Method and Theory* 3(2):159–88.

Dawdy, Shannon Lee

2002 *La comida mambisa*: Food, Farming, and Cuban Identity. *(NWIG) New West Indian Guide Nieuwe West-Indische Gids* 76(1–2):47–80.

Dawdy, Shannon Lee, and Richard Weyhing

2008 Beneath the Rising Sun: "Frenchness," and the Archaeology of Desire. *International Journal of Historical Archaeology* 12:370–87.

Deagan, Kathleen

1987 *Artifacts of the Spanish Colonies of Florida and the Caribbean, 1500–1800*. Vol. 1 of *Ceramics, Glassware, and Beads*. Smithsonian Institution Press, Washington, D.C.

2002 *Artifacts of the Spanish Colonies of Florida and the Caribbean, 1500–1800*. Vol. 2 of *Portable Personal Possessions*. Smithsonian Institution Press, Washington, D.C.

Deagan, Kathleen, and José María Cruxent
2002 *Columbus's Outpost among the Taínos: Spain and America at La Isabela, 1493–1498*. Yale University Press, New Haven, Conn.
DeCorse, Christopher
2001a *An Archaeology of Elmina: Africans and Europeans of the Gold Coast, 1400–1900*. Smithsonian Institution Press, Washington, D.C.
DeCorse, Christopher R. (editor)
2001b *West Africa during the Era of the Atlantic Trade: Archaeological Perspectives*. Leicester University Press, London.
DeCorse, Christopher R., Francois Richard, and Ibrahima Thiaw
2003 Toward a Systematic Bead Identification System: A View from the Lower Falemme, Senegal. *Journal of African Archaeology* 1(1):77–110.
Deetz, James
1990 Prologue: Landscapes as Cultural Statements. In *Earth Patterns: Essays in Landscape Archaeology*, edited by William M. Kelso and Rachel Most, 1–4. University Press of Virginia, Charlottesville.
Delle, James
1998 *An Archaeology of Social Space: Analyzing Coffee Plantations in Jamaica's Blue Mountains*. Plenum, New York.
2014 *The Colonial Caribbean: Landscapes of Power in the Plantation System*. Cambridge University Press, New York.
DeMarrais, Elizabeth, Chris Gosden, and Colin Renfrew
2005 Introduction. In *Rethinking Materiality: The Engagement of Mind and the Material World*, edited by Elizabeth DeMarrais, Chris Gosden, and Colin Renfrew, 1–7. McDonald Institute for Archaeological Research, Cambridge, UK.
DeWolf, Thomas N.
2008 *Inheriting the Trade: A Northern Family Confronts Its Legacy as the Largest Slaveholder Family in the United States*. Beacon, Boston.
Dimock, Joseph
1998 *Impressions of Cuba in the Nineteenth Century: The Travel Diary of Joseph J. Dimock*. Edited by Louis A. Pérez. Scholarly Resources, Wilmington, Del.
Domínguez, Lourdes S.
1986 Fuentes arqueológicas en el estudio de la esclavitud en Cuba. In *La Esclavitud en Cuba*, edited by Academía de Ciencias de Cuba, 266–79. Editorial Academia, Havana.
1999 *Los collares en la santería cubana*. José Martí, Havana.
2005 Historical Archaeology in Cuba. In *Dialogues in Cuban Archaeology*, edited by L. Antonio Curet, Shannon L. Dawdy, and Gabino La Rosa Corzo, 62–71. University of Alabama Press, Tuscaloosa.

Domínguez González, Lourdes S.
1991 Las ruinas de los cafetales de la Sierra del Rosario, Pinar del Río, Cuba. In *Arqueología de Cuba y de otras áreas antillanas*, 264–70. Editorial Academia, Havana.
2004 Guanabacoa: "Una experiencia india" en nuestra colonización. *Gabinete de Arqueología Boletín* 3:4–11.
Du Bois, W.E.B.
[1908] 1969 *The Negro American Family*. Negro Universities Press, Westport, Conn.
Dumont, Alejandro B. C.
[1823] 1833 *Consideraciones sobre el cultivo del café en esta Isla*. Havana. Reprinted in Guatemala, Gobierno Supremo del Estado.
Egerton, Douglas R.
2010 Slave Resistance. In *The Oxford Handbook of Slavery in the Americas*, edited by Robert Paquette and Mark M. Smith, 447–64. Oxford University Press, New York.
Ekunsanmi, Toye
2010 *What Africans Eat: Traditional Foods and Food Traditions of West Africa*. Outskirts Press, Denver.
Ellis, Clifton
2010 Building for "Our Family, Black and White": The Changing Form of the Slave House in Antebellum Virginia. In *Cabin, Quarter, Plantation: Architecture and Landscapes of North American Slavery*, edited by Clifton Ellis and Rebecca Ginsburg, 144–55. Yale University Press, New Haven, Conn.
Ellis, Clifton, and Rebecca Ginsburg
2010 Introduction. In *Cabin, Quarter, Plantation: Architecture and Landscapes of North American Slavery*, edited by Clifton Ellis and Rebecca Ginsburg, 1–15. Yale University Press, New Haven, Conn.
Ellis, Clifton, and Rebecca Ginsburg (editors)
2010 *Cabin, Quarter, and Plantation: Architecture and Landscapes of North American Slavery*. Yale University Press, New Haven, Conn.
Ely, Roland T.
[1963] 2001 *Cuando reinaba su Majestad el Azúcar: Estudio Histórico-Sociológico de una Tragada Latinoamericana: El Monocultivo en Cuba. Origen y Evolución del Proceso*. Imagen Contemporánea, Havana.
Epperson, Terrence
1990 Race and the Disciplines of the Plantation. *Historical Archaeology* 24(4):29–49.
Fairbanks, Charles, H.
1972 *The Kingsley Slave Cabins in Duval County, Florida, 1968*. Conference on Historic Site Archaeology Papers, 1971 7:62–93.

Fennell, Christopher C.
2007 *Crossroads and Cosmologies: Diasporas and Ethnogenesis in the New World.* University Press of Florida, Gainesville.
Ferguson, Leland
1992 *Uncommon Ground: Archaeology and Early African America, 1650–1800.* Smithsonian Institution Press, Washington, D.C.
Fesler, Garrett
2004 From Houses to Homes: An Archaeological Case Study of Household Formation at the Utopia Slave Quarter, ca. 1675 to 1775. PhD dissertation, University of Virginia, Charlottesville.
Fidelzait, Sarah, and Juan Pérez de la Riva
[1973?] 1987 *San Jose de Sumidero: Demografia social en el campo cubano.* Editorial de Ciencias Sociales, Havana.
Figueras, Francisco
1959 *Cuba y su evolución colonial.* Editorial Cenit, Havana.
Fischer, Sibylle
2004 *Modernity Disavowed: Haiti and the Cultures of Slavery in the Age of Revolution.* Duke University Press, Durham, N.C.
Foster, Helen Bradley
1997 *"New Raiments of Self": African American Clothing in the Antebellum South.* Oxford University Press, New York.
Foucault, Michel
1979 *Discipline and Punishment: The Birth of the Prison.* Translated by Alan Sheridan. Vintage Books, New York.
Franco, José Luciano
1973 *Los Palenques de los Negros Cimarrones, Colección Historia.* Comisión de Activistas de Historia, Havana.
Galle, Jillian
2010 Costly Signaling and Gendered Social Strategies among Slaves in the Eighteenth-Century Chesapeake: An Archaeological Perspective. *American Antiquity* 75(1):19–43.
Galle, Jillian, and Amy Young (editors)
2004 *Engendering African American Archaeology: A Southern Perspective.* University of Tennessee Press, Knoxville.
Garcell Domínguez, Jorge F.
2009 Cueva del Agua y del Hueso: patrimonio arqueológico en La Habana. *Cuba Arqueológica* 2(2):108–10.
García, Gloria
2003a *Conspiraciones y revueltas: La actividad política de los negros en Cuba (1790–1845).* Editorial Oriente, Santiago de Cuba.

2003b *La Esclavitud desde La Esclavitud*. Editorial de Ciencias Sociales, Havana.

García Melero, José Enrique.

1992. Arquitectura: Juan de Villanueva y los nuevos planes de estudio. In *Renovacion, crisis, continuismo: La Real Academia de San Fernando en 1792*, edited by Real Academia de Bellas Artes de San Fernando, 13–55. Calcografía Nacional INEM-FSE, Madrid.

García Rodríguez, Gloria

2011 *Voices of the Enslaved in Nineteenth-Century Cuba: A Documentary History*. Translated by Nancy L. Westrate, with a foreword by Ada Ferrer. University of North Carolina Press, Chapel Hill.

García Santana, Alicia

1999 *Contrapunteo Cubano del arco y el hórcon*. Instituto Cubano del Libro, Havana.

2000 La Habana, crisol de arquitecturas. *Opus Habana* 4(2):4–15.

2012 A puntes sobre el bohío manera de presentación. In *Vivienda esclava rural en Cuba: bohíos y barracones*, by Lisette Roura Álvarez and Silva T. Angelbello Izquierdo, xi–xxii. Editorial Unicornio, San Antonio de los Baños, Cuba.

Gebelein, Jennifer

2012 *A Geographic Perspective of Cuban Landscapes*. Springer, New York.

Georgia Writers' Project

1940 *Drums and Shadows*. University of Georgia Press, Athens.

Gibson, Heather

2007 Daily Practice and Domestic Economies in Guadeloupe: An Archaeological and Historical Study. PhD dissertation, Department of Anthropology, Syracuse University, Syracuse, N.Y.

Gil Recio, Laura, and Bartolo Cardenas Alpízar

1993 *Cocina criolla cubana*. Editorial Oriente, Santiago de Cuba.

González Fernández, Doria

1991 La economía cafetalera cubana: 1790–1860. *Arbor: Ciencia, Pensamiento y Cultura* 547–48:161–80.

González-Ripoll Navarro, Maria Dolores

1999 *Cuba, la isla de los ensayos: Cultura y sociedad (1790–1815)*. Consejo Superior de Investigaciones Científicas, Madrid.

Goody, Jack

1982 *Cooking, Cuisine, and Class*. Cambridge University Press, Cambridge, UK.

Gordon y Acosta, Antonio

1896 *Una responsabilidad de nuestros cafés*. El Figaro, Havana.

Gott, Richard

2004 *Cuba: A New History*. Yale University Press, New Haven, Conn.

Guerra Sánchez, Ramiro
[1948] 1974 *Mudos testigos: Crónica del ex-cafetal Jesús Nazareno.* Editorial de Ciencias Sociales, Havana.
Gutiérrez Domech, Roberto, and Manuel Rivero Glean
1999 *Regiones naturales de la isla de Cuba.* Instituto Cubano del Libro Editorial Científico-Técnica, Havana.
Hall, Gwendolyn Midlo
2005 *Slavery and African Ethnicities in the Americas.* University of North Carolina Press, Chapel Hill.
Handler, Jerome
1997 An African-Type Healer/Diviner and His Grave Goods: A Burial from Plantation Slave Cemetery in Barbados, West Indies. *International Journal of Historical Archaeology* 1(2):114–20.
2009 The Middle Passage and the Material Culture of Captive Africans. *Slavery and Abolition: A Journal of Slave and Post-Slave Studies* 30(1):1–26.
Hauser, Mark W.
2008 *An Archaeology of Black Markets: Local Ceramics and Economies in Eighteenth-Century Jamaica.* University Press of Florida, Gainesville.
2011 Routes and Roots of Empire: Pots, Power, and Slavery in 18th-Century British Caribbean. *American Anthropologist* 113(3):431.
Heath, Barbara J.
1999 *Hidden Lives: The Archaeology of Slave Life at Thomas Jefferson's Poplar Forest.* University Press of Virginia, Charlottesville.
2004 Engendering Choice: Slavery and Consumerism in Central Virginia. In *Engendering African American Archaeology: A Southern Perspective*, edited by Amy Young and Jillian E. Galle, 19–38. University of Tennessee Press, Knoxville.
Hegel, Georg W. F.
[1931] 1967 *The Phenomenology of Mind.* Translated with introduction and notes by J. B. Baillie. Introduction to Harper Torchbook edition by George Lichtheim. Harper and Row, New York.
Henry, Daniel Edward
1995 *Collins: Machetes and Bowies, 1845–1965.* Krause Publications, Iola, Wisc.
Hernández de Lara, Odlanyer
2010 *De esclavos e imigrantes: arqueología histórica en una plantación cafetalera cubana.* Centro de Investigaciones Precolombinas, Instituto Superior del Profesorado Dr. Joaquín V. González, Buenos Aires.
Hernández de Lara, Odlanyer, Boris Rodríguez Tápanes, and Carlos Arredondo Antúnez
2012 *Esclavos y cimarrones en Cuba: Arqueología histórica en la cueva el Grillette.*

Centro de Investigaciones Precolombinas, Instituto Superior del Profesorado Dr. Joaquín V. González, Buenos Aires.

Higman, Barry W., with George A. Aarons, Karlis Karlins, and Elizabeth Reitz

1998 *Montpelier Jamaica: A Plantation Community in Slavery and Freedom, 1739–1912.* University Press of West Indies, Kingston, Jamaica.

Hilliard, Kathleen M.

2010 Finding Slave Voices. In *The Oxford Handbook of Slavery in the Americas,* edited by Robert Paquette and Mark M. Smith, 685–701. Oxford University Press, New York.

2014 *Masters, Slaves, and Exchange: Power's Purchase in the Old South.* Cambridge University Press, New York.

Hodder, Ian

2006 *The Leopard's Tale: Revealing the Mysteries of Çatalhöyük.* Thames and Hudson, London.

Hodder, Ian, and Scott Hutson

2004 *Reading the Past: Current Approaches to the Interpretation in Archaeology.* Cambridge University Press, Cambridge, UK.

Howe, Julia Ward

[1860] 1969 *A Trip to Cuba: Source Books and Studies on Latin America.* Praeger, New York.

Hurlbert, Henry

1854 *Gan-Eden or Pictures of Cuba.* John P. Jewett, Boston.

Instituto Cubano de Geodesia y Cartografía (ICGC)

1978 *Atlas de Cuba: XX Aniversario del Triunfo de la Revolución Cubana.* Havana.

Irwin, David

1997 *Neoclassicism.* Phaidon, London.

Isidro Méndez, Manuel

1952 *Biografía del Cafetal Angerona.* Biblioteca Nacional José Martí, Havana.

Iturralde-Vinent, Manuel

1967 Preliminary Report on the Distribution of Karst Landscapes in Cuba and Their Relationship to Geology. *Professional Geographer* 29(4):208–9.

Johnson, Sherry

2001 *The Social Transformation of Eighteenth-Century Cuba.* University Press of Florida, Gainesville.

Johnson, Walter

2013 *River of Dark Dreams: Slavery and Empire in the Cotton Kingdom.* Belknap Press of Harvard University Press, Cambridge, Mass.

Jopling, Carol F.

1988 *Puerto Rican Houses in Sociohistorical Perspective.* University of Tennessee Press, Knoxville.

Joseph, J. W., and Stephen Bryne

1992 Socio-Economics and Trade in Viejo San Juan, Puerto Rico: Observations from the Ballaja Archaeological Project. *Historical Archaeology* 26(1):45–58.

Kaye, Anthony E.

2007 *Joining Places: Slave Neighborhoods in the Old South*. University of North Carolina Press, Chapel Hill.

Kelly, Kenneth G.

2008 Creole Cultures of the Caribbean: Historical Archaeology in the French West Indies. *International Journal of Historical Archaeology* 12(4):388–402.

Kelso, William

1984 *Kingsmill Plantations, 1619–1800: Archaeology of Country Life in Colonial Virginia*. Academic Press, Orlando.

1997 *Archaeology at Monticello: Artifacts of Everyday Life in the Plantation Community*. Monticello Monograph Series. Thomas Jefferson Memorial Foundation, Charlottesville, Va.

Kopytoff, Igor

[1986] 2000 The Cultural Biography of Things: Commoditization as Process. In *Interpretative Archaeology: A Reader*, edited by J. Thomas, 377–97. Leicester University Press, London.

Kreamer, Christine Mullen

1995 Practical Beauty: Headgear for Daily Wear. In *Crowning Achievements: African Arts of Decorating the Head*, edited by Mary Jo Arnoldi and Christine Mullen Kreamer, 83–98. Fowler Museum of Cultural History, Los Angeles.

Laborie, Pierre Joseph

1798 *The Coffee Planter of Saint Domingo*. R. Cadell and W. Davies, London.

Landers, Jane G.

2010 *Atlantic Creoles: In the Age of Revolutions*. Harvard University Press, Cambridge, Mass.

Langarika, Enrique

[1862] 1996 *El Cocinero de los enfermos, convalecientes y desganados: Manual de Cocina Cubana*. Editorial Betania, Madrid.

La Rosa Corzo, Gabino

1989 *Armas y tácticas defensivas de los cimarrones en Cuba*. Reporte de investigación del Instituto de Ciencias Históricas, no. 2. Academia de Ciencias de Cuba, Havana.

1991a La Cueva de la Cachimba: Estudio arqueológico de un refugio de cimarrones. In *Estudios arqueológicas*, 57–84. Editorial Academia, Havana.

1991b *Los Palenques del Oriente de Cuba: Resistencia y acoso*. Editorial Academia, Havana.

1999 La huella africana en el ajuar del cimarrón arqueológica. *El Caribe Arqueológico* 3:109–15.
2002 *Exposición: Fragmentos de un pasado mestizo*. Arqueología Lajera. Oficina del Historiador de la Ciudad de La Habana, Havana.
2003 *Runaway Slave Settlements in Cuba: Resistance and Repression*. Translated by Mary Todd. University of North Carolina Press, Chapel Hill.
2005 Subsistence of Cimarrones: An Archaeological Study. In *Dialogues in Cuban Archaeology*, edited by L. Antonio Curet, Shannon L. Dawdy, and Gabino La Rosa Corzo, 163–80. University of Alabama Press, Tuscaloosa.
2008 Aproximaciones antropológicas a las bandas cimarronas de las ciénagas de Cuba. *Gabinete de Arqueología Boletín* 7:4–18.
2010 La arqueología histórica en el estudio de la resistencia esclava. *Gabinete de Arqueología Boletín* 8:15–20.
2012 Cafetal Angerona: La más famosa plantación esclavista de Cuba. Una mirada desde la Arqueología. *Gabinete de Arqueología Boletín* 9:15–37.

La Rosa Corzo, Gabino, and Joaquín Pérez Padrón
1994 La resistencia esclava en la Sierra de Grillo: Estudio arqueológico. In *Estudios arqueológicos: Compilación de temas 1990*, edited by Editorial Academia, 101–28. Editorial Academia, Havana.

Law, Robin
1998 Barracoons. In *Macmillan Encyclopedia of World Slavery*, edited by Paul Finkelman and Joseph Miller, 102–3. Macmillan Reference, New York.

Lefebvre, Henri
1991 *The Production of Space*. Translated by N. Donaldson-Smith. Basil Blackwell, Oxford, UK.

Leone, Mark
2005 *The Archaeology of Liberty in an American Capital: Excavations in Annapolis*. University of California Press, Berkeley.

Llanes, Lillian
1999 *The Houses of Old Cuba*. Thames and Hudson, London.

Loren, Diana DiPaolo
2010 *The Archaeology of Clothing and Bodily Adornment in Colonial America*. University Press of Florida, Gainesville.

Lowell, Mary Gardner
2003 *New Year in Cuba: Mary Gardner Lowell's Travel Diary, 1831–1832*. Edited with introduction by Karen Robert. Massachusetts Historical Society and Northeastern University Press, Boston.

Lugo Romera, Karen Mahé, and Sonia Menéndez Castro
2003 *Barrio de Compeche: Tres estudios arqueológicos*. La Fuente Viva series no. 27. Fundación Fernando Ortíz, Havana.

Mack, Angela D., and Stephen G. Hofficus (editors)

2008 *Landscape of Slavery: The Plantation in American Art*. University of South Carolina Press, Columbia.

Madden, Richard R.

1853 *The Island of Cuba: Resources, Progress, and Prospects, Considered in Relation Especially to the Influence of Its Prosperity on the Interests of the British West India Colonies*. Partridge and Oakey, London.

Mann, Mary Peabody

[1887] 2000 *Juanita: A Romance of Real Life in Cuba Fifty Years Ago*. Edited and introduction by Patricia M. Ard. New World Studies. University Press of Virginia, Charlottesville.

Manzano, Juan

[1840] 1996 *The Autobiography of a Slave/Autobiografía de un esclavo*. Bilingual ed. Introduction by Ivan A. Schulman. Translated by Evelyn P. Garfield. Wayne State University Press, Detroit.

Marrero, Levi

1985 *Cuba: Economía y sociedad*. Vol. 11. Playor, Madrid.

Martin, Ann Smart

2008 *Buying into the World of Goods: Early Consumers in Backcountry Virginia*. Johns Hopkins University Press, Baltimore.

McDaniel, George

1982 *Hearth and Home: Preserving a People's Culture*. Temple University Press, Philadelphia.

McGuire, Randall

[1992] 2002 *A Marxist Archaeology*. Peacheron Press, Clinton Corners, N.Y.

2007 Marxism. In *Handbook of Archaeological Theories*, edited by R. Alexander Bentley, Herbert D. G. Maschiner, and Christopher Chippindale, 73–93. AltaMira Press, Lanham, Md.

Méndez Rodenas, Adriana

1998 *Gender and Nationalism in Colonial Cuba: The Travels of Santa Cruz y Montalvo, Condesa de Merlin*. Vanderbilt University Press, Nashville.

Meskell, Lynn

2005 Introduction: Object Orientations. In *Archaeologies of Materiality*, edited by Lynn Meskell, 1–17. Blackwell, Malden, Mass.

Miller, George

1991 A Revised Set of CC Index Values for Classification and Economic Scaling of English Ceramics from 1787 to 1880. *Historical Archaeology* 25(1):2–36.

1994 English Shell-Edged Earthenware. *Antiques* 145(3):432–43.

Mintz, Sidney W.

1974 *Caribbean Transformations*. Columbia University Press, New York.

1985 *Sweetness and Power: The Place of Sugar in Modern History*. Penguin Books, New York.

Mintz, Sidney W., and Douglas Hall

1960 *Origins of the Internal Marketing System*. Yale University Publications in Anthropology 57. Yale University Press, New Haven, Conn.

Mohl, Raymond A.

1972 A Scotsman in Cuba, 1811–1812. *The Americas: A Quarterly Review of Inter-American Culture History* 29(2):232–45.

Moore, Robin D.

1997 *Nationalizing Blackness: Afrocubanismo and Artistic Revolution in Havana, 1920–1940*. University of Pittsburgh Press, Pittsburgh.

Moreno Fraginals, Manuel

1977 Africa in Cuba: A Quantitative Analysis of the African Population in the Island of Cuba. In *Comparative Perspectives on Slavery in New World Plantation Societies*, edited by Vera Rubin and Arthur Tuden, 189–201. New York Academy of Sciences, New York.

1978 *El ingenio: complejo económico social cubano del azúcar*. 3 vols. Editorial de Ciencias Sociales, Havana.

Morris, Christopher

1998 The Articulation of Two Worlds: The Master-Slave Relationship Reconsidered. *Journal of American History* 85(3):982–1007.

Mullins, Paul R.

2012 *The Archaeology of Consumer Culture*. University Press of Florida, Gainesville.

Nicholls, David

1985 *Haiti in Caribbean Context: Ethnicity, Economy, and Revolt*. St. Martin's Press, New York.

Niell, Paul

2010. El Templete and Cuban Neoclassicism: A Multivalent Signifier as Site of Memory. *Bulletin of Latin American Research* 30(3):344–65.

2013a Introduction. In *Buen Gusto and Classicism in the Visual Cultures of Latin America, 1780–1910*, edited by Paul B. Niell and Stacie G. Widdifield, xiii–xxxv. University of New Mexico Press, Albuquerque.

2013b Rhetorics of Place and Empire in the Fountain Sculpture of 1830s Havana. *Art Bulletin* 95(1):440–64.

Niell, Paul B., and Stacie G. Widdifield (editors)

2013 *Buen Gusto and Classicism in the Visual Cultures of Latin America, 1780–1910*. University of New Mexico Press, Albuquerque.

Norman, Benjamin

1845 *Rambles by Land and Water, or Notes of Travel in Cuba and Mexico*. Paine and Burgess, New York.

Nussbaum, Arthur.
1957 *A History of the Dollar.* Columbia University Press, New York.
Ochoa, Todd Ramón
2010 *Society of the Dead: Quita Manaquita and Palo Praise in Cuba.* University of California Press, Berkeley.
Oficina del Gobierno Constitucional
1821 Cafetal Valiente: Tradición y venta del cafetal en el partido de Güines y de las estancia de Refugio de Regla, con todos sus edificios Oficina del Gobierno Constitucional. La Biblioteca Nacional José Martí, Havana.
Orser, Charles E., Jr., and Pedro P. A. Funari
2001 Archaeology and Slave Resistance and Rebellion. *World Archaeology* 31(1):61–72.
Ortega, Elpidio J.
2000 *Expresiones Culturales del Sur Publicaciones de la Academia de Ciencias de la Republica Dominicana.* Academia de Ciencias de la República Dominicana y Fundación Ortega Álvarez, Santo Domingo, Dominican Republic.
Ortiz, Fernando
[1916] 1988 *Los Negros Esclavos.* Editorial de Ciencias Sociales, Havana.
1992 *Los cabildos y la fiesta afrocubanos del Día de Reyes, Colección Fernando Ortiz.* Editorial de Ciencias Sociales, Havana.
[1947] 1995a *Cuban Counterpoint: Tobacco and Sugar.* With a new introduction by Fernando Coronil. Duke University Press, Durham, N.C.
[1906] 1995b *Los negros brujos, Pensamiento cubano.* Editorial de Ciencias Sociales, Havana.
Orwa, C., A. Mutua, R. Kindt, R. Jamnadass, and S. Anthony
2009 *Agroforestree Database: A Tree Reference and Selection Guide.* Version 4.0. World Agroforestry Centre, Nairobi. http://www.worldagroforestry.org/sites/treedbs/treedatabases.asp.
Otto, Solomon John
1984 *Cannon's Point Plantation, 1794–1864: Living Conditions and Status Patterns in the Old South.* Academic Press, Orlando.
Pabón, Arleen
2003 *Por la encendida calle antillana:* Africanisms and Puerto Rican Architecture. *CRM: The Journal of Heritage Stewardship* 1(1):14–32.
Palma, Ramón de
1838 Una pascua en San Marcos. In *Cuentos cubanos por Ramon de Palma,* edited by A. M. Eligio de la Puente, 19–102. Librería Cervantes, Havana.
Palmer, David T.
2011 Archaeology of Jim Crow–Era African American Life on Louisiana's Sugar Plantations. In *The Materiality of Freedom: Archaeologies of Postemancipation*

Life, edited by Jodi A. Barnes, 136–57. University of South Carolina Press, Columbia.

Paquette, Robert L.

1988 *Sugar Is Made with Blood: The Conspiracy of La Esclera and the Conflict between Empires over Slavery in Cuba*. Wesleyan University Press, Middletown, Conn.

Penningroth, Dylan

2003 *The Claims of Kinfolk: African American Property and Community in the Nineteenth-Century South*. University of North Carolina Press, Chapel Hill.

Pérez, Louis, A., Jr.

1990 *Cuba and the United States: Ties of Singular Intimacy*. University of Georgia Press, Athens.

2000. *Winds of Change: Hurricanes and the Transformation of Nineteenth-Century Cuba*. University of North Carolina Press, Chapel Hill.

Pérez, Louis A., Jr. (editor)

1992 *Slaves, Sugar, and Colonial Society*. Scholarly Resources, Wilmington, Del.

Pérez, Louis A. Jr., and Rebecca J. Scott (editors)

2003 *Los archivos de Cuba/The Archives of Cuba*. University of Pittsburgh Press, Pittsburgh.

Pérez de la Riva, Francisco

1944 *El café: historia de su cultivo y explotación en Cuba*. Edited by J. Montero. Vol. 16 of *Biblioteca de historia, filosofía y sociología*. Marticorena, Havana.

1952 La habitación rural en Cuba. *Revista de arqueología y etnología* 7:295–392.

Pérez de la Riva, Juan

1975 El barracón de ingenio en la êpoca esclavista. In *El barracón y otros ensayos*, 15–74. Editorial de Ciencias Sociales, Havana.

Pichardo, Esteban

1860–72 *Isla de Cuba: Carta geo topográfica*. Dirección de la Capitanía General, Havana.

1953 *Pichardo novísimo; o, Diccionario provincial casi razonado de vozes y frazes cubanas*, edited by Esteban Rodríguez Herrera. Editorial Selecta Librería, Havana.

Portuondo Zúñiga, Olga

1992 *Santiago de Cuba: Los colonos franceses y el Formento Cafetalero (1798–1809)*. Editorial Oriente, Santiago de Cuba.

Posnansky, Merrick

1999 West Africanist Reflection on African-American Archaeology. In *"I, Too, Am America": Archaeological Studies of African-American Life*, edited by Theresa A. Singleton, 21–37. University Press of Virginia, Charlottesville.

Prado Flores, Aneli, Joyce Rossi Álvarez, and Roger Arrazcaeta Delgado

2004 Rescate arqueológico en Mercaderes no. 15. *Gabinete de Arqueología Boletín* 3:31–40.

Pulsipher, Lydia M., and Conrad M. Goodwin
1999 Here Where the Old Time People Be: Reconstructing the Landscapes of the Slavery and Post-slavery Era in Montserrat, West Indies. In *African Sites: Archaeology in the Caribbean*, edited by Jay B. Haviser, 9–37. Markus Wiener, Princeton, N.J.
Ramírez Pérez, Jorge Freddy, and Fernando Antonio Paredes Pupo
2004 *Francia en Cuba: Los cafetales de la Sierra del Rosario (1970–1850)*. Ediciones Unión, Havana.
Ramos Zúñiga, Antonio
1984 *Las armas del ejército Mambi*. Editora Política, Havana.
Rebelledo, Don José.
1910 *Manual de Constructor*. Madrid.
Reeves, Matthew B.
2014 Mundane or Spiritual? The Interpretation of Glass Bottle Containers Found on Two African Diaspora Sites. In *Materialities, Meanings, and Modernities of Rituals in the Black Atlantic*, edited by Akinwumi Ogundiran and Paula Saunders, 176–96. Indiana University Press, Bloomington.
Reynoso, Álvaro
1861 *Estudios progresivos sobre varias materias científicas, agrícolas e industriales: Colección de escritos sobre los cultivos de la cana, café, tobaco, maiz, arroz*. Vol. 1. Imprenta del Tiempo, Havana.
Roura Álvarez, Lisette
2002 Enterramientos humanos en la casa de Obrapía no. 55. *Gabinete de Arqueología Boletín* 2:4–9.
2006 Valle de los Ingenios, Campana, 2006. *Gabinete de Arqueología Boletín* 5:212.
Roura Álvarez, Lisette, Roger Arrazcaeta Delgado, and Carlos Hernández Oliva
2006 La cerámica de tradición aborigen: ejemplos habaneros. *Gabinete de Arqueología Boletín* 5:16–34.
Roura Álvarez, Lisette, and Teresa Angelbello Izquierdo
2007 El bohío: Vivienda esclava en las plantaciones cubanas del siglo XIX. *Gabinete de Arqueología Boletín* 6:136–57.
Roura Álvarez, Lisette, and Silva T. Angelbello Izquierdo
2012 *Vivienda esclava rural en Cuba: Bohíos y barracones*. Editorial Unicornio, San Antonio de los Baños, Cuba.
Salas y Quiroga, Jacinto
1840 *Viages: Isla de Cuba*. Edited by I. Boix. Madrid.
Samford, Patricia M.
2007 *Subfloor Pits and the Archaeology of Slavery in Colonial Virginia*. University of Alabama Press, Tuscaloosa.

Samson, R.

1992 Knowledge, Constraint, and Power in Action: The Defenseless Medieval Wall. *Historical Archaeology* 26(3):36–44.

Sarmiento Ramírez, Ismael

2006 Fuentes para el Estudio de la Cultura Material en La Cuba Colonial. *Annals del Museo de América* 14:285–326.

2009 Del funche al ajiaco: la dieta que los amos imponen a los esclavos africanos en Cuba y la asimilación que éstos hacen de la cocina criolla. *Annals del Museo de América* 16:126–54.

Scarpaci, Joseph L., and Armando H. Portela

2009 *Cuban Landscapes: Heritage, Memory, and Place.* Guilford Press, New York.

Schávelzon, Daniel

1998 Catálogo de cerámicas históricas de Buenos Aires (Siglos XVI–XX): Con notas sobre la región del Río de la Plata. Fundación para la Investigación del Arte Argentino, Buenos Aires.

Schulman, Ivan A.

1996. Introduction. *The Autobiography of a Slave/Auto biografía de un esclavo.* Wayne State University Press, Detroit.

Scott, James C.

1985 *Weapons of the Weak: Everyday Forms of Peasant Resistance.* Yale University Press, New Haven, Conn.

1990 *Domination and the Arts of Resistance: Hidden Transcripts.* Yale University Press, New Haven, Conn.

Scott, John F.

1999 *Latin American Art: Ancient to Modern.* University Press of Florida, Gainesville.

2012 Latin American Art. In *Encyclopedia Britannica: Hispanic Heritage in the Americas.* http://www.britannica.com/hispanic_heritage/article-253332 (accessed July 1, 2012).

Scott, Rebecca

[1985] 2000 *Slave Emancipation in Cuba: The Transition to Free Labor, 1860–1899.* 2nd ed., with a new afterword. University of Pittsburgh Press, Pittsburgh.

Seale, Don, Lee Florea, Beth Fratesi, Limaris Soto, and Manuel A. Iturralde-Vinent

2004 Karst of Western Cuba: Observations, Geomorphology, and Digenesis. *12th Symposium on the Geology of the Bahamas and Other Carbonate Regions.* http://digitalcommons.wku.edu/geog_fac_pub/13.

Serrano, Francisco de Paula

1829 Memoria sobre cultivo y beneficio del café en 1829. *Memorias de la Real Sociedad Económica de Amigos del País* 9:77–120.

1837 *Agricultura cubana o Tratado sobre las Ramas principales de su Industria rural.* Vol. 1. Oficios del Gobierno y Capitanía General por S.M., Havana.

Shackel, Paul A.

2011 *The Archaeology of American Labor and Working-Class Life.* University Press of Florida, Gainesville.

Shepherd, Verene A., and Kathleen E. A. Monteith

2002 Pen Keepers and Coffee Farmers in a Sugar-Plantation Society. In *Slavery without Sugar: Diversity in Caribbean Economy and Society since the Seventeenth Century*, edited by Verene A. Shepherd, 82–104. University Press of Florida, Gainesville.

Singleton, Theresa A.

1991 The Archaeology of Slave Life. In *Before Freedom Came: African American Life in the Antebellum South*, edited by Edward D. C. Campbell with Kym Rice, 155–75. University Press of Virginia, Charlottesville.

2001 Slavery and Spatial Dialectics on a Cuban Plantation. *World Archaeology* 33(1):99–114.

2003 Archaeology and Material Culture of Santa Ana de Viajacas: A Coffee Plantation in Western Cuba. In *Proceedings of the International Congress for Caribbean Archaeology*, edited by Clenis Tavárez María and Manuel A. García Arévalo, 725–30. Museo del Hombre Dominicano and Fundación García Arévalo, Santo Domingo, Dominican Republic.

2005a An Archaeological Study of a Cuban Coffee Plantation. In *Dialogues in Cuban Archaeology*, edited by L. Antonio Curet, Shannon Dawdy, and Gabino La Rosa Corzo, 181–99. University of Alabama Press, Tuscaloosa.

2005b Landscape, Archaeology, and Memory of Cuban Coffee Plantations, 1800–1860. In *Proceedings of the International Association for Caribbean Archaeology (IACA)*, edited by Basil Reid, Henri Petitjean, and Antonio Curet, 654–60. University of the West Indies, School of Continuing Studies, St. Augustine, Trinidad and Tobago.

2006 African Diaspora Archaeology in Dialogue. In *Afro-Atlantic Dialogues: Anthropology in the Diaspora*, edited by Kevin A. Yelvington, 249–87. School of American Research Press, Santa Fe, N.M.

2010 Reclaiming the Gullah-Gheecee Past: Archaeology of Slavery in Coastal Georgia. In *African American Life in the Georgia Lowcountry: The Atlantic World and the Gullah Geechee*, edited by Philip Morgan, 151–87. University of Georgia Press, Athens.

Singleton, Theresa A., and Marcos André Torres de Souza

2009 Archaeologies of the African Diaspora: Brazil, Cuba, and the United States. In *International Handbook of Historical Archaeology*, edited by Teresita Majaweski and David Gaimster, 449–69. Springer, New York.

Smith, Frederick H.
2008 *The Archaeology of Alcohol and Drinking*. University Press of Florida, Gainesville.
Smith, S. D.
2002 Coffee and the "Poorer Sort of People": Jamaica during the Period of African Enslavement. In *Slavery without Sugar: Diversity in Caribbean Economy and Society since the Seventeenth Century*, edited by Verene A. Shepard, 102–28. University Press of Florida, Gainesville.
Sosa Rodríguez, Enrique
1978 *La economía en la novela cubana del siglo XIX*. Editorial Letras Cubanas, Havana.
Stine, Linda F., Melanie Cabak, and Mark Groover
1996 Blue Beads as African-American Cultural Symbols. *Historical Archaeology* 30(3):49–75.
Suárez y Romero, Anselmo
1859 *Colección de Articulos de Anselmo Suárez y Romero*. La Antilla, Havana.
Tabío, Ernesto E., and Rodolfo Payarés
1968 *Sobre los cafetales coloniales de la Sierra del Rosario*. Series Pinar del Río, no. 17. Academia de Ciencias de Cuba, Havana.
Tomich, Dale
1988 The "Second Slavery": Bonded Labor and the Transformation of the Nineteenth-Century World Economy. In *Rethinking the Nineteenth Century: Movements and Contradictions*, edited by Francisco O. Ramírez, 103–17. Greenwood Press, Westport, Conn.
2003 The Wealth of Empire: Francisco Arango y Parreño, Political Economy, and Second Slavery in Cuba. *Comparative Study of Society and History* 20(4):4–28.
Torres de Souza, Marcos André, and Camilla Agostini
2012 Body Marks, Pots, and Pipes: Some Correlations between African Scarifications and Pottery Decoration. *Historical Archaeology* 46(2):102–23.
Trouillot, Michel-Rolph
1993 Coffee Planters and Coffee Slaves in the Antilles: The Impact of a Secondary Crop. In *Cultivation and Culture*, edited by Ira Berlin and Philip D. Morgan, 124–37. University Press of Virginia, Charlottesville.
Turnbull, John
[1840] 1969 *Travels in the West Cuba; with Notices of Porto Rico and the Slave Trade*. Negro Universities Press, New York.
Upton, Delle
[1985] 2010 White and Black Landscapes of the Eighteenth Century. In *Cabin, Quarter, Plantation: Architecture and Landscapes of North American Slavery*, edited by Clifton Ellis and Rebecca Ginsburg, 121–39. Yale University Press, New Haven, Conn.

Van Beek, Gus W., with Ora Van Beek

2008 *Glorious Mud! Ancient and Contemporary Earthen Design and Construction in North Africa, Western Europe, the Near East, and South Asia.* Smithsonian Institution Scholarly Press, Washington, D.C.

Van Norman, William C.

2005 Shade Grown Slavery: Life and Labor on Coffee Plantations in Western Cuba, 1790–1845. PhD dissertation. University of North Carolina, Chapel Hill.

2013 *Shade-Grown Slavery: The Lives of Slaves on Coffee Plantations in Cuba.* Vanderbilt University Press, Nashville, Tenn.

Villapol, Nitza

1997 *Cuban Cuisine.* Editorial José Martí, Havana.

Villaverde, Cirilo

[1882] 1977 *Cecilia Valdes.* 2 vols. Editorial de Arte y Literatura, Havana.

Vlach, John Michael

1993 *Back of the Big House: The Architecture of Plantation Slavery.* University of North Carolina Press, Chapel Hill.

Von Humboldt, Alexander F.

[1856] 1969. *The Island of Cuba.* Translated from Spanish by J. S. Thrasher. Negro Universities Press, New York.

Voss, Alexa, and Karsten Voss

2008 Al margen de la esclavitud: una cultura propia. El enterramiento de un afrocubano en Cuba del siglo XIX: Una contribución arqueológica. *Boletín—Museo del Hombre Dominicano* 35(42):159–72.

Weik, Terrance M.

2012 *The Archaeology of Antislavery Resistance.* University Press of Florida, Gainesville.

Wilkie, Laurie A.

1996 Glass-Knapping at a Louisiana Plantation: African-American Tools? *Historical Archaeology* 30(4):37–49.

Wilkie, Laurie A., and Paul Farnsworth

2005 *Sampling Many Pots: An Archaeology of Memory and Tradition at a Bahamian Plantation.* University Press of Florida, Gainesville.

Wurdemann, John G. F.

[1844] 1971 *Notes on Cuba: An Account of Its Discovery and Early History.* Edited by Robert M. Goldwyn. Arno Press, New York.

Yun, Lisa

2008 *The Coolie Speaks: Chinese Indentured Laborers and African Slaves in Cuba.* Temple University Press, Philadelphia.

Index

The letter *f* following a page number denotes an illustration; the letter *t* following a page number denotes a table.

Theresa Singleton is on the faculty of the Department of Anthropology, Syracuse University, Syracuse, New York. She was elected a member of the American Antiquarian Society in 2013 and received the J. C. Harrington Award from the Society for Historical Archaeology for her lifetime contributions to historical archaeology in 2014. She is the editor of *Archaeology of Slavery and Plantation Life* and of *"I, Too, Am America": Archaeological Studies of African-American Life*.

Cultural Heritage Studies
Edited by Paul A. Shackel, University of Maryland

The University Press of Florida is proud to support this series devoted to the study of cultural heritage. This enterprise brings together research devoted to understanding the material and behavioral characteristics of heritage. The series explores the uses of heritage and the meaning of its cultural forms as a way to interpret the present and the past.

Books include important theoretical contributions and descriptions of significant cultural resources. Scholarship addresses questions related to culture and describes how local and national communities develop and value the past. The series includes works in public archaeology, heritage tourism, museum studies, vernacular architecture, history, American studies, and material cultural studies.

Heritage of Value, Archaeology of Renown: Reshaping Archaeological Assessment and Significance, edited by Clay Mathers, Timothy Darvill, and Barbara J. Little (2005)
Archaeology, Cultural Heritage, and the Antiquities Trade, edited by Neil Brodie, Morag M. Kersel, Christina Luke, and Kathryn Walker Tubb (2006)
Archaeological Site Museums in Latin America, edited by Helaine Silverman (2006)
Crossroads and Cosmologies: Diasporas and Ethnogenesis in the New World, by Christopher C. Fennell (2007)
Ethnographies and Archaeologies: Iterations of the Past, by Lena Mortensen and Julie Hollowell (2009)
Cultural Heritage Management: A Global Perspective, by Phyllis Mauch Messenger and George S. Smith (2010; first paperback edition, 2014)
God's Fields: An Archaeology of Religion and Race in Moravian Wachovia, by Leland Ferguson (2011; first paperback edition, 2013)
Ancestors of Worthy Life: Plantation Slavery and Black Heritage at Mount Clare, by Teresa S. Moyer (2015)
Slavery behind the Wall: An Archaeology of a Cuban Coffee Plantation, by Theresa A. Singleton (2015)
Excavating Memory: Sites of Remembering and Forgetting, edited by Maria Theresia Starzmann and John R. Roby (2016)
Mythic Frontiers: Remembering, Forgetting, and Profiting with Cultural Heritage Tourism, by Daniel R. Maher (2016)